SUSTAINABLE TOURISM DEVELOPMENT

Sustainable Tourism Development

Edited by
HARRY COCCOSSIS
and
PETER NIJKAMP

Avebury

Aldershot • Brookfield USA • Hong Kong • Singapore • Sydney

Published by
Avebury
Ashgate Publishing Limited
Gower House
Croft Road
Aldershot
Hants GU11 3HR
England

Ashgate Publishing Company
Old Post Road
Brookfield
Vermont 05036
USA

British Library Cataloguing in Publication Data

Sustainable Tourism Development
    I. Coccossis, Harry   II. Nijkamp, Peter
    338.4791

ISBN 1 85972 177 X

Library of Congress Catalog Card Number: 95-78523

Typeset by
Dianne Beiderberg
Contact Europe
Buyskade 39 E
1051 HT Amsterdam
The Netherlands

Printed and bound by Athenæum Press Ltd.,
Gateshead, Tyne & Wear.

Contents

Figures and tables

Contributors

G.J. Ashworth
Urban and Regional Planning Department
University of Groningen
P O Box 72
9700 AB Groningen
The Netherlands

H. Briassoulis
National Center for Scientific Research 'Demokritos'
P O Box 60228, Ag. Paraskevi 15210
Athens
Greece

D. Buhalis
173 Walnut Tree Close
Guildford GU1 4UB
England

H. Coccossis
Department of Environmental Studies
University of The Aegean
17 Karadoni Street
81100 Mytilene
Greece

G. Dickinson
Department of Geography and Topographic Science
University of Glasgow
Glasgow G12 8QQ
Scotland

A. Edwards
Department of Geography
University College of Swansea
Singleton Park
Swanswea SA2 8PP
England

J. Fletcher
173 Walnut Tree Close
Guildford GU1 4UB
England

T.Z. de Haan
Department of Tourism and Recreation Studies
Netherlands Institute of Tourism and Transport Studies
Breda
The Netherlands

H. Janssen
Ministry of Transportation
Plesmanweg 1-6
The Hague
The Netherlands

M. Kiers
TNO-FEL
P O Box 96864
2509 JG The Hague
The Netherlands

A. Lanza
Fondazione Eni Enrico Mattei
Via S. Sofia 27
I-20122 Milano
Italy

B. Nitsch
Department of Leisure Studies
European Centre for Nature Conservation
P O Box 1352
5004 BJ Tilburg
The Netherlands

P. Nijkamp
Economics Faculty
Free University
De Boelelaan 1105
1081 HV Amsterdam
The Netherlands

A. Parpairis
Department of Environmental Studies
University of The Aegean
17 Karadoni Street
81100 Mytilene
Greece

F. Pigliaru
Fondazione Eni Enrico Mattei
Via S. Sofia 27
I-20122 Milano
Italy

G. Priestly
Departament of Geography
University of Barcelona
Belaterra 08193
Barcelona
Spain

J. van der Straaten
European Center for Nature Conservation
P O Box 1352
5004 BJ Tilburg
The Netherlands

S. Verdonkschot
Department of Regional Economics
Free University
De Boelelaan 1105
1081 HV Amsterdam
The Netherlands

J. Westlake
173 Walnut Tree Close
Guildford GU1 4UB
England

Preface

Tourism has been a rapidly growing sector and a wide-sweeping socioeconomic phenomenon with broad economic, social, cultural and environmental consequences. It is likely that tourism will continue to dominate the international scene for many years to come. Nevertheless, there seem to be significant structural changes in tourist demand which are likely to influence the traditional model of 'mass tourism', as the sector has been experiencing dramatic changes over the last few years in response to broader patterns of globalization of economic activities. There is growing evidence of an emerging new tourist 'profile' in connection with the change in view and behavioural patterns of all 'actors' involved in planning and management of the tourist industry as well as new trends taking place not only in the area of demand but also in the interrelated area of supply.

Tourism is not only a rapidly rising economic activity, on all continents, in countries and regions, but it is also increasingly recognized that this new growth sector has many adverse effects on environmental quality conditions. In the context of the worldwide debate on sustainable development there is also an increasing need for a thorough reflection on sustainable tourism, where the socioeconomic interests of the tourist sector are brought into harmony with environmental constraints, now and in the future. Tourism is intricately involved with environmental quality, as it affects directly the natural and human resources and at the same time is conditioned by the quality of the environment. Such a relationship has important implications from the point of view of policies, management and planning.

The subject is of utmost importance in Europe, as the European Union does not have an explicit policy on tourism, an idea which is gradually being developed. It lasted until spring 1994 when the Presidency of the Union announced that tourism and the environment is a priority issue. In fact, in May 1994, an Informal Council of European Environment Ministers was organized on this theme on Santorini Island, Greece. In addition, in the new Programme for the Environment (1994-1997) of the European Union, the basic strategy outlined refers to the issue of sustainable development, a priority perspective following the Global Meeting on Environment and Development in Rio (1992).

Furthermore, tourism is the largest single sector in the European Union. Particularly for the Mediterranean countries it represents a large proportion of their GDP. One third of all tourist arrivals in the world concentrates on the Mediterranean. Tourism is rapidly becoming a leading sector in most other European countries, for example, in the United Kingdom, the Netherlands, Denmark, France and several central European countries.

The purpose of the book is to provide insight into the relationship between tourism and the environment, highlighting the fact that tourism is a complex socioeconomic phenomenon, multidimensional in character, which has significant effects on the environment but depends also on environmental quality. It is this feedback mechanism which has to be understood and incorporated into policy making.

It goes without saying that multiple disciplines are to be involved in a dedicated theme on environment and tourism. This book is intended for those working in the area of policy making, teaching or undertaking research in tourism, regional development and environmental protection. It brings together new and refreshing ideas, reflections and methods for studying the complex issue of sustainable tourism development.

The book comprises two parts:
- The first part presents general views on the relationship between tourism and the environment with seven chapters on issues which are currently considered as being of primary concern: environmental economic, cultural and socioeconomic change, the economic importance of the tourist sector and sustainable development.
- The second part is more concerned with applied fieldwork and policy case studies and presents also some analytical tools for policy making with regard to tourism and the environment through a series of European cases regarding various types of tourism and related facilities.

The editors wish to thank Dianne Biederberg (Contact Europe, Amsterdam) who did a professional job in text editing this volume.

May 1995   Athens, Harry Coccossis
                                                            Amsterdam, Peter Nijkamp

Part A
SUSTAINABLE TOURISM: THEORY AND PLANNING

1 Environmental impacts on tourist destinations: An economic analysis

D. Buhalis and J. Fletcher

1.1 Introduction: environmental concern and tourism

Environmental protection has become a major issue in the recent years. In general, most people realize that the planet has quite limited resources and therefore attempt to identify various methods which will enable its preservation. "Despite the recognition of the long history of the environmental problem, it should be noted that until the beginning of the twentieth century, in general only relatively modest environmental changes were taking place, as the prevailing technological and economic was unable to alter environmental condition on earth dramatically" (Nijkamp, 1992, p.1).

An idea is emerging that people have the right to live in a protected environment and that this right should apply to our children and grandchildren. The feeling that people have borrowed this world and they need to return it in a similar or better condition to the new generation is growing rapidly in the modern world. However, quite often, environmental concern is against the short term economic benefit of numerous organizations and corporations which increase their profits with little, if any, regard to the environment.

In modern societies a coherent and integrated approach has often been adopted in order to strive towards harmonic development of both economy and ecology (Nijkamp, 1992, p.2). "The challenge is to find an acceptable level and pattern of development which is compatible with the maintenance or even enhancement of the environment" (Goodall and Stabley, 1992, p.61).

Tourism as an economic activity has an inevitable effect on the environment, especially at the destination level. "Environment is a core feature of the tourist product. Tourists are therefore, 'consumers of environment' travelling to producers' locations, the tourist destination, in order to consume the product" (Goodall, 1992, p.60).

However, tourism as an 'industry' is often under attack for a number of abuses to the physical nature of destinations. Consequently, it increasingly attracts the attention of environmentalists protesting against the negative effects that have invariably accompanied tourism development. Most of the attacks are against the anarchic and chaotic tourism development which is observed in many destinations, and especially in the Mediterranean.

This chapter attempts to demonstrate the relationship between tourism and

3

environment and to illustrate the major actors which effect the environmental assets at a destination level, namely locals, tourists, local enterprises, tour operators and National Tourist Organizations. Moreover, it identifies the major economic factors which influence the environment in the tourism destination and finally outlines some of the major trends, responsibilities and strategies which are adapted worldwide.

1.2   Environmental impacts of tourism: symbiotic or antagonis - tic relationships

The environment is probably one of the most important contributors to the desirability and attractiveness of a destination. Scenic sites, amenable climates and unique landscape features have an important influence in tourism development and the spatial distribution of tourist movements. Consequently, **sustainable development,** which for the purposes of this chapter can be defined as "development that meets the needs of the present without compromising the ability of future generations to meet their own needs" (Eber, 1992, p.1), is required in order to preserve the environment as an asset for the tourism industry. Thus, some researchers suggest that there may be a symbiotic relation between tourism and the environment (Mathieson and Wall, 1982, p.96).

However, tourism has been responsible for a great number of environmental problems. The major problems arise because the environment (at least in the short term) is a zero-priced public good, and as with any zero-priced good, is subject to excess demand and over-utilization. This over-utilization of the natural resources, especially during the peak periods of tourist activity as well as often ill planned tourism development, have provided a number of examples where tourism is in conflict with the environment (Mathieson and Wall, 1982, p.101).

Consequently, the nature of the tourism-environment relationship is quite difficult to analyze and the estimation of environmental impacts associated with tourism development is an extremely complex issue. Clearly, one of the reasons that tourism stands out as an export industry which creates environmental problems is because of the 'visibility' of the consumers who must visit the destination in order to consume the industry's output. Indeed, tourism seems to receive more than its fair share of criticism from the environmentalist camp. Islands have sometimes been devastated by mining industries with little regard to environmental preservation, whilst the possibility of increasing tourist numbers meets with growing concern. Any form of economic development will bring with it economic, environmental and sociocultural change and the damage which currently sits on the doorstep of the tourism industry must be kept in perspective.

Apart from the positive and negative environmental impacts, which are caused directly by the tourism industry, there are several impacts which can be indirectly attributed to tourism activity within a destination. These impacts result from the tourism supporting industries, which supply the destination with essential products to meet the tourist demand.

4

1.2.1. The symbiotic relation

Once the environment is recognized as an asset to the tourism industry, an emerging need for its preservation becomes apparent. Thus, tourism development is dependent on environment and therefore essential measures should be taken in order to maintain and even improve the quality of the natural resources. The General Secretary of the WTO suggests that there is a peaceful coexistence of tourism and the environment, which is illustrated by the following propositions (Savignac, 1992, p.2):

1 Travel promotes environmental awareness.
2 Well managed tourism is a good friend of the environment.
3 A successful tourism industry needs a high quality environment.

Consequently, "conservation and preservation of natural areas, archaeological sites and historic monuments have emerged as important spillover benefits of tourism. In turn,the protection of these prime tourist resources enhances and perpetuates tourism by maintaining its very foundation" (Mathieson and Wall, 1982, p.97).

Increased environmental concern is probably the most important benefit arising from tourism activities. Industry understands the importance of the surrounding environment as an asset for their operation and attempt to protect it. It is straight forward that in the absence of an attractive environment there would be little or less beneficial tourism. Consequently, "tourism development assigns natural resources to a determinate use and ensures that more harmful and perhaps polluting industrial development does not occur" (WTO, 1983a, p.18).

National Tourist Organizations also recognize the importance of natural resources for incoming tourism and, therefore, concentrate their efforts on preserving and enhancing attractions. A number of administrative and planning controls are often adopted while numerous projects are initiated. As a result, "tourism provides the incentive for 'cleaning up' the overall environment through control of air, water and noise pollution, littering and other environmental problems and for improving environmental aesthetics through landscaping programmes, appropriate building design, sign controls and better building maintenance" (Inskeep, 1991, p.343).

In addition, most of the tourists themselves are becoming increasingly **environmentally conscious**. Apart from the alternative forms of tourism which have traditionally been searching for unspoiled natural settings, the trend for 'green considerations' is emerging in the mass tourism market as well.

Moreover, the **protection, conservation, renovation and transformation of historical sites, buildings, heritage and monuments** has also been stimulated by tourism activity. As tourists express their demand for these sites they, in so doing, partly finance their preservation. Quite a lot of the existing attractions would never have survived without the tourists contributions (Mathieson and Wall, 1982, p.98, Inskeep, 1991, p.343, WTO, 1983a, p.29). Some of these building and sites have been completely renovated and transformed into new tourism facilities. Old castles in Mani, Greece, for example, have been transformed to small accommodation and catering units and therefore manage to survive and offer a superb

5

environmentally friendly activity.

In addition, tourism often stimulates the **creation of natural parks, manmade attractions and marine conservation units**. In various projects worldwide, millions of plants have been planted, while wild animals and rare species have been protected. The Everglades National Park in Florida,USA is an example of symbiosis on a far larger scale (Mathieson and Wall, 1982, p.99, WTO, 1983a, p.17, Inskeep, 1991, p.342).

Finally, the constant demand for **an unspoilt and well protected environment** is a leading movement within the tourism industry. Tourists are no longer prepared to spend their holidays at crowded, spoilt and unhealthy destinations. This trend influences local people who realize the importance of conservation to the economic success of tourism (Inskeep, 1991, p.344). As a consequence the preservation of the natural life in a destination is a prime consideration for the entire tourism industry and the bodies which regulate it.

1.2.2 The antagonistic relation

However, tourism has often been blamed for negative impacts on the environment. The accommodation of increasing tourism demand, especially during the peak tourist period, cannot normally be satisfied by the limited natural resources in a destination. Therefore, a number of problems are generated. Two major types of impacts can be illustrated: Those which are associated with structures (hotels, roads, and aircrafts) and those resulting from the tourists themselves (May, 1991, p.113). Table 1.1 illustrates a comprehensive list of the environmental damages which tourism or its excesses may cause, which has been prepared by the OECD (1980, p.24-25):

Another type of undesirable environmental impacts is the **visual pollution** which may result from several sources (Inskeep, 1991, p.345):

*Poorly designed hotels and other tourist facility buildings that are not compatible with the local architectural style and scale or well integrated into the natural environment,
*use of unsuitable building materials on external surfaces,
*badly planned layout of tourist facilities
*inadequate or inappropriate landscaping
*use of large and ugly advertising signs
*overhead utility (electric and telephone) lines and poles,
*obstruction of scenic view by development and,
*poor maintenance of buildings and landscaping.

The **increased danger of fire** is another environmental impact emerging from tourism activity. As more people are gathered in a destination the fire risks are greatly increased. Careless actions have ruined the vegetation and wildlife of particular areas. In addition, fire can arise from the variety of indirect tourist activities in a destination (WTO, 1983a, p.12).

6

Table 1.1
Impact of tourism on the environment:
short and long term effects

a Effects of pollution

I **Air pollution** mainly due to motor traffic and to the production and use of energy (More in Inskeep, 1991, p.344; WTO, 1983a, p.13; Mathieson and Wall, 1982, p.102).

II **Water pollution** (sea, lakes, rivers, springs), due to:
- discharge of untreated waste water due to the absence or malfunction of sewage treatment plants;
- discharge of solid waste from pleasure boats; and
- motor boating (discharge of hydrocarbons).
    (More in Inskeep, 1991, p.344; WTO, 1983a, p.9; Mathieson and Wall, 1982, p.103).

III **Pollution of sites** by littering (picnic, etc.) and the absence or inadequacy of waste disposal facilities (mainly household waste).

IV **Noise pollution**, mainly due to motor traffic or the use of certain vehicles used for recreational purposes (snow mobile, cross country motorcycles, motor boats, private planes, etc.) but also to the crowds of tourists themselves and the entertainments provided for them (publicity stands, beach contests etc.).

b Loss of Natural landscape: Agricultural and pastoral lands

I The growth of tourism brings with it the **construction of housing,** facilities and infrastructure **for tourists** which inevitably encroach on previously open spaces, ie natural landscapes or agricultural and pastoral lands.

II Some **valuable natural sites (beaches, forests) are often barred to public access** because they become privately owned by hotels or individuals.

c Destruction of flora and fauna

I The various kinds of pollution mentioned above, together with loss of natural landscape and agricultural and pastoral lands, are responsible for the **disappearance of some of the flora and fauna**.

II Excessive access to and use of natural sites also result in the **disappearance of various plants and animal species**, owning to tourist behaviour (trampling, excessive picking of fruit or flowers, carelessness, vandalism, or the kind of thoughtless conduct sometimes leading to forest fires, for example) (More in Mathieson and Wall, 1982, p.105).

d Degradation of landscape and of historic sites and monuments

I The installation of modern tourist related facilities and infrastructure often leads to **aesthetic degradation** of the landscape or sites: the style and architecture of such new installation may thus not always be in harmony or on a scale with traditional buildings, moreover tourist facility development is often disorderly and scattered, giving the landscape a 'moth eaten' look.

II An **excessive number of visitors to historical or exceptional natural sites** may also result in degradation (graffiti, pilfering etc.).

Table 1.1 (cont)
Impact of tourism on the environment:
short and long term effects

e   **Effects of Congestion**

  I The **concentration in time and space of tourists on holiday** leads to
     congestion of beaches, ski slopes, resorts and overloading of tourist
     amenities and infrastructure, thus causing considerable harm to the
     environment and detracting from the quality of life.

  II One major consequence is **traffic congestion** on roads at weekends and at the
     beginning and the end of peak holiday periods, leading to loss of leisure
     time, high fuel consumption and heavier air and noise pollution.

f   **Effects of conflict**

     During the tourist season, the **resident population** not only has to put up
     with the effects of such congestion, unknown during the rest of the year, but
     often has to change its way of life completely (faster work, pace, an extra
     occupation etc.), and to live cheeks by jowl with people of a different,
     largely urban kind in search of leisure pursuits. This 'coexistence' is by no
     means always easy and social tensions, particularly acute in places where
     there are many tourists, may occur.

g   **Effect of competition**

     Since the development of tourism uses up a great deal of space and siphons
     off a fairly large proportion of local labour, **competition is bound to occur,**
     usually to the detriment of traditional activities, (for instance, less land
     under cultivation and less manpower means agriculture). Competition of this.
     kind generally tends to result in the exclusive practice of tourist related
     activities, which may be economically undesirable for the regions concerned
     (More in Inskeep, 1991, p.347).

Source : OECD, 1980, p.23-24.

   However, all these impacts of tourism activity on the environment return as a
boomerang against the tourism industry. People avoid the ruined destinations
and head to new, unspoilt areas where they can enjoy their holidays in a safer
way. A comprehensive analysis of the environmental impacts of tourism is
offered in Jenner and Smith (1992, p.13-40) while a general overview of
environmental conservation in the context of the global economic activity is
outlined in Dasmann (1984).

1.3   Five major actors influencing the environmental assets at destination

Most of the natural resources in a destination are public. They rarely belong to
someone and they are available for the existence and recreation of their users.
In this chapter, a five actors framework is adopted in order to analyze the
environmental impacts of tourism, namely: locals, tourists, local tourism
enterprises, Tour Operators, and National Tourism Organizations (Figure 1.1).

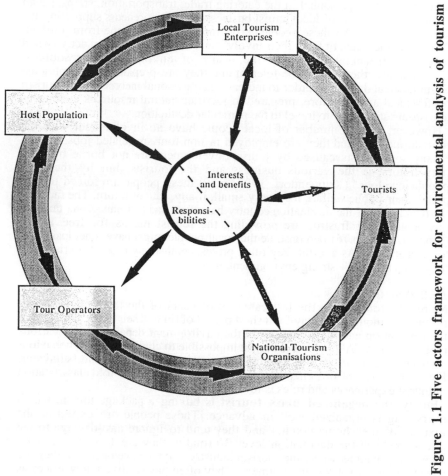

Figure 1.1 Five actors framework for environmental analysis of tourism

Local Tourism
Enterprises

Host Population

Interests
and benefits

Tourists

Responsi-
bilities

Tour Operators

National Tourism
Organisations

9

Two major users of the destination environment can be initially identified: the local people and the visitors or tourists who stay in the destination for a short period of time. Thus, the natural resources should be able to satisfy the demand for both. The problems occur when there are insufficient resources to support the demand and when users act carelessly against the environment.

1.3.1 Local people

Local people can be divided into two main categories. Firstly, people who have a direct relation with tourism, i.e. people who are serving or supplying the tourism industry, personnel in the catering trade, transportation, shops, travel agencies, proprietors of local tourist business and entrepreneurs supporting the tourism industry. All these people derive most of their income from tourism. Therefore, they benefit from their involvement within the tourism activity and receive a financial return on the usage of environmental resources. Consequently, they tend to be tolerant and they are prepared to accept some environmental damage in order to increase their personal income. Most tourism professional are, therefore, prepared to sacrifice natural resources as long as tourists are still happy to travel to the particular destination.

However, a great number of local people have no involvement with the tourism industry and they are employed in non-tourism related jobs. As the "many social costs caused by tourist development are not borne by their perpetrators, ie the various business and the tourists, but by the local population alone" (Krippendorf, 1987, p.50) these people are forced to lose part of their public welfare for a very small, if any, rate of return. The fact that the population of the destination country has often had to finance, via taxation payments, the infrastructure providing the tourist means for free access (Sinclair, 1992, p.76) demonstrate that local people might have a net loss from tourism activity. As a result they often protest against any type of tourism and they often tend to be strong environmentalists.

1.3.2 Tourists

Moreover, tourists are the last category of users of the local environment resources although they stay for a short period of time. Their expectations from the destination and their impacts on the environment depend on the various types of tourists. Although it is almost impossible to classify tourism behaviour accurately, there are various typologies describing tourist roles and behaviour. For the purposes of this chapter Cohen's (1972, p.167) four-fold classification of tourist experiences and roles is followed.

Firstly, the **organized mass tourist** is buying a package tour in which everything is organized well in advance. These people are expecting the luxuries of their home country and they tend to ignore any damage to the environment at the destination level. Normally, they are travelling to well known destinations where the tourism industry is quite developed and they are used to a not-so-natural environment. They often pay relatively low prices as most arrangements have been made through powerful Tour Operators who manage to achieve large discounts. As a consequence they pay little or no contribution to the 'social costs' involved in their consumption of the natural resources.

Secondly, the **individual mass tourists** are similar to the previous ones, except that their tour is not rigidly packaged. Although all arrangements have been made through travel agencies, there is some flexibility and some decisions are taken independently. More environmentally conscious than the previous categories, the individual mass tourist are usually going to a destination in the early days of its tourism development. They are looking for the similar security level offered by Tour Operators and they are prepared to accept a little environmental pollution. These tourists have slightly better behaviour towards the environment while they often make a greater contribution to the local economy which tends to balance the social costs.

Thirdly, the **explorers** arrange their trip independently. Comfortable accommodation and reliable means of transportation are often required. Explorers are usually choosing destinations with little or no tourism development. As soon as the minimal facilities are provided, they are happy to visit the areas. They tend to avoid ruined destinations and they are environmentally conscious. However, these tourists normally have similar environmental impacts as the local people while they tend to have a higher expenditure. Therefore, they partially contribute to the preservation of the environment and they might have positive impacts.

Finally, the **drifters**, make all their travel arrangements independently while they have a tendency to meet local people, eat local food and live in the 'native way'. They rarely travel to mass tourism destinations and they tend to discover new pioneer destinations. Drifters have minimum environmental impacts and they often contribute to its preservation by involving themselves in local environmental projects. As almost all their expenditure stays within the destination, they probably have greater contribution to the local economy per unit of expenditure than any other type of tourists.

As a result of environmental consciousness, a great number of alternative forms of tourism have been developed in the last decade. Various names are utilized to demonstrate the typologies of the environmentally friendly tourist. 'Green', 'soft', 'eco', 'sustainable', 'responsible' or 'alternative' tourism are some of the terms used in the literature (Nash and Butler, 1990, p.263). Ecotourism is a form of "tourism which directly or indirectly promotes conservation and supports sustainable economic development" (Pleumarom, 1990, p.12). Goodall (1992, p.61) suggests that "sustainable tourism requires that the demand of increasing numbers of tourists are satisfied in a manner which continues to attract them, whilst meeting the needs of the host population with improved standards of living, yet safeguarding the destination environment and cultural heritage". All of these types of tourism are, therefore, against mass tourism which reacts regardless of the environmental impact. Brackenbury (1991, p.6) suggests that "it is now fashionable to criticize mass tourism. Research has revealed that consumers do expect destinations to be clean and 'green' and will make choices to avoid places that are perceived to fail to meet this image".

However, the innocence of the alternative types of tourism is often questioned (Cohen, 1987). On the one hand, researchers suggest that tourism trade uses the green issues as a prime message in their campaign simply because 'it sells'. Quite a lot of authors have been suggesting that "responsible tourism seems to be adopted more as a marketing tool rather than as a sensitive planning mechanism" (Wheeller, 1991, p.94 and 1992, p.141).

11

In addition, some enterprises try to avoid the 'hysterical' legislative restrictions and prohibitions by integrating environmental issues into their business policies and publications. "Ironically those who contribute most to environmental damage, are becoming the most active elements in the field of tourism and environment" (Pleumarom, 1990, p.14). The fact that the International Federation of Tour Operators (IFTO) is trying to control the HELMEPA, which is responsible for rewarding the cleanest beaches with the 'Blue Flag' and the 'Golden Stars', is probably a good example of this case.

The third criticism is that alternative tourism, essentially, opens the destination to mass tourism. As soon as alternative tourists arrive to the destination they stimulate their friends to visit the area and the destination ends up as being just another mass tourism area. Wheeller (1991, p.92) suggests that these types of tourism inevitably and inexorably pave "the way for the package tour" in the "new, exotic, unspoiled and vulnerable" destinations. That explains why alternative tourism is often referred to as 'Trojan Horse' (Butler, 1989 and 1990). The mechanics of the mass tourism invasion example are thoroughly analyzed in Allen (1985) and Josephides (1992).

1.3.3 Tourism enterprises and supporting industries in a destination level

The environmental impacts should also be examined with respect to the spectrum of economic relations which underline the tourism industry. The different parties involved therefore, should be examined and their effects on the natural resources should be illustrated. Hitherto, two major actors, the locals and the tourists, have been investigated. Three more actors which comprise the major business forces of the tourism industry, namely local tourism enterprises, international travel trade and particularly the tour operators, and the public sector or National Tourism Organizations, should be investigated.

Normally, tourist destinations are composed of a wide network of small and medium tourism enterprises (SMTE) which independently offer a great variety of tourism, hospitality and leisure products. These SMTE provide accommodation, catering, entertainment, transportation and financial services for the tourists. Quite often SMTE have an unfriendly behaviour towards the environment, as they attempt to maximize their financial benefits in the short term. Especially, if the businessman/woman is not a local investor, his/her behaviour might be described in the following way: "His investment is constructed for maximum capacity or density as close to the environmentally highly valued attractions point as possible; his contribution is often for high rate of depreciation and he aims for maximum utilization of his facilities. Aiming for recovering his capital quickly, maintenance expenditure is often kept to a minimum and capital gains are realize in the shortest possible time" (OECD, 1980, p.55). In general, the minimization of costs and the maximization of benefits principles govern SMTE operations. However, often investments or costs are involved in order to maintain the quality of the environment and to preserve the natural resources. Sewage systems are a classical example of conflict between the short term cost and the environmental conservation. The environmentally unfriendly behaviour of the tourism enterprises often results in the rapid deterioration of the physical and environmental capital at the destination, while it rarely achieves a reasonable return on the social cost generated by using the public natural sources.

As a result the enterprises may maximize their short term benefits at the expense of public welfare. In the long term, however, they are losing their business and their ability to attract up-market visitors. Consequently, they are forced to operate with lower profit margins and thus make small contribution to local wealth. Buhalis (1991, p.69) suggests that one of the major strategic threats for the SMTE is environmental pollution as it might jeopardize their long term survival.

In addition, the environmental damage, so often discussed in articles, relates only to the direct environmental damage. The full environmental cost of tourism development, like the full economic activity, can only be truly estimated if the direct and indirect impacts are assessed. If tourism development is 'sold' to destinations on the basis of its strong backward linkages with other sectors of the economy, then the environmental damage emanating from these supporting industries, as a result of tourism activity must also be brought into the equation.

1.3.4 Tour operators and the environment

Tour Operators have played a controversial role with respect to the environment in the destination level. Firstly, they are regarded as responsible for the **tourist concentration** in particular resorts.Since they operate under the 'economies of scale' principle they attempt to maximize the number of tourists in a resort in order to gain economies of large scale production. Consequently, Tour Operators are often blamed for sending enormous numbers of tourists to destinations and therefore overuse and abuse the natural resources of the area.

Secondly, as a result of this action they are normally stimulating a **rapid and irrational development** where no consideration of the environment is taken. Majorca is probably a good example where "local people were able to exercise little influence over the pace of development. What the Tour Operators wanted, the Tour Operators got - throw the hotels up quickly, worry about sewage, water supply, roads and other amenities later. Who cared about architecture or niceties such as fire regulations" (Barrett, 1992a, p.43).

Stimulation of **the growth of tourism supply** has occurred through the means of prepayment or 'commitment' of a bulk number of rooms in hotels under construction. As a result, hoteliers rush to expand their properties and, therefore the total capacity of the destination increases at very rapidly. The expansion of supply increases the competition between the local hotelier which effectively reduces the prices of the tourism products. Thus, tourists are able to get much cheaper holidays and therefore, they do not pay adequately for the natural resources they use.

Thirdly, Tour Operators may be in **direct conflict with environmental preservation**. Quite often they demand amenities which cannot be met by the natural resources of the destination or they stimulate environmental consuming activities. A recent example of such a conflict is the closure of the Zakynthos airport at night by the Greek Tourism Authorities, during the breeding season of the endangered loggerhead turtle from Summer 1993. The noise and the lights of the airport confuse the baby loggerheads and instead of scampering to the safety of the sea, they head inland to almost certain death. However, the Tour Operators' Study Group (TOGS) was not prepared to find alternative solutions and suggested that if the Greeks would ban night flights to Zakynthos a 50% reduction in tourism arrivals should be expected. The inflexibility of the international airports timetables in the countries of origin and specifically the unwillingness of the British Authorities to allow night flights into Gatwick, Luton, or Manchester airports led the TOSG to suggest that if the Greeks want tourists they should not ban night flight and consequently they should kill the baby loggerheads (Ottaway, 1992).

Finally, relatively few Tour Operators have made significant contributions to conservation of the natural areas to which they offer tours. Some park managers, surveyed during the WWF-Germany study, often complained that private operators took protected areas for granted (Jenner and Smith, 1992, p.156) and they were unprepared to do anything to support the environment. Instead their policy, hitherto, is to drain a destination and then pass to another (Allen, 1985, p.86 and Josephides, 1992). Brackenbury (1992, p.26) suggests that "the tourist industry developed its Magalufs and when they became too down market moved on to Greece, Turkey, Africa and the Caribbean".

1.3.5. National tourist authorities - the public sector

Traditionally, National and Regional Tourist Authorities are responsible for the destination's tourism planning and development. Aiming to improve the balance of payments for the particular country they take all essential steps to attract tourists. Quite often the assumption that "more tourist arrivals mean more economic benefits for the destination" is proven not to be the case. As a consequence, NTOs have to create and execute a strategic plan for the destination, where its aims and environmental concerns should be explained.

However, since most NTOs actions have been limited in maintaining the trends in tourist arrivals and bednights, as well as in promoting the destination abroad, they often downgrade the importance of the environment in the destination. In addition, until recently, they avoid getting involved with individual tourism projects, leaving the environmental control to the rest of the public sector. "The absence of planning and failure by the public sector to assume responsibilities leaving private enterprises with the task of developing tourism according to the logic of the marketplace, which does not always reflect the interests of the community has been responsible for most of the negative results of tourism development" (WTO, 1983b, p.10).

However, private sector operators in the tourism industry are primarily concerned with the short term profit and loss account of their particular business and, hence there is no obvious and direct need to take on board conservation and preservation issues. The end result of private sector led development, particularly on the Mediterranean Seaboard, is irreversible damage which not only reduces the quality of life of the host population, but also affects the consumer's welfare by reducing choice in future time periods and producers' profit and loss account in the long term. No form of friendly persuasion will alter the producer's economic behaviour. Therefore, the solution must rest within the close cooperation of the public and private sectors to create a sustainable development framework in which the producers are required to operate.

1.4 Trends/responsibilities/future

The economic aspects of the environmental impacts of tourism has been analyzed. An examination of the current trends on the different actors involved, along with an outline of their responsibilities is attempted in this section. The main principle which should govern the action throughout the tourism industry cannot be different than the maximization of effort to preserve and improve the biggest asset of the tourism industry - the environment.

Ethical issues, such as the responsibility to the next generation are combined with pure economic practices, such as the long term survival and return on investment in order to provide a pragmatic approach and a viable model of tourism development. It is more likely that environmental damage associated with tourism development may be determined and can be reduced by the degree of public and private sector cooperation and coordination.

Krippendorf proposes 10 principles for achieving a tourism development in harmony with nature (Lanquar, 1990, p.51-51):

1   Recognize the need to take action
2   Support weak elements/destinations/communities
3   Set the objectives of development in a restrictive way
4   Exercise control over property and land and pursue an active policy towards landownership and land development
5   Adopt a policy of restrictions on materials and facilities according to integrated objectives
6   Protect nature and the countryside effectively by managing it dynamically in a way in which nature can evolve positively
7   Strengthen agriculture and forestry and use as allies
8   Widen the range of economic activities
9   Help preserve local architecture, traditions and cultural and folk heritage
10 Put tourism marketing and promotion at the service of integration

These principles could probably act as a platform for each particular destination, enterprise or individual in order to incorporate the environmental concern in their strategic planning. More specifically, an outline of trends, responsibilities and actions for most of the parties involved in the tourism activities is provided.

1.4.1 Trends and responsibilities for local people

Most host populations should realize that their environment, apart from supporting their survival and enjoyment, is the primary attraction for the tourists. Therefore, they should try to maintain and improve it. Ways of reducing the natural resources consumption should be identified and promoted amongst the population. Of course, the nature of public source usage by tourists should be understood. A certain amount of tolerance might be required, especially during peak periods, when congestion and probably competition is occurring for the limited natural resources.

However, local people should make sure that they can get a sufficient return on the usage of their public facilities. Moreover, tourism activities should offer a contribution to the maintenance and improvement of the natural resources.

The financial benefits might be direct income for people related to the tourism industry and indirect for people with unrelated to tourism jobs. A fair contribution of the financial benefits among the host population should be ensured.

1.4.2 Trends and responsibilities for tourists

Evidence suggests that modern tourists are quite environmentally conscious. They may avoid areas with saturated tourism development and littered beaches. In addition to this, a responsibility is emerging for new tourists to behave respectably towards the environment. Krippendorf (1987, p.132) offers the following description of the mature tourist: "The mature tourist is always a critical consumer - both in everyday life and in making decisions about his holidays. He is discerning in his choices of what to take from the many travel offers and critical towards himself. He analyses, compares and examines before making decision what to buy. He tries to see through the seductive promises made by tourist publicity. He chooses his travel destination advisedly. He doesn't accept the philosophy of tourist trade competition which says that prices are more important than countries. He considers the consequences that his visits and his behaviour may have, as well as who can benefit from or be damaged by his journey. He doesn't always go for the lowest price, and once there, doesn't always try to pay even less or bargain harder, because he knows that low prices are often the result of exploitation of other people. He applies the idea underlying the action "jute instead of plastic" to travel. This implies that he chooses those forms of travel which are least harmful to the environment, which are least disturbing for the people and cultures of the tourist areas and from which they get the greatest benefit. He spends his money on those products and services about which he knows the origin and who will profit from their sale. He observes these principles choosing accommodation, food, means of transport, visiting institutions, buying souvenirs. He takes time to prepare his journey and he stays as long as possible in the places he visits so that the experience may be a lasting one an that he may really identify with it. The mature tourist resists the thoughtless exploitation and standardization that are part and parcel of the usual tourist business. He opposes the big machine by trying, at least in his personal behaviour, not to exploit but to assume responsibility. The critical tourist will increasingly find the courage, even during his holidays, to protect against activities which blatant disregard all these principles".

As there is a growing international tendency towards these prototypes, it is believed that a new, experienced, sophisticated, demanding, and environmentally conscious tourist is emerging in the market. This tourist will be accommodated through individual arrangements and will probably make a large contribution to the tourism industry and the destination.

However, on the other hand, mass tourism will continue to grow. People will always benefit from the security offered by Tour Operators and enjoy their low prices in the market. The low-income segments of the market will increasingly search for special offers. But these people will be directed to the well established - saturated tourist destinations, which cannot easily attract other types of tourism.

16

1.4.3 Tourism enterprises' and supporting industries' responsibilities

An alternative approach of operating tourism related enterprises should be employed. The size of the enterprise needs to take in consideration the destination's carrying capacity limits. Emphasis should be given in the aesthetics of the buildings and the decoration, which should me made according to the local architecture and culture. Furthermore, necessary expenditures for environmental preservation should be incorporated into the feasibility study of any prospective tourism enterprise.

Long term survival and profitability should be one of the major strategic directions of tourism enterprises (Buhalis, 1991, p.86; OECD, 1980, p.53). Although these directions can often be in conflict with environmental conservation, enterprises should realize that one of the major factors for survival, in the long term, is to maintain and develop the destination area, particularly its environmental assets. This would enhance tourist satisfaction and, consequently, will ensure the prosperity of tourism enterprises. These principles should also be applied to those enterprises indirectly related to tourism, which support and supply the tourism industry.

In addition, the enterprises' responsibility to the local people should be emphasized. As tourism enterprises utilize the public natural resources in order to make profits, they are ethically obliged to return some of this 'value' back to host community. In this way, a sustainable economic development will benefit both local people and enterprises.

Close cooperation between tourism enterprises at the destination level is regarded as essential for harmonic development. Buhalis (1991, p.97) suggested the emergence of a supporting agency for local tourism enterprises, which would provide technical support and advice. In cooperation with the public sector, this agency could ensure that all steps are taken to maintain and improve the natural resources of the destination. Joint projects should be encouraged and the coordination of the various organization and authorities involved could be facilitated.

Scientific and technological developments are expected to make a major contribution to environmental preservation. Therefore, "the resultant increase in environmental quality will stimulate demand and supply for leisure activities in natural environments" (Moutinho, 1992, p.14 and Coccossis and Paparairis, 1992, p.3). New technology has an important role to play by providing "innovations resulting in the substantial reduction of energy consumption such as new materials, construction techniques and computerized energy management systems"(WTO, 1988, p.27). The less energy consumed, the less pollution created. "Water recycling technology will also prove vital important as almost all countries, not just those with an existing acute water shortage, will face a clean water crisis in the near future based on current consumption patterns"(Jenner and Smith, 1992, p.169).

In conclusion, Krippendorf (1987, p.138) calls "on all suppliers of tourist services to acknowledge their responsibility towards travellers, the host population and the environment, to state clearly what contribution they are prepared to make to a more human tourism and what regulations they are willing to observe. I propose that they should formulate and make a public code of practise and the principles of their internal and external business conduct. Not in a few beautifully worded and vague sentences, but in concrete and practicable policy statements, to which they would be answerable".

1.4.4 Tour Operators trends, responsibilities and future

A new 'green' trend has been observed recently in the Tour Operators' behaviour towards the environment. Thomson Holidays, for example, has for the first time published the manifestation of the company's new found environmental concern. 'Caring for your holiday environment' is a small section given a prominent billing in the brochure, offering an eight-point guide to greener travel (Figure 1.3). It reminds prospective travellers not to litter, to save water and energy, to respect the peace and quiet of others and so on. The brochure goes on to suggests that the chapter used is made from trees grown as "a commercial renewable resource: for every tree felled at least two are planted to replace it" (Barrett, 1992b, p.39). Moreover, the Association of Independent Tour Operators (AITO) provides 'Green Tips' throughout their brochure while other companies produce codes of environmentally acceptable tourist behaviour.

A number of reasons can explain the tour operators movement towards environmental friendly tourism. Firstly, the **growing public concern on 'green' issues**, especially during their leisure time. It is suggested that the destinations which do not satisfy the 'clean and green' features will become unattractive (Brackenbury, 1991, p.6). Although tour operators use the 'green' image, they keep sending people to 'landscape disfiguring tower block hotels' the fact that the environmental concerns are published increase the sales (Barrett, 1992b, p.39).

Secondly, the **new EC directive** (990/314/EC) on Package Travel, Package Holidays and Package Tours (to be implemented from 31 December 1992) which clearly imposes certain responsibilities on tour operators (and/or travel agents) regarding their products, will encourage European tour Operators to be more environmentally conscious (Goodall, 1992, p.71 and Barrett, 1992b, p.39)

Thirdly, and probably more importantly, **Tour Operators are running out of destinations**. Brackenbury (1992, p.26) suggests, that it is no longer possible to shift destinations as soon as one becomes saturated and down-market. "The reason is simply because they have nowhere else to move on to". That essentially means that "the places they have got, which they've invested an awful lot of time developing, are the ones that they are going to stick with if they are going to have a business for the future. That lies at the centre of the concern with environmental issues. It's nothing to do with altruism and long term views on the planet. The only way we can make this business work is if people are satisfied when they get there.It's entirely to do with self interest".

1.4.5 Responsibilities for public sector

The public sector in general, and the National Tourism Organizations in particular, should realize the importance of the environment as an asset for the destination. In addition, the significance of natural resources on tourism decision making and especially in destination selection has to be recognized and understood.

OBJECTIVE	Formulated by :	Implemented by :
(i) Development of environmentally friendly tourism products, e.g. eco-tours, walking and cycling holidays	Destination tourism boards and offices. Individual tourism firms, e.g. tour operators, hoteliers	Firms supplying tourism products, i.e. tour operators, hoteliers, transport carriers, souvenir shops, etc.
(ii) Compliance with environmental legislation and development of reasonable and workable environmental regulations, e.g. aircraft noise levels at take-off	Destination (national) public sector agencies and planning authorities	Tourism firms (monitored via public sector inspection)
(iii) Reduction of any negative environmental impacts of current tourism activities and avoidance of such impacts from proposed tourism developments, e.g. installation of sewage treatment in place of disposal of untreated sewage directly into the sea; phasing out use of CFC-based aerosols and detergents / cleaners containing phosphates	Destination planning agencies and tourism firms	Destination public agencies and tourism firms jointly
(iv) Increasing the efficiency of resource use, including waste minimisation, and substitution of environmentally benign inputs and equipment wherever feasible, e.g. by recycling rubbish such as paper, glass, cooking oil; tourist promotional literature, etc. printed on recycled paper; consideration of energy efficiency of buildings	Tourism firms	Tourism firms, e.g. hoteliers, restauranteurs, car hire firms, tour operators, theme parks, zoos, etc.
(v) Fostering of an understanding of environmental issues amongst tourism entrepreneurs and employees, destination residents and tourists, e.g. codes of conduct advising tourists on behaviour at a destination issued by tour operators	Destination tourism boards and planning authorities Tour operators	Destination tourist information services and offices Tour operators

Source: Goodall and Stabler 1992

Figure 1.2 Sustainable tourism policy objectives: formulation and implementation

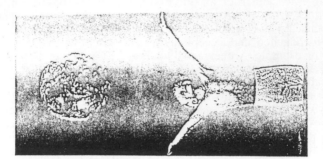

Caring for Your Holiday Environment

You can help us care for your holiday environment. You'll enjoy your holiday more - and you'll be helping to keep a pleasant resort preserved for future visitors.

○ DON'T LITTER

Discarded rubbish is an eye-sore, so even if you see others litter, be sure to take yours away for proper disposal.

○ DO SAVE WATER

Water is a precious resource in hot climates, so take care to use water sparingly.

○ DON'T WASTE ENERGY

Always switch off lights and electrical or gas appliances when not in use.

○ DO GUARD AGAINST FIRE

In hot, dry countries, a carelessly discarded cigarette or unquenched picnic fire could easily start a fire.

○ REMEMBER THE COUNTRYSIDE CODE

Fasten all gates, keep to paths when crossing farmland, avoid damaging fences, walls or hedges, and respect the life of the countryside.

○ DO RESPECT THE RIGHTS OF OTHERS

We all enjoy some peace and quiet on holiday. Loud noise can be annoying, so please think of your fellow guests.

○ DO PROTECT LOCAL WILDLIFE

Don't collect coral, shells, reef animals or other marine 'treasures'. Remember many animals are protected by law.

Please don't buy souvenirs made of tortoiseshell, ivory, reptile skins, furs or exotic feathers.

If you have any comments or suggestions, please let us hear from you. Write to:

The Environment Manager – SS
Thomson Holidays
Greater London House
Hampstead Road
London NW1 7SD

The paper used in the production of this brochure has been carefully selected with due consideration for the environment. It is made from trees grown as a commercial, renewable resource: for every tree felled at least two are planted to replace it.

Source: Thomson Summer Brochure 1993

Figure 1.3 Thomson's environmental reminder

In order to estimate the full environmental impact of tourism development it would be possible to construct an environmental index based on an input-output framework, which could demonstrate the environmental requirements associated with tourism demand. The basic framework of input - output is well documented and accepted by researchers in the field of economics (see for example Archer and Fletcher, 1990). True, it has its limitations as any modelling technique does, but it has proven itself to be a robust and adaptable tool for impact analyses and answering "What if...?" policy issues. The conversion of this framework to an environmental model is no easy task. It would be necessary to estimate the environmental impact of each sector of the economy in order to produce a matrix of environmental impact coefficients which could then be driven by tourism demand (expenditure) and the intersectoral linkages within the economy. If such a model is constructed it will enable researchers to identify the primary perpetrators of negative environmental impacts and, in the shortterm, minimize them by seeking alternative production channels and, in the long term, by finding alternative production techniques. For instance, if particular forms of tourism activities are associated with lower environmental impact damage at the direct and indirect level of impact than others, it may be possible to focus marketing attention on that segment of the market in preference to other segments which may have lower direct environmental impacts but overall larger environmental impacts when the knock-on effects are taken into account.

Moreover, National Tourist Authorities should make every effort in order to maintain and enhance the natural resources. A shift towards the environmentally friendly tourist who is prepared to pay for the usage of the public facilities and contribute to resource preservation should be undertaken. Such a policy would to a degree, ensure that a 'price' is charged for environmental resources, that funds are available for environmental services and that the rate of development is consistent with physical and fiscal resources available in the region. In addition, a number of incentives should be offered to reward the best environmental friendly enterprises, destinations, villages and tourists. The publicity achieved through these incentives could stimulate the rest of the enterprises to adopt environmentally conscious procedures and thereby contribute to environmental preservation.

Finally, National Tourist Organizations should launch promotional campaigns, to both local people and tourists, explaining why they should behave responsibly and what would be the direct benefit to them. Part of this task could be achieved through the conventional educational system where people can learn from their early years 'the code of the good tourist'. Figure 1.2 illustrates the sustainable tourism policy objectives among with the responsibilities for its formulation and implementation. In this sense NTOs should have a coordinating and enforcing role.

1.6   A word of conclusion

In conclusion, tourists' 'right to holidays' can some times be in conflict with 'the right for improving the quality of life' of the host population. As people in developing countries and particularly in the South, are in vulnerable economic positions and desperate to improve their balance of payments they are often forced to sell some of their natural resources to temporary visitors. In return, the tourism industry's development usually stimulates a general economic growth within the destination. As a result of this growth there are numerous, both positive and negative, environmental impacts on the destination. This chapter suggests that the environmental impacts of tourism can be generated by the activities of both directly and indirectly related economic sectors to the tourism industry. Consequently, an integrated examination of the economy and the environment should be undertaken.

The environmental impacts of tourism can be assessed with an input - output model, similar to the models used for the economic impacts analysis, which could demonstrate the environmental requirements associated with tourism demand. Clearly, given the formidable difficulties associated with constructing an environmental index for even one sector of the economy, the task of building a sectoral environmental interdependence model for the whole economy is not one that is likely to be taken on easily by researchers, but is, nevertheless, an essential ingredient for successful tourism development into the next century.

Furthermore, through an economic analysis of the actors influencing the environmental resources in a destination level, it is argued that natural resources should be regarded as an invaluable asset and they need to be preserved and improved. Closer cooperation between the private and the public sectors is essential in order to achieve this task.

Finally, users of environmental resources should pay for the 'social cost' of their activities. A balance or equilibrium between the various and sometimes conflicting interests associated with tourism activity should be identified, for the benefit of tourists, host populations and the tourism industry in general.

References

Allen, T. (1985), Marketing by a small Tour Operator in a market dominated by big operators, *European Journal of Marketing*, vol.19 (5), pp.83-90.

Archer, B. and Fletcher, J. (1990), Multiplier Analysis in Tourism, In *Cahier de Tourisme*, Centre des Hautes Etudes Touristiques, Universite de Droit, d'Economie et de Sciences

Barrett, F. (1992a), Majorca: sceptred or septic isle?, *The Independent*, Saturday 6 June, p.43.

Barrett, F. (1992b), A case of enlarging the small prints, *The Independent*, Saturday 17 October,p.39.

Brackenbury, M. (1991), The preferences of tourists in the European Market, Presentation in Conference: "Strategic Development of European Tourism towards 2000", Crete, 18-20 May.

Brackenbury, M. (1992), The broad mind of travel, Monday interview, *Financial Times*, 24 August, pp.26.

Buhalis, D., (1991), Strategic marketing and management for the small and medium tourism enterprises in the periphery of the European Community. A case study for the Aegean Islands in Greece, M.Sc. Dissertation, University of Surrey, UK.

Butler, R. (1989), Alternative Tourism: Pious Hope or Trojan Horse, World Leisure and Recreation, vol.31 (4), pp.9-17.

Butler, R., 1990, Alternative Tourism: Pious Hope or Trojan Horse, Journal of Travel Research, vol. 28(3), pp.40-45.

Coccosis, H. and Parpairis, A. (1992), Assessing the interactions between environment and tourism: Case study of the island of Myconos, Proceedings of IV World Congress of Regional Science International, University of Balearic Islands, Palma de Mallorca, 26-29 May.

Cohen, E. (1972), Towards a sociology of international tourism, Social Research, vol. 39, pp.164-182.

Cohen, E. (1987), Alternative Tourism - A critique, Tourism Recreation Research, vol. 12(2), pp.13-18.

Dasmann, R., 1984, Environmental Conservation, 5th ed., John Wiley & Sons, New York.

Eber, S. (ed.) (1992), Beyond the Green Horizon: Principles for sustainable tourism, World Wide Fund for Nature, England.

Goodall, B. (1992), Environmental auditing for tourism, in Cooper, C. and Lockwood, A. (eds.), *Progress in Tourism, Recreation and Hospitality Management*, vol.4, Belhaven Press, London, pp.60-74.

Goodall, B. and Stabler, M. (1992), Environmental Auditing in the quest for sustainable tourism: The destination perspective, *Conference proceedings: Tourism in Europe*, Newcastle Polytechnic, 8-10 July, pp.G1-G13.

Inskeep, E. (1991), *Tourism planning: an integrated and sustainable development approach*, New York, Van Nostrand.

Jenner, P. and Smith, C. (1992), The tourism industry and the environment: *Special report No 2453*, The Economist Intelligence Unit, London.

Josephides, N. (1992), Environmental concerns - what's in it for the tourism industry, Conference Proceedings, *Tourism and the Environment: Challenges and Choices for the 90's*, The Queen Elizabeth II Conference Centre, London, 16-17 November, pp. 51-56.

Krippendorf, J. (1987), *The holiday makers: Understanding the impact of leisure and travel*, Heinemann, London.

Lanquar, R. (1990), Integration of the environment in tourism planning for the Mediterranean coast, *Tourism Reports*, vol.2, pp.49-62.

Mathieson, A. and Wall, G. (1982), *Tourism: economic, physical and social impacts*, Longman, London.

May, V. (1991), Tourism environment and development values, *Tourism Management*, vol. 12 (2), pp.112-118.

Moutinho, L. (1992), Tourism: the near and future future from 1990s to 2030s or from sensavision TV to skycycles, Conference proceedings: Tourism in Europe, Newcastle Polytechnic, 8-10 July.

Nash, D. and Butler, R. (1990), Towards sustainable tourism, *Tourism Management*, vol.11 (3), pp.263-264.

Nijkamp, P. (1992), Regional science and environmental sustainability, Proceedings of IV World Congress of Regional Science International, University of Balearic Islands, Palma de Mallorca, 26-29 May.

OECD (1980), The impact of tourism on the environment: General reports, Paris.

Ottaway, M. (1992), Turtle Power, *The Sunday Times*, 28 June.

Pleumarom, A. (1990), Alternative Tourism: A viable solution?, Contours, vol. 4(8), pp.12-15.

Savignac, A. (1992), Address by the Secretary General of the World Tourism Organisation to the United Nation Conference on Environment and Development, Rio de Janeiro. Brazil, 4 June.

Sinclair, T. (1992), Tourism economic development and the environment: Problems and policies, in Cooper, C. and Lockwood, A. (eds.), *Progress in Tourism, Recreation and Hospitality Management*, vol.4, Belhaven Press, London, pp.75-81.

Wheeller, B. (1991), Tourism's troubled times: Responsible tourism is not the answer, *Tourism Management*, vol. 12(2), pp.91-96.

Wheeller, B. (1992), Alternative tourism-a deceptive ploy, in Cooper, C. and Lockwood, A. (eds.), *Progress in Tourism, Recreation and Hospitality Management*, vol.4, Belhaven Press, London, pp.140-145.

WTO (1983a), Workshop on environmental aspects of tourism: Joint UNEP and WTO meeting, Madrid, 5-8 July.

WTO (1983b), Study of tourism's contribution to protecting the environment, Madrid.

WTO (1988), Guidelines for the transfer of new technologies in the field of tourism, Madrid.

2 The environmental internalities of tourism: Theoretical analysis and policy implications

H. Briassoulis

2.1 Introduction

The enthusiasm of the 1960s and 1970s with the economic benefits brought about by tourism development was soon followed by a growing concern about its detrimental economic, environmental and sociocultural impacts. The environmental impacts of tourism especially, are currently being intensively discussed as they represent another facet of contemporary environmental problems. Several analyses and studies have appeared since the late 1970s on the relationship between tourism and the environment (OECD 1980; Mathieson and Wall 1982; Farrell and McLellan 1987; Farrell and Runyan 1991; Briassoulis 1992). The main thesis of most of them is that tourism causes negative environmental externalities on other economic activities and on human welfare. The following analysis will attempt to demonstrate, however, that several of these externalities are not external to tourism but, on the contrary, are internal to it, hence the term 'internalities'. The purpose of the chapter is to conceptualize the issue of tourism's internalities, to offer a theoretical analysis of the tourism-environment relationship in this perspective and to suggest appropriate planning and policy approaches to achieve sustainable tourism development. The first section defines tourism and discusses its characteristics and differences from conventional economic sectors. The second section analyzes the tourism-environment relationship and clarifies the distinction between the environmental externalities and internalities of tourism. The third section outlines the basic shape of public and private sector policies needed for effective tourism planning and management. Finally, future research directions are discussed in the last section.

2.2 Tourism - characteristics and particularities

Tourism involves a complex of interlinked and interdependent activities, the most important of which are: travel, accommodation, catering, sightseeing and entertainment, shopping and services (Baud-Bovy and Lawson 1977; UNEP 1982). Hence, tourism cannot be considered either as an economic sector or as an industry although both terms are widely used for lack of better ones. This

25

analysis posits that tourism is a **complex** of economic activities whose **collective** operation determines the quantity and quality of the tourist product provided in an area. Several supply- and demand-side particularities of tourism are presented in the following and tourism is contrasted to conventional economic sectors to support the thesis that only the conceptualization of tourism as an activity complex avoids misplaced and misspecified analyses of tourism-related issues, including the tourism-environment relationship. An important consequence of this conceptualization is that the analytical tools of mainstream environmental economics are inappropriate for studying the environmental impacts of tourism as they assume economic activities with more or less homogeneous production and consumption structure (de Kadt 1990).

Supply-side characteristics. Tourism is multiactivity and multisectoral, its various constituent activities following interdependent patterns. The sectors constituting tourism contribute differently to the production and consumption of the tourist product but even the least important sectors must exist in an area in order for this product to be complete.

Tourism-related enterprises are numerous, offering various types of products and each one making its own, particular contribution to, and affecting the quality of, the tourist product. With the exception of large multinational hotel chains and related enterprises, they are small in scale given the relatively free entry status of tourism, the relatively little capital required, tourist preferences for small, humane enterprises and the generous governmental support which is frequently available, making the competitive advantages provided by large scale to be of secondary importance in the case of tourism. The small and many tourism-related firms represent a large number of **centres of decision** which are frequently in conflict making difficult the control of the aggregate result of their actions; an instance of the "tyranny of small decisions" (Kahn 1968).

As a result of the multiactivity and multisectoral nature of tourism, the tourist product is multidimensional and multiattribute with material (tangible) - the various sectoral products and the natural and cultural resources with which a tourist area is endowed - and immaterial (intangible) - landscape aesthetics, sociocultural values, tourist satisfaction, etc. - components. The tourist product does not include all characteristics and attributes of a tourist place but, rather, it is a 'packaged selection' of those elements the interested tourist agent - producer and/or consumer - considers important (Ashworth 1992).

Due to this particular composition - quantifiable items which can be sold at the market and unquantifiable, unpriced ones - the tourist product, unlike typical commodities, does not have a **single** price, a fact with important analytical and practical implications. As an aggregate of variously priced and unpriced elements, the tourist product can be neither treated with the traditional tools of economic analysis nor can it be subjected to price controls and other regulations. Consumers face a multipriced product for which they do not have perfect information and free choice and, thus, they make suboptimal decisions. Producers also do not respond efficiently to demand shifts since they cannot gauge changes in consumer preferences from changes in a single product price. Because of the presence of unpriced component products - such as the environmental resources of an area, the 'price' of the tourist product does not reflect all costs and benefits associated with its production and consumption

(Ashworth 1992).

The tourist product consists of reproducible - services offered by hotels, shops, etc. - and nonreproducible - natural and cultural resources - components. The participation of nonreproducible components differentiates the tourist product from other products in that: (a) the nonreproducible elements are not controlled by either producers or consumers and (b) if they are damaged or irreversibly altered, the product looses its original quality. Inputs originating in nature especially are overused and eventually abused because they are unpriced the result being environmental degradation, or, as Hardin (1968) has called it, "tragedy of the commons".

Finally, the tourist product is a mix of private and public goods making difficult the application of purely public or purely private sector policies for the control of its quality and impacts.

Space and spatial interaction take on an added importance in tourism. The production and consumption of the tourist product take place frequently in the same place and at the same time. The conflicting demands placed on local resources result in negative impacts of one tourist activity on the other. Moreover, once a component tourist activity suffers damages or the natural and/or cultural resources are destroyed, correction cannot be postponed to a later date neither can the damage be relocated. Remedial action must be immediate to preserve the economic health of tourist enterprises.

Demand-side characteristics. The tourist market has many domestic and international segments, depending on the characteristics of tourists and the nature of tourist activities, which generate different patterns of demand for and effects on local natural and cultural resources as well as conflicting demands for the same tourist resources.

Seasonality of tourist demand gives rise to discontinuous impacts which tend to be ignored in the off-tourist season. Viewed in a longer term perspective, tourist demand and the associated environmental impacts are dynamic, fluctuating over space-time with changes in tourist preferences and marketing.

The multiactivity character of tourism implies that tourist demand, unlike demand for typical commodities, is not necessarily spatially concentrated but covers a wide territory, the transportation network being a catalyst in this respect. In addition, tourism uses resources which are used by other activities serving mostly the local population while also tourist facilities are frequently shared in common by both tourists and locals.

Tourism induces urban development in host areas, a phenomenon associated with other economic activities as well, although in the case of tourism the process is usually more rapid and intense. Activities benefitting from tourism or the related infrastructure concentrate in tourist areas increasing, thus, the burden on local environmental resources and capacity.

The particular characteristics of tourism imply that its relationship with the environment differs in important ways from the general economy-environment relationship assumed for typical economic activities, a theme discussed next.

27

2.3 The tourism-environment system: externalities and internalities

Economic activities interact with the environment in the framework of a two–way process as shown in Figure 2.1 which is a simplified version of the materials balance model. On the one hand, the environment provides resources for the production and consumption of economic goods while, on the other, it offers sink services to the economy; the unwanted byproducts of production and consumption are disposed of to the various environmental media modifying variously the quality and quantity of the associated resources. The materials balance principle states that the sum of matter and energy entering the economic system equals the sum of matter and energy which comes out of it. However, resources taken up by the economy undergo modifications during the production and consumption processes and what is left of them returns in a different, usually undesirable, form back to the environment. Conflicts arise when the disposal of undesirable byproducts by an economic agent modifies the quality and quantity of environmental resources needed by another. This is, in general, the case of environmental externalities.

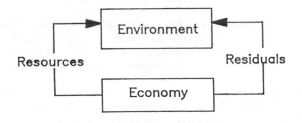

Figure 2.1 A simplified version of the materials balance model

When all economic activities are taken together, their demand for environmental services is depicted in Figure 2.2. Frequently, the same medium provides resources and serves as a sink for unwanted byproducts. Figure 2.2 applies, however, to the case of conventional economic sectors which have a more or less homogeneous product and production structure. When a complex of economic activities like tourism is considered, the relationship with the environment is better approximated by a different scheme as shown in Figure 2.3. Its central characteristic is that for economic activities contributing to the production and consumption of a multifaceted and multidimensional product such as the tourist product, environmental resources constitute 'common property' and 'common capital'. Any conflicts arising out of contemporaneous demand for the resources and sink services of the environment by these activities are not external to them any more, i.e. externalities, but they are **internal** to their collective operation, i.e. they are internalities. Because this is exactly the core argument of the present chapter, the rest of this section takes a

28

closer look at the environmental externalities and internalities of tourism and discusses the related methodological issues. This analysis purports to contribute to the resolution of the central question in tourism policy making and planning in relation to the environment of how to apportion the total burden of environmental protection to the parties involved in proportion to their contribution to the environmental problems.

From the producer viewpoint, an environmental externality exists whenever an output of one economic agent to the environment (disposal of undesirable byproducts or excessive resource extraction) appears as an input in the consumption or production function of another without accompanying compensation (Baumol and Blinder 1979, Hafkamp 1984). From the consumer viewpoint, the same is true except that the utility function of the affected economic agent is considered now. In this sense, alterations of the environment caused by activities participating in the tourism complex and affecting negatively the production and consumption functions of nontourist activities are properly considered as externalities (Figure 2.3). These alterations - excessive resource use (e.g. land, water) by tourist-related sectors or uncontrolled disposal of byproducts to the environment or both - render the environmental resources of an area unsuitable for nontourist uses. Of course, the reverse is also true; i.e., nontourist activities may affect negatively the environmental resources used for tourism.

Internalities arise when the actions of economic agents belonging to the **same** industry or sectoral grouping and participating in the production or consumption of the **same** good alter the quality and quantity of resources needed by other agents in the **same** group. As early as 1910, Alfred Marshall had drawn the distinction between internal and external (dis)economies for a firm when he first introduced the concept of 'externality' (Hafkamp 1984). In the present context, however, groups of firms and/or industries are considered, a common situation in the tertiary sector. For the case of tourism specifically, Emannuel de Kadt puts it succinctly: "in tourism development, the cost of protecting the environment needs to be treated as an internality, viz. a cost of doing business" (de Kadt 1990). Figure 2.3 depicts roughly the incidence of internalities.

Although in theory the distinction between externalities and internalities seems straightforward, in practice several issues must be resolved to make it operational and applicable. At the sectoral level, distinguishing between externalities and internalities of tourism requires a clearcut definition of which sectors belong to the tourism complex and which do not. This is not a very easy task since: (a) certain sectors cater to both tourists and nontourists, at least for some periods within a year; (b) some sectors contribute directly to the tourist product while some others contribute indirectly and (c) tourism-induced urban and regional development introduces sectors which are difficult to categorize as tourist/nontourist leaving, thus, open the question whether this development has to be considered an externality (positive or negative does not matter) of tourism or not. In any event, because environmental resources and services are **shared in common** by several activities, it is important to differentiate the tourist sectors which must bear **collectively** the burden of environmental protection within their territory, for their own good, from the other sectors on which they impact and are impacted from. The choice of the proper sectoral level at which to draw the distinction - e.g. the individual firm or the industrial sector level - depends on how easy it is to identify, monitor, and control environmental problems caused by tourist establishments taken individually or in groups.

From the spatial point of view, the environmental impacts of tourist activities and tourism-induced development are spatially diffused creating, thus, problems in determining the spatial extent and coverage of externalities and internalities. Tourism-related activities usually intermingle with nontourist ones rendering, thus, problematic the exact spatial delineation of the resources used and affected by the former, an important issue for tourism planning and policy making. The proper spatial scale for determining internal and external impacts will depend on the specific character and spatial structure of the study area and the degree of spatial aggregation desired for policy making and planning.

At the temporal level, several issues must be accounted for in determining the temporal duration of tourism's externalities and internalities. Firstly, in most cases, the touristic resources of an area - inputs to the production of the tourist product - are **simultaneously** receptors of the undesirable byproducts of economic activities (the tourist ones included). This lack of spatiotemporal separation between the resources and sink services of the environment in tourist areas raises two questions: (a) what part of the environment is used and affected by tourism and, thus, must be treated as an internality for tourism and an externality for the rest of the sectors and (b) what part of the environment is used and affected by other sectors and, thus, constitutes an externality for tourism; i.e tourism suffers uncompensated damages from other sectors.

Secondly, some of the environmental impacts of tourism are immediate and occur in the short-term while some others have lagged manifestations. The seasonality of tourism complicates things further, even within the tourism complex, if enterprises and sectors operate at different seasons. On the one hand, it is difficult to establish causality links and assess the related impacts and, on the other, it is difficult to distinguish with certainty the impacts of tourist from those of nontourist sectors and those resulting from natural processes. The carrying capacity of the environment plays a critical role in this respect. If some activities occur when and where the carrying capacity of the environment is high, their impacts may not be as salient as it would be the case otherwise. Or, some impacts may dissipate quickly after the tourist season if the carrying capacity of the area is high in contrast to environmentally sensitive areas where impacts carry over into the nontourist season.

Sectoral changes, changes in tourist preferences or promotional activities as well as more general spatial redistributions of activities may induce shifts in the spatiotemporal distribution of tourism's internalities and externalities as well. Consider the case of a rural area adjacent to a tourist resort. Tourism-related activities may damage agricultural production; an externality situation. If agrotourism is promoted, this damage is not a damage to a party external to tourism any more but it is internal to it; a case of internality. It is, therefore, necessary to monitor the process of regional change to detect shifts in impacts from external to internal (and, vice versa perhaps) and adjust the related policies accordingly. The appropriate level of aggregation for this purpose depends on the specific spatial and sectoral structure of the study area as well as on its particular rate of change.

30

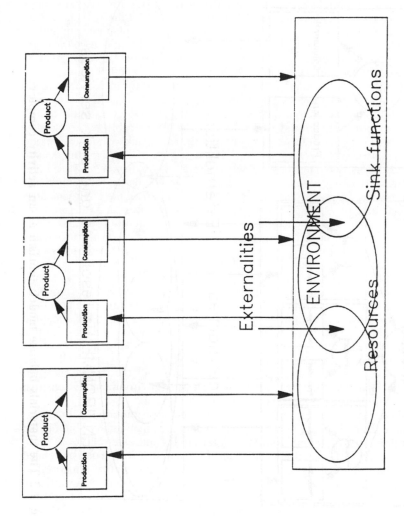

Figure 2.2 The materials balance model: many conventional sectors

31

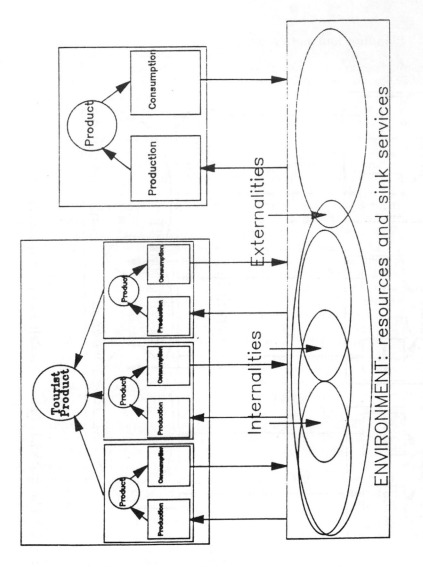

Figure 2.3 The materials balance model: tourism as an activity complex

The methodological issues discussed so far and many more perhaps which were not covered here represent important questions which must be addressed systematically since the distinction between tourism's externalities and internalities has important planning and policy implications as it is discussed in the following.

2.4 Planning and policy implications

Mainstream economic analysis is not adequate to support tourism policy decisions because tourism is not a typical economic sector or activity assumed by this type of analysis. When tourism is conceptualized as an activity complex, more integrated analytical approaches are required to represent the interrelatedness among the tourism-related economic sectors and the environment. One consequence of this view is that several of the environmental impacts of tourism are not externalities but internalities whose control requires the coordinated application of both public and private sector policies and planning actions. The previous analysis provides a basis for outlining the basic shape of these policies.

The principal purpose of public sector policies will be to coordinate the economic activities occurring within a given territory so that their demands for environmental services are met within the limits of local environmental carrying capacity. Coordination requires integrated planning at the local and regional level, one component of which will be tourism planning. This holistic approach is necessary since tourism cannot develop profitably and successfully when it competes with other nontourist sectors for environmental services and suffers negative impacts in the form of limited quantities of quality inputs (land, water, views, etc.). In addition, the impacts tourism causes on nontourist sectors must be properly controlled as well. Integrated local and regional planning should provide: (a) the broad framework for controlling the **externalities** arising among sectors, treating tourism as an activity complex and (b) the infrastructure needed in common by all sectors (Figure 2.4). These two functions of public planning are briefly discussed below.

Several planning tools are available for controlling externalities. Land use planning and regulation are the most important and widespread while the price mechanism is the usual prescription of economists. **Land use planning** aspires for spatial arrangements which reduce interactivity conflicts and are sustainable, i.e. within the limits of the social, economic and environmental capacity of the area (Pearce and Kirk 1986). Tourism-induced urban and regional development is an important externality of tourism which may be tackled satisfactorily via land use planning. **Regulation**, a common control approach in the case of many centres of decision, dispersed demand for policy and high information costs (Lowi 1964; Salisbury and Heinz 1970), specifies principally the limits to the functioning of activities (e.g. area occupied, use density, maximum pollution levels permissible) to reduce conflicts among them and attain desired planning outcomes. Finally, the **price mechanism** is a means to 'internalize' the externalities arising among activities (Fisher 1981). Despite its theoretical soundness, however, it is not so widely used, because significant practical difficulties are encountered in determining proper prices for

33

environmental goods and services and setting the corresponding levels of taxation or charges. In the case of tourism these difficulties are compounded by the fact that it is an activity complex, each activity having its particular cost and price structure. Because the tourist product consists of priced and unpriced elements, market prices do not reflect adequately all tourism-related costs and benefits and, thus, cannot balance demand and supply efficiently. Consequently, the price mechanism can be used as a partial policy tool only for controlling tourism's externalities.

Each of the above planning tools necessarily are suitable for certain but not all facets of tourism development. Combinations of these tools may prove to be more effective in achieving environmentally sound and balanced development in tourist areas than reliance on just one of them.

The second function of public planning, infrastructure provision to support both tourist and nontourist activities (e.g. wastewater treatment plants, roads, etc.), is justified on two fronts: (a) it is a public good which the private sector has no incentive to provide and (b) activities intermingle frequently in space and time and their separation for cost allocation is rather problematic although not impossible (e.g. by means of user fees, charges, taxes).

Private sector policies target primarily the environmental **internalities** of tourism (Figure 2.4). A 'bubble policy' approach is suggested, an idea borrowed from the field of air pollution control (Liroff 1986), which aims at achieving cost-efficient and equitable allocation of environmental control costs. A 'bubble' is assumed to encompass all economic activities offering tourism services in one form or another in an area and they are considered to represent a single economic unit (Figure 2.5). Tourism management and planning is undertaken on a common, holistic basis within the bubble, each activity applying environmental protection measures which are cost-efficient from its particular point of view. The rationale behind this approach is that the environment constitutes common property for the tourist firms, common capital stock used for the production of the tourist product. Touristic entrepreneurs constitute, whether they perceive it or not, a common interest group for which the protection of the environment is of first priority. Thus, they may be willing to undertake common action to safeguard their 'property', the environment, although in the most cost-efficient manner. In this case, **self-regulation** may be an appropriate policy type since it is employed usually when demand for policy is concentrated, the decision making system is solid and information costs are high (Salisbury and Heinz 1970). Self-regulation within the tourism complex will purport to regulate tourist firms to reduce or eliminate potential conflicts among them (demand for environmental resources and sink services) as well as to protect these firms against the externalities caused by nontourist interests. Land use planning, regulatory measures and pricing can be used to this purpose as before. The only difference is that now these tools are implemented within the tourism complex to achieve equitable and balanced functioning of the constituent activities. 'Codes of environmental conduct' should be devised and adopted by all tourist firms. In addition, selfprotective measures against the adverse impacts of other sectors should be taken collectively to safeguard the common interests of tourist enterprises. The result of self-regulation within the tourism complex will be 'cooperation economies'; i.e. input and pollution control cost reduction achieved when sectors cooperate to control collectively their internalities and act collectively against the externalities caused by nontourist sectors.

Naturally, elaborating the details of self-regulation within the tourism complex will not be easy given the methodological problems mentioned already. For example, delineating the spatial boundaries of tourist activities, to determine their individual contributions for just allocation of pollution abatement costs, may not be as straightforward as it is desirable since these activities intermingle among them and with nontourist ones. However, approximate delineations should be made to facilitate making decisions for the use of resources (land, water, sea, etc.) and the control of pollution by tourist firms. In addition, these firms should assume responsibility for regulating their internalities and externalities during the tourist season mainly as well as the externalities which persist for longer time periods. It is probable that, by controlling their internalities, tourist firms achieve, at the same time, control of their externalities in the long run (e.g. control of the ski activity during the ski season reduces soil erosion for the rest of the year).

The preceding discussion described roughly the shape of public and private policies needed to control the total environmental impact of tourism and ensure equitable cost allocation among the parties involved. Accepting officially the conceptualization of tourism adopted in the present analysis may require revisions and changes in the institutional and legislative setting within which planning and policy decisions are taken currently. New economic, legal and planning instruments may have to be devised to address the issue of tourism's externalities and internalities if the current ones ignore this distinction. State intervention should be greatly confined to the control of intersectoral externalities only leaving enough room to tourist actors to care for their internalities. This is particularly important in countries where excessive state support for tourism development does not encourage the private sector to act responsibly and pay its share of environmental protection. Moreover, state subsidies to tourist firms may be made conditional on their proper environmental conduct as well as on the existence of self-regulatory mechanisms which ensure cooperation among them. By redistributing the environmental protection burden and requiring certain environmental costs to be considered as production costs of tourist firms, the latter will set prices and control the quantity of the product to be supplied accordingly. In their turn, tourists will adjust their behaviour to the price and quantity of the product supplied. The degree of environmental protection achieved will be partly determined ultimately by the adequacy of these decisions and actions.

In addition to the above main actions, several complementary actions are indispensable for effective and equitable environmental protection in tourist areas. Education of tourism producers and consumers and suitable environmental advertising are among the most important perhaps as contributing to consciousness-raising which, for tourist entrepreneurs especially, is a critical prerequisite for achieving unanimity among them on the need to act collectively and cooperate for environmental protection in their territory.

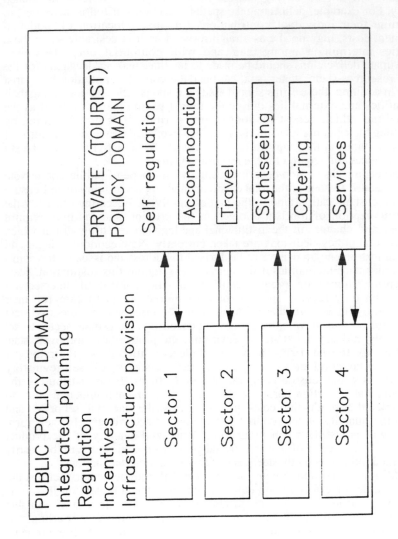

Figure 2.4 Public and private sector policies

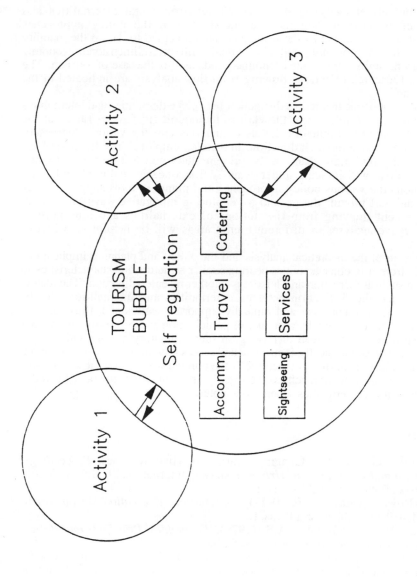

Figure 2.5 The 'bubble' policy approach for tourism

2.5   Conclusions

The theoretical analysis of tourism's environmental externalities and internalities introduced in the present study and the policy approaches suggested were dictated by the inadequate attention paid to date to the inability of mainstream economic analysis to deal with multidimensional economic phenomena and multiattribute economic goods as it is the case of tourism. The principal research directions flowing from this analysis are indicated in the following.

Refinement of the theoretical distinction between externalities and internalities of tourism and resolution of the various methodological issues raised at the sectoral, spatial and temporal levels of analysis and for various degrees of aggregation is one research direction. In parallel, empirical investigation of the theoretical propositions made in the present study will test their validity and applicability, will indicate under what socioeconomic, political and other conditions the various policy approaches and planning tools suggested may work and will provide the ground for exploring innovative ways for tourism management drawing from the notions of externalities and internalities. Comparative analyses of different tourist areas will be helpful also in this respect.

Extension of the theoretical analysis and the policy and planning implications derived from it to other activities bearing similar structure and characteristics to tourism such as recreation and leisure is another research direction. The idea is to introduce the distinction between externalities and internalities into the operation of interdependent and mutually supported sectors and, thus, achieve environmental protection by more active participation and responsive behaviour of the private sector instead of relying on state regulatory activity and support which may be economically inefficient and practically ineffective. An important research question in this perspective is the comparative economic analysis of environmental protection achieved currently and that which can be achieved if the internalities/externalities schema is adopted.

References

Ashworth, G. (1992), Managing Tourism in Historic Cities, *Proceedings, International Congress on Urban Tourism*, International Cultural Centre, Krakow, Poland, June 27 - July 1.

Baud-Bovy and Lawson, F. (1977), *Tourism and Recreation Development*, London: The Architectural Press, Ltd.

Baumol, W.J. and Blinder, A.S. (1979), *Economics; Principles and Policy*, New York: Harcourt Brace Jovanovich, Inc.

Briassoulis, H. (1992), Environmental Impacts of Tourism: A Framework for Analysis and Evaluation, in, Briassoulis, H. and van der Straaten, J. (eds.), *Tourism and the Environment: Regional, Economic and Policy Issues*, Kluwer Academic Publishers, Dordrecht, pp. 11-22.

de Kadt, E. (1990), Making the alternative sustainable: Lessons from development for tourism, in, *Environment, Tourism and Development: An Agenda for Action?*. Workshop papers. Aberdeen: Centre for Environmental

Management and Planning.

Farrell, B.H. and McLellan, R.W. (1987), Tourism and Physical Environment Research, *Annals of Tourism Research*, 14(1): pp. 1-16.

Farrell, B. H. and Runyan, D. (1991), Ecology and Tourism, *Annals of Tourism Research*, 18(1), pp. 26-40.

Fisher, A.C. (1981), *Resource and Environmental Economics*, Cambridge University Press, Cambridge.

Hafkamp, W.A. (1984), *Economic-Environmental Modeling in a National–Regional System*, North-Holland, Amsterdam.

Hardin, G. (1968), The Tragedy of the Commons, *Science*, vol.162, pp. 1243–1248.

Kahn, A.E. (1966), The Tyranny of Small Decisions: Market Failures, Imperfections, and the Limits of Economics, *Kyklos*, 19(1), pp. 23-47.

Liroff, R.A. (1986), *Reforming Air Pollution Regulation: The Toil and Trouble of EPA's Bubble*, The Conservation Foundation, Washington D.C.

Lowi, T. (1964), American Business, Public Policy, Case Studies, and Political Theory, *World Politics*, July 1964, pp. 677-715.

Mathieson, A. and Wall, G. (1982), *Tourism: Economic, Social and Physical Impacts*, Longman, London.

OECD (1980), *The Impact of Tourism on the Environment*, Organization for Economic Cooperation and Development, Paris.

Pearce, D.G. and Kirk, R.M. (1986), Carrying Capacities for Coastal Tourism. *Industry and Environment*, vol.9, pp. 3-6.

Salisbury, R. and Heinz, J. (1970), A Theory of Policy Analysis and Some Preliminary Applications, in, Sharkansly, I. (ed.), *Policy Analysis in Political Science*, Ch.3, pp.39-59, Markham Publishing Company, Chicago.

UNEP (1982), Tourism, in, *The World Environment 1972-1982*, Holdgate, M.W. and Kassas, M. (eds.), Ch. 14, Tycooly International Publishing, Dublin, pp. 545-559.

3 New trends in leisure and tourism affecting the tourist industry and destination areas

T.Z. de Haan

3.1 Introduction

This chapter is about recent new trends in tourism and leisure as they affect the demand and supply for holidays and tourist facilities in tourist origin and tourist destination areas.

Many different trends can be seen in demand for leisure and holidays which results in many different types of holidays that are offered on the market in North West Europe. Environment and nature are rapidly gaining core-attention status in holiday consumption, production and marketing.

The tourist industry responds to the changing demand in the tourists generating regions through which a steady change in what is expected of the destination areas. The possible responses by the tourist industry and governmental bodies in destination areas are many. A very thoughtful and sensitive response is needed because environmental issues are obtaining increasing attention in tourist-generating regions.

This chapter is based on the situation in the Netherlands and on trends that can be seen there. Trends and developments that take place in the Netherlands can more or less be generalized to trends and developments in North-West Europe. However, the Netherlands is a small country with specific holiday behaviour and peculiarities albeit only because of its size.

Differences can br seen for exampl in the holiday intensity. The Netherlands had a long holiday intensity of 69% in 1990, whereas neighbouring Belgium had a percentage of 49%, and the UK of 61%. There are a significant differences, but also a lot of similarities as well.

3.2 Trends in demand

Some trends and developments in demand are especially significant. Holiday intensity in North-West Europe has been growing constantly, especially since the sixties and seventies. In the Netherlands holiday intensity was 76,2% in 1991, with a percentage of 70,6 for long, and a percentage of 32,2 for short holidays. These are ever-growing figures, of which a further increase is anticipated to almost 75% for long, and to about 36% for short holidays in

41

1995 (De Haan, 1992).

In relation to this, the number of holidays is continuing to increase, especially in the segments long holidays abroad (from more than 9,3 million in 1991 to 10,5 in 1995), short domestic holidays (from 7,39 to about 9 million in 1995) and short holidays abroad, which will probably have the relatively largest growing number (from 2,08 million in 1991 to 2,5 million in 1995) (De Haan, 1992).

Connected with this, there is a long existing trend for people to go more often on holidays. In 1991, compared to 1990, 250,000 more Dutch people went on a holiday. The 10,7 million holidaymakers 'produced' an extra number of 750,000 holidays to a total of 26 million (NRIT, 1992).

The holiday frequency, that is the number of holidays per holidaymaker, is such that all holidaymakers went on a holiday 2,44 times in 1991.

Another development is that all holidays become shorter. Especially holidays of two weeks and longer are becoming less important.

Ever-increasing holiday spending is another trend. This can be said for the spending on holidays in total as well as for the spending per day, even if we take into account that holidays are becoming shorter. It is not only due to the fact that travelling takes a larger part of holiday costs with a shortening of the holiday period itself. Of every holiday guilder spent by the Dutch, 80% is spent on holidays abroad, of which 47% goes on hotel holidays. However, much of this 80% goes to Dutch tour operators, travel agencies and transport facilities (NRIT, 1992).

Also the percentage of self-catering holidays is still growing at the expense of the full or partly catered type of holiday.

Seasonality in the holiday pattern is losing its strong character. The shoulder seasons are becoming broader, a phenomenon warmly welcomed by the tourist industry. Fewer people are restricted to one major vacation in the summer and instead, are electing for shorter vacations with greater frequency.

According to a recent NHTV study (1991) holidaymakers also generally prefer more distant destinations, and significantly more varying holidays: not only Greece, but next time Florida, Turkey, or Belgium, not only sea, sand and sun holidays for the individual, but next year up to the mountains or to the lakes with a group.

A consequence of this is that the supply side can expect less loyalty from its usual group of customers. Of course, the loyalty of customers has already been put under pressure by the destination areas themselves, because of the massive 'concretization' of resorts. If people can escape the concrete environments they already have at home, they certainly will! And of course: the travel industry offers these escape possibilities.

Another reason why loyalty to destinations is coming under increasing pressure, is the holiday experience that holidaymakers now have. In earlier days it was enough if you were on holiday, just being somewhere else. Nowadays being somewhere else is not a subsequent condition any more. What holidaymakers can do in the place where they are is becoming much more important.

This results in a situation in which the requirements regarding the possibilities for activities on a possible holiday site are much higher.

Added to this, the holidaymakers know the market, know the offer, know the destinations, know the possibilities for activities. Because of this, holidaymakers will certainly make the choice for the most attractive offer, because price is not as important as it was. Quality counts more and more: the performance of the entire holiday product including the buildings and natural environment is becoming increasingly important. Holiday experience and information has made the market transparent.

3.3   Environmental issues

The above-mentioned developments result in variation in choice of destination and kinds of holidays, but what role does the environment play in the decisionmaking of tourists?

Although tourists in the Netherlands think that the environment is an important issue (93%), they do not seriously consider the environment when choosing a holiday location (NHTV, 1991).

However, this will is not a stable situation and varies across countries. For example in Germany, there is a growing awareness about the environment which is reflected in the decisionmaking process for holiday choice. Generally speaking, it is expected that environmental issues in relation to holidays will be given more and more attention by the public, with rapid, fundamental impacts. Tour operators in the Netherlands are especially taking this into account!

3.4   Different types of holidays

Some existing trends in demand have been pointed out, trends which are leading to a number of new types of holidays.

The first to be mentioned is the so-called 'green tourism'. There is a growing tendency for people to want to go to - environmentally seen - unspoiled areas and no longer to the polluted Mediterranean, nor to the eroding Alps. Holiday–makers are heading to the agricultural areas in North West Europe, for example, in Germany and Scandinavia and even in the Netherlands!

What this growing reaction will lead to, depends mainly on the quickness in the responses in regions presently considered to be polluted areas, as well as in the 'unspoiled' regions!

City tourism and cultural tourism are two other relatively new kind of holidays. Both take a growing share of the market. This is not totally inexplicable. If people are looking for more variation and tend to take more and shorter holidays, a special city or a special event are easily chosen. Cities can benefit from this and events of all kind are given an extra stimulus. National and regional tourist boards are structuring tourist development and marketing with an open eye to these developments.

Another trend in new kinds of holidays are 'active holidays', but 'active' in two different ways. One is that holidaymakers tend to choose holidays with one main activity, which could be biking, climbing, diving, walking holidays: a great variation is needed in whatever experience holidaymakers want to get on their vacation.

The other choice that holidaymakers make is for more variation per holiday.

This means an expanding demand for more kinds of activities, organized or non–organized, during the same holiday.

3.5 Reactions of the tourist industry

The tourist industry responds to all these different trends in many different ways. This is not only because there are different trends resulting in different responses, but also because the tourist industry is a very broad sample of many different businesses varying in scale, size, interest and possibilities.

The offers made by the tourist industry change, resulting in a shift in destinations and the number of destinations: a growing expanding offer. This can be illustrated with the changing offer in charter flights from the Netherlands to Spain and Greece in 10 years time.

Table 3.1
Dutch holiday-charters to Spain and Greece

		1982	1991
Spain	Destinations	18	18
	Passengers	1.052.056	872.559
	Flights	6.334	4.797
Greece	Destinations	8	17
	Passengers	193.625	601.288
	Flights	1.393	4.081

Source: Schiphol Airport,
Terminal Marketing Services, 1992.

In Spain, the number of destination airfields for Dutch charter flights` remained the same, the number of flights and passengers decreased in the same period. During the same 10 year period, the number of destinations in Greece doubled, the number of flights more than doubled and the number of passengers tripled.

The expanding offer from the tourist industry results in a situation that per tour operator there will be more different kinds of holidays, not only beach holidays, but also city tours, self-drive holidays, etc. This means that a more diversified product offer will reach the market.

Contrary to this, more specialized tour operators covering special interest segments of the market will try to develop a special position in market: specialization as a tool against the large generalist tour operators with 'something of everything'.

Another response by the 'industry' and the market is that higher quality standards are required, which will reflect especially on destination areas.

44

In the Netherlands, a quality label for active holidays already exists! Even a real 'keurmeester', a quality-controller, employed by the Stichting Recreatie in The Hague, has been given the challenge to check if the labelled organizations keep to self-imposed regulations (Bos, 1992).

It is also expected that many tour operators will soon show the public a 'green image' or have already started with the implementation of this in their marketing policies. We can expect that tour operators will take this very seriously and of course this will also have very serious consequences for destinations.

Large tour operators will also try to encourage the spreading of holidays for environmental reasons, like for example Dutch tour operator ARKE in the Federation of Dutch tour operators ANVR.

Also promotion of the internal and external use of non-chlorified paper for use in the office itself and for brochures has evolved in a short period of time.

Certainly the above-mentioned developments will affect destination areas and tourist facilities.

3.6   Impacts of changes: sustainability

Many tour operators will start to select their accommodations, resorts and desti - nation areas with an eye on three close related items: sustainability, quality and variation.

Tour operators increasingly will pay attention to sustainability, which means that they will have in mind the long term health of the resource base on which their product and in general tourism depends.

Many items can be viewed considering sustainability. But one of the main and underestimated issues in 'sustainability' is 'water', to my opinion an important one. Pigram (1992) writes about this: "A key constraint in the establishment, operation and expansion of tourist developments is the availability of water."

Already "in arid zones the availability of water resources to sustain tourism development is often seen as a major constraint in the planning process." (Pigram, 1992). However, in coastline developments, like in Greece, this is hardly ever recognized in time. Water quality as swimming water is a well known issue, but the availability of water for nature, vegetation itself, for the local population as well as for agriculture providing the local and the tourists food and beverage needs is hardly ever taken in consideration.

In summertime, with August as a peak, the water use in the Netherlands in spite of all those millions of Dutchmen being abroad for their holiday, is the highest of the year (NIPO, 1992; VEWIN, 1992). The North West European holidaymakers take their ever growing water use habits with them abroad, where they even add a swimming pool nearby to their not very modest wishes. Result is a lack of water supply for tourism, agriculture, the local population and of course an ever drier and drier holiday landscape.

Rivers that dry up, do not complain, landscapes and vegetation do not either, and local people always have trouble to be heard in time or at all with the developers! Maybe they all will find an unexpected ally in tour-operators when they bring up the issue of spoilt, dried out coastal zones on 'their' destinations!

3.7 Quality improvement

Important conditions for a sustainable tourism product are quality improvement and variation.

The recognition of the necessity of quality will result in certain pressure for quality in accommodation and will mean that tour operators demand quality improvement of the environment. In the near future, more and more accommodation suppliers will be placed under pressure by tour operators to avoid production of unnecessary waste, to stop using excessive energy and water and to ensure cleaner waste-water disposal.

3.8 Variation

In addition to quality, another important condition for sustainability is variation: if destinations want to have and to maintain an attractive tourism product, they must pay attention to variation in many ways.

A variation in types of accommodation is needed: not a monoculture of one kind, but a mixture of hotels, apartment buildings, campings, self-catering.

Variation in attractions and primary attractivities. Attractions like amusements, sporting facilities, historic buildings and attractivities like landscapes, 'cityscapes', nature etc.

Also variation is needed in opportunities for various leisure activities. More and more holidaymakers want the opportunity to choose from all kinds of offered organized activities. Club Med ideas, with a more voluntary, less forced participation. Many variations are already in operation.

"Leisure activities have to be seen as an inseparable part of marketing instruments in tourism" (Nijs, 1989). Therefore, hotels have to offer, on their own or together with their competitors, a full scale amusement activities pro - gramme and resorts must create possibilities for such a competitive programme if the accommodation is equipped to do so!

Variation in the visual appearance of resorts and resort regions, just as a variation in kinds of resorts is necessary.

A variation in landscape and vegetation is an essential factor which cannot be overestimated. It belongs to the possibilities and responsibilities of those who can influence. What is a dried-up waterfall in a tourist guide? Just a disappointment in every way. A determination of optimum capacities is essential because it can help to "prevent overuse, deterioration and destruction" (McIntosh, R.W. and C.R. Goeldner, 1990).

If variation as described before exists in the destination areas, tour operators and tourists may be loyal customers!

3.9 Conclusion

Destination areas, resorts and individual entrepreneurs have to develop schemes on creating quality destinations, with sufficient activity possibilities and with enough variation, to be able to attract different target groups to ensure their sustainable future.

References

Bos, R. (1992), 'Sportvakanties worden in de gaten gehouden', in *De Volkskrant*, 23 May.

Haan, T.Z. de (1992), 'The Netherlands' in Ritchie, J.R. Brent and Hawkins, D.E., *World Travel and Tourism Review Volume 2 1992*, C.A.B International.

McIntosh, R.W. and Goeldner, C.R. (1990), *Tourism principles, practices, philosophies*, John Wiley and Sons, New York, pp. 327-328.

NHTV (1991), Vakantie: verleden, heden en toekomst, Breda.

NIPO (1992), Het waterverbruik thuis, eindrapport. No. T-353.

Nijs, D. (1989), Leisure and animation. Paper (unpubl.) Cyprus.

NRIT (1992), Trendrapport toerisme 1991, Breda.

Pigram, J. (1992), Water resources planning for ecologically sustainable tourism, Paper Vienna, Armidale.

VEWIN (1992), Watergebruik over eerste halfjaar in 1992 1,5% hoger, in H2O (25) no.20.

4 Environmental quality and tourism and the environment

G. J. Ashworth

4.1 Assertions and arguments: the existence of a crisis

The general relationship between environmental quality and tourism development is increasingly a subject of concern of governments and citizens alike. An investigation of this multifaceted topic is intrinsically too extensive and complex for detailed consideration here. Therefore one specific type of environmental resource, namely the historic resources of the built-environment, and one type of tourism activity, namely heritage tourism, have been chosen to serve as an example of the product - resource relationship which will have wider applications.

The argument followed in this chapter will proceed by an elucidation of the following statements;

- A major tourism industry has been developed on a world-wide scale based upon sets of environmental resources. Of these resources historic and cultural artifacts are notable as supporting a major and still growing tourism sector.

- The neglect of the study of the resource base of tourism by both the tourism industry and by academic observers is explainable in part by the structure of the tourism industry and in part through the difficulty of applying to this phenomenon the dominant paradigms of tourism studies as a whole.

- There is in addition a third assertion that underlies the critical importance of pursuing the first two and provides much of the motivation for preceding with this argument. Tourism in general and heritage tourism in particular, shows many signs of approaching a point of crisis, caused by intrinsic weaknesses in the understanding of the relationship of increasing demand to resources.

This third assertion needs further description. It is undeniable that tourism, based upon historic resources is an activity that has conveyed demonstrable economic and social benefits: its very success, however, has generated costs that can no longer be dismissed as a marginal and acceptable inconvenience. The point may well have been reached in the development of this form of tourism where continued success threatens the quality and even continued existence of the resources upon which this and other uses of them, depend.

These misgivings are supported by warning signs detectable in many quite different fields. There is an increasing chorus of complaint, for example, to be found in the literature of cultural anthropology about the damage inflicted by the presence of tourists on vulnerable local cultures (see the many examples included by contributors to Smith, 1977): historians, curators and archivists show a growing concern about tourism's selectivity and distortion of what they regard as the authenticity of the records of the past (see for example Horne's, 1984, complaint about the conversion of Europe into 'the great museum', largely by tourists which he clearly regards as undesirable). Most serious of all perhaps is the challenge that is being mounted to tourism's central claim that it furthers local economic development. Hewison (1987) for example takes an opposite position by linking Britain's 'climate of decline' to its increasing economic dependence upon an essentially backward looking heritage industry. More seriously Mossetto's (1990;1991) series of economic models claim to demonstrate the essential economic sterility of tourism based upon urban cultural resources that it uses but does not, and cannot, create.

Such doubts about the value of tourism in general and cultural tourism in particular have only rarely been echoed from within tourism studies (Cheng, 1990; and Hughes, 1991 are notable exceptions). If, as seems likely, from a cursory review of those academic observers most concerned with the resources upon which heritage tourism depends, there is a widespread impression that tourism offers more threats than promises, especially in heritage rich localities, then the industry faces a major problem of which it seems not to be aware. A solution to what is in essence a resource depletion problem is thus an urgent necessity for those responsible for managing cultural resources, sites and places, and equally for tourism itself, whose further development of heritage is likely to evoke stiffening resistance from many quarters and yet whose customers are demanding more varied and spatially diverse heritage tourism experiences. The argument here is that the recognition that a problem exists and the description of its dimensions is thus an urgent necessity and precondition for the shaping of tourism policy.

4.2 Why have academic observers and the tourism industry not averted this impending crisis?

The study of tourism is, and during its short history almost always has been, the study of an economic activity. This immediately limits the scope and approaches adopted and to a large extent predetermines the answer to many questions posed by tourism specialists not least about heritage resources (see Hughes, 1991). If the prevailing paradigms are economic and these are operationalized through what is often termed 'an industrial approach' (see the recent structuring use of this approach in Sinclair and Stabler, 1991) then even defining heritage tourism becomes exceptionally difficult and what is difficult to define, isolate and study will tend to be neglected in favour of those aspects of tourism that can.

This ostensibly rather sweeping accusation of tourism studies can be tested by trying to incorporate heritage tourism into the descriptive and explanatory structures currently dominant. Analysis from the side of the supply of facilities results in an inventory of historical objects, sites, associations and symbols experienced or used by tourists that is lengthy, vague, extremely diverse, non - exclusive to tourism uses, and necessarily incomplete. An attempt to construct a composite heritage tourism product from an assemblage of such elements is so difficult, and so unsatisfying when it is performed, that it has generally deterred the attempt. Similarly the demands of the customer, the heritage tourist, are motivated by a diverse mixture of as yet only dimly understood objectives which result in complex patterns of tourist behaviour which simple market mechanisms fail to adequately reflect. In short neither the heritage tourist nor the heritage product is identifiable or traceable in practice. Some of these difficulties may be equally present in other forms of tourism but they are intrinsic to the nature of heritage tourism and thus to the resource problem discussed here.

If the academic study of tourism has proved incapable of recognizing the existence, let alone the appreciating the dimensions, of a resource-activity problem then it might be expected that the tourism industry would be aware of the threats to the resources upon which it depends. This has proved not to be the case largely because of the peculiar structure of tourism in comparison to other industries.

The organizational structure of tourism is marked by an extreme fragmentation both horizontally between suppliers and vertically between stages in the production and delivery of the final product. Simply those responsible for managing the resources, shaping and promoting the product, and servicing the consumer are many, diverse and fragmented. No organization is capable of exercising an overall management, which in any event would be difficult as there is little consensus between producers over objectives, and many of the heritage resource management agencies are either unaware of their role in tourism or discount its importance to them. The resources of both the built and the natural environments have inevitably been regarded as being largely in free, ubiquitous and inexhaustible supply. Thus the industry itself has had little reason to be aware of their existence let alone encourage their study.

If this observation seems harsh then reference should be made to the recent rash of defensive publications issued by the tourism agencies in many Western Countries in response to the groundswell of popular sentiment that increasingly sees tourism development as an environmental threat. In Britain alone the industry (represented by a consortium of the English Tourist Board, Countryside Commission and Rural Development Commission) and government, though its 'Tourism and the Environment Task Force', have produced quantitatively impressive documentation (ETB et al. 1992; Tourism and the Environment Task Force, 1991) ostensibly designed to tackle the problem. In fact they do nothing of the sort. They are composed of little more than general statements of 'environmentally friendly' intent together with defensive declarations of the economic importance of a growing tourism industry (Ashworth, 1992). There is no appreciation that tourism demands upon environmental resources, can or even should be, directed let alone reduced. In other words, as Wheeller (1991) has succinctly pointed out, the tourism industries response to the rising tide of misgivings of its use of resources is to deal with the criticisms not the underlying problem that gave rise to them. It is viewed as a public relations promotional problem, a field in which the tourism industry is particularly familiar, not a problem of resource maintenance.

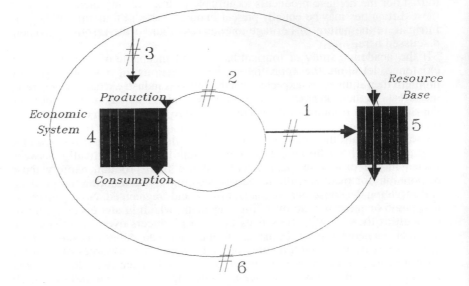

'VALVES'
1. Emissions
2. Reuse
3. Material input
4. Products
5. Material effects
6. Recovery

Figure 4.1 Model of sustainable use of natural resources

Thus solutions to the resource crisis are unlikely to be found or even actively sought for, within the present dominant paradigms of tourism study or the approaches of the agencies, whether private or public operating in the tourism industry. Solutions to these difficulties must be sought be bypassing them with a significantly different working definition which leads to an explanation of what is occurring as the basis for shaping new policy approaches.

4.3 Sustainable historic resources and heritage tourism development

The idea of commodification, that is the treatment of, in this case, selected elements from the past (see Ashworth, 1991), can be used to explain how heritage is created within a closed production system. It does not however contribute to the resolution of the central problem posed here which stems from the closed nature of such a model. An appreciation of the threat to the resource base itself requires the placing of this closed production system within a wider context, thereby accepting that resources may be effected by their use in tourism and may even be exhaustible. In addition it must be appreciated that the production and consumption of the tourism heritage product has substantial impacts outside the closed system. In other words some sort of sustainable development must be sought which links the production process with the resources that it uses, in this case historical resources which, it must be remembered, have important uses other than in tourism. A central tenet of such sustainable models (see Opschoor and van Straaten, 1991) is certainly that development occurs rather than mere resource representation, but that such development is capable of serving a variety of social goals over the long rather than short term.

Such models, and the concepts underlying them, have been developed principally for natural rather than man-made resources. Indeed it is possible to apply the idea of sustainability to urban systems as a whole (Nijkamp (1990) where development is seen as securing the 'long term survival of the system' by encouraging 'its regenerative capacity for renewal'. It is thus not difficult to import this type of approach from the management of aspects of the natural environment to the use of heritage elements within tourism. The idea of environment frequently combines philosophically and organizationally both natural and cultural elements. For example both natural and historical resources are handled together within Canada's environmental 'Green Plan', (Government of Canada, 1990). North American organizational structures and management practices make no fundamental distinction between historical and natural resources (see Ashworth and Sijtsma, 1992, for an account of US and Canadian conservation planning practice).

Therefore simple diagrams borrowed from models of natural resource exploitation can be applied to the case of the historical resources used in tourism. Figure 4.1 is the basic model recently devised in the Netherlands (Ministry of Housing and Physical Planning, 1989) for supporting national policies for the sustainable use of natural environmental resources. A particularly notable aspect of this simple model is the identification of specific so-called 'valves'. These are access points in the system where deliberate intervention is possible with the objective of maintaining an overall balance. This system can be quite easily transposed to heritage by placing the tourism heritage 'industrial' system within a broader context of a 'total heritage system', which traces the flows of costs and incomes between production and resources. Such a model focuses attention on the consequences of the exclusion of the resources used within heritage tourism from the tourism production system. In simple terms the historic resources of buildings, cityscapes, artifact collections and the like have been preserved, and are currently managed dominantly by agencies other than the producers of the tourism product. Many of these are in the public sector and publicly financed. Such resources are thus for various reasons usually accessible without charge to the user. Historic cities can be freely enjoyed by visitors who do not finance their maintenance and most museum collections and historic sites and monuments have either no user charges or below cost charges. This results in a number of fundamental difficulties which policy must confront.

Heritage tourism is in competition for the resources it uses with other heritage users and cannot exclude other competing users. Of course the multi-use of the same resources is possible and historical resources, in contrast to many natural resources can sustain a multiplicity of simultaneous users. They are not however inexhaustible.

Space for example is obviously finite and urban space most evidently so. Actual physical land-use conflict between tourism and other users of historical sites and monuments is the most obvious and some cases are described below. Most of such conflicts are amenable to solution through the exercise of existing planning controls and management policies. Less obvious but probably more important are the problems caused by conflicting products on offer simultaneously to quite different markets. For example heritage is a major component of local cultural identities and thus local regional or national place images. The selection and interpretation of heritage for these purposes is likely to be different from that for tourism if only because tourists differ from residents in their knowledge, expectations and requirement of the same local history. Numerous examples of such conflicts are discussed in various urban contexts in Ashworth and Tunbridge (1990). The difficulty is not that using historical resources for heritage tourism inevitably distorts or trivializes, causing offence to some higher authenticity by staging a version of what Boorstin (1963) termed a 'pseudo-event': it is more simply that different markets require different products. Different 'pasts' are being constructed from the same history and it is not always practical to separate the different market segments.

A second difficulty arises from the location of the resources largely outside the system of tourism accounts.

The flows of costs and benefits between producers and consumers of the tourism product must be supplemented by the costs and benefits that are external to this production system. The seriousness of this failure of the accounting system is the probability that external costs and benefits are not in balance. Tourism imposes costs upon the heritage resources that are more direct and probably larger than the compensating flow of benefits accruing to these resources through either user charges or indirect taxation contributions. There are many possible examples where the presence of the wide variety of

54

secondary support facilities required by tourists frequently imposes costs on other land-uses serving local needs. Even the visual intrusion of tourists en masse is a local cost and the dilemma posed by the need for modern tourism accommodation built to house the visitors to historic cities largely incapable of integrating such developments without damage to the quality of the cityscape is discussed at length in Ashworth (1988).

Finally there is a set of external costs that are obvious to many observers and provoke much of the opposition to heritage tourism development. These are the costs that arise from the simple spatial coexistence of tourists and historic buildings, monuments and sites which lead to physical damage, whether intentional or not, and more subtly the destruction of ambience. In addition the costs incurred may be less direct in the form of additional public facility provision in historic places as a result of the presence of tourists. Compensation in the form of flows of revenues from heritage tourists to historic resources are most likely to be indirect and delayed as well as wholly inadequate to cover the costs incurred. The resource is not activated by tourism: it already exists and will most probably continue to exist regardless of any payments from the tourism users who are therefore in the curious position of being cross-subsidised by other local uses. There are various non-quantifiable benefits to local promotional images and perhaps just the increased consciousness of visitors of the value of preserving and enhancing aspects of the past. Such political support gained from the visitor as potential voter is extremely indirect when tourists are drawn from distant political systems.

4.4   Applicable concepts for sustainable development

Some of the central concepts implicit in sustainability models derived from natural resources can now be examined in more detail with the intention of using them as instruments for shaping management strategies that resolve some of the difficulties outlined above. The six points of potential intervention in the system outlined in Figure 4.1 can be simplified and regrouped into four most relevant to the heritage system. The discussion of each of these points of intervention needs some exemplification but heritage tourism is such a pervasive phenomenon that illustrations of it can be found in every city and almost every village in Europe and beyond. Not all, or even most, cities in Europe experience the problem with the same intensity but the lessons of the extreme cases may well be more clearly and starkly demonstrated. Available space prevents justice being done to any case studies which have therefore been avoided. Detailed studies of the tourism resource problem in major historic cities can be found for Bruges (Jansen-Verbeke, 1990; Decker, 1991), Norwich (Ashworth and de Haan, 1986), Venice (Borg, 1992) and in any event almost any reader can substitute his own national experience.

Resource valuation
The way resources are valued is common to all definitions of sustainable development. Cultural resources are required to satisfy both a demand for participation in various ways and demand for possession or only continued existence. The concept of heritage implies not merely an inheritance from the

past but a passing on of that inheritance intact to future generations. This valuation of resources at the very least is likely to complicate their use within tourism and may often result in conflict. A complication in reconciling these quite different types of demands upon cultural resources may be that they occur at different spatial scales. There is, for example, a demonstrable world-wide option demand for many well known cultural artifacts that can be expressed through the mobilizing of world opinion, often through international organizations in defence of 'world heritage'. This in turn may conflict with local development plans to use the same resources for tourism. Clearly sustainable tourism development will have to reconcile a range of quite different types of valuation of the resources it wishes to use.

In the exploitation of natural resources a distinction is made between renewable and non-renewable resources: this may have some relevance here to management for the resolution or avoidance of such conflicts. An advantage of many cultural resources is that they are not in such a fixed supply as are many natural resources. It has already been argued that the conservation movement can create the resources it conserves, in so far as its stimulation of an awareness of historicity endows value to objects or buildings which previously had no such ascribed value. Equally conflicts over many cultural resources can be resolved by moving, rearranging and even within limits duplicating them.

Most strategies for sustainable natural resource exploitation stress the possibilities offered by renewal, recycling and recuperation. The relevance of the first two of these ideas to cultural resources is obvious. Much that is encompassed within the culture industries is in essence a recycling of the past, and renewal, in the sense of repair and reconstruction is clearly essential. Recuperation however implies the operation of natural regenerative processes which will have only limited significance to a few cultural historical landscapes and sites.

A major feature of urban heritage resources is their spatial concentration usually in a compact area of the inner city which may be difficult to expand in situ. Within this restricted area there is often competition from other urban functions for the same heritage resources and for the same physical space which further complicates resource management (Ashworth and Tunbridge, 1990).

Output equity
Sustainable development also requires a revaluation on the output side of the model. Production is assessed against a series of output goals that aim at attaining certain equities or balances. The importance of intergenerational equities is inherent in the idea of heritage as argued above and as it is in policies for natural resources. Past, present and future uses are at least in theory brought into harmony although in practice this would be difficult to achieve. There is in addition, as suggested earlier, a necessity for 'intersectoral equity' reconciling the variety of contemporary uses through policies that prevent the depletion of the resource upon both tourism and other activities depend.

Frequently there is a conflict in objectives between heritage as a tourism resource for an export market and as a major component in local place identity and civic consciousness that is so sharp as to lead to conflict expressed politically and even, on occasion, physically. It is worth noting that the

56

magnitude of the differences in objectives between visitors and residents is likely to be determined by the existing economic and social differences between the two groups, and thus, if such conflicts are evident in European cases, they are likely to be that much more intense in the case of heritage tourism in less developed countries.

Carrying capacities
The link between resource valuation, at one end of the model, and equity outputs, at the other, can be made through the two concepts of 'carrying capacity' and 'homeostatic adjustment'. The concept of carrying capacity, long used as a management tool in pastoral agriculture, has a superficial attraction for the management of recreationists in recreation areas. In fact the search for optimum carrying capacities is such a simple yet powerful idea for the relating of visitor numbers to resources that it has assumed among recreation planners some of the intensity of the search for the 'holy grail' (see among others Wall, 1983; Graefe et al. 1984; Westover and Collins 1987). It assumes that visitors have many of the behavioral characteristic of pastoral animals and tourism areas, whether rural or urban, many of the resource characteristics of pastures with the objective being the maximizing of numbers while maintaining the long term sustainability of the resource base. Heritage sites and cities can then be managed through controlling the size of the 'herd' and also, although less usually, increasing the carrying attributes of the sites. Under-utilization, capacity and saturation can then be applied particularly within such tourism development models as recreation product life-cycles.

However the basic analogy very easily becomes itself unsustainable. The first problem encountered is that capacity is not determined by the characteristics of the resource base alone. It is clear from the above discussion that visitors vary greatly in their valuation of heritage resources and thus their uses of them. For some preservational users a single visitor is too many while for some tourists, even on the same site, many thousands of fellow visitors would not detract from the quality of the individual experience.

A second difficulty is that in cultural tourism in particular resources are more strictly managed than is the case in many natural environments. The places where heritage tourism occurs, mainly multifunctional cities, are extremely physically robust and characterised by a varied and diverse economy and society, subject to management and capable of absorbing large tourist influxes with few problems. Historical resources in particular, once they have been transformed into heritage by interpretation, as argued above, can be moved, extended and even replicated to a considerable degree in a way that many natural resources cannot. The carrying capacity therefore is not only capable of being influenced by its management but is in practice largely determined by that management.

In short carrying capacity is an optimizing model which thus depends for its outcome on a prior determination of what is to be optimised (Mathieson and Wall, 1982) and in the case of heritage tourism there is a wide variety of possible outcomes depending upon the compromises reached between the aims of the tourism industry, the individual tourist, the custodians of the historical resources and the public interests of the city itself. Carrying capacity is in practice not so much seeking an answer to the question, 'how many visitors can the resources bear?' but, 'what do the actors involved want to achieve?'

However carrying capacity can be a specific rather than general management tool if objectives have been previously determined. There may be no valid general statements of the capacity of a heritage city but hotels, car parks, and even museums, cathedrals, piazzas and boulevards do have physical capacities at specific times which in practice may determine, or can be used to determine, the physical capacity of a heritage site or city. The danger with this of course is that such manageable physical capacities may not coincide with other optima such as the limits of existing societies to absorb the demands of tourism without provoking negative reactions. There is in addition a serious danger that any general capacity figures used as the basis of overall management neglects the specific capacity of particular locations or sites. In particular it is frequently the secondary supporting tourism services (most usually accommodation or vehicle circulation and parking space) that are most easily used to provide controllable capacity figures rather than the primary heritage facilities that are often more difficult to monitor and control visitor access. Thus there may be surplus capacity in the city as a whole while simultaneously specific heritage sites are suffering irreparable damage.

Thus this deceptively attractive management idea provides general statements which have little logical foundation and, worse, are of limited value in most heritage tourism situations and even when used to determine the incidence of specific problems of congestion, needs considerable care in its application.

Homeostatic systems adjustment
A question that could be, but rarely is, posed by a discussion of carrying capacities is whether they are self-regulating, for if they are, then this becomes not so much a management tool but an argument for non-intervention in the tourism system. Indeed it has to be argued for heritage tourism in general that management in a collective public interest is necessary for this commercial activity when such arguments are not made for other commercial activities whose locations, size and customer numbers are left to the workings of a free market which adjusts supply and demand without such intervention.

A heritage tourism site or city that receives more visitors than it can accommodate will deliver a quality of experience to the customer that is lower than expected for the price charged. This then influences subsequent consumer decisions in favour of competing sites or cities or the same site at different times. The argument thus has to be clearly made why a heritage tourism product operating within a highly competitive market, which in general is more afflicted by over-supply of possibilities rather than any shortage, should not be allowed the automatic homeostatic adjustment of supply and demand through the market that applies to other free market products. This is in fact the central question that stems from much of the preceding discussion of resources, outputs and capacities. Similarly the nature of the answers will indicate not merely that intervention in general is needed but more precisely intervention at which point to correct which malfunction of the system.

Part of the argument may revolve around the consequences of the commodification of environmental resources. The operation of the system may be too sluggish or delayed to prevent irretrievable damage to the resource. The nature of tourism does not encourage rapid feedback between customers to producers of the sort experienced with other products. The purchase of a holiday is a rare event, and the decision to buy is made long before the product is consumed and on the basis of very imperfect knowledge of the product. The customer is not able to adjust his behaviour according to his degree of satisfaction with the product except over the very long term. In addition because heritage resources are valued in different ways by different users who obtain different levels of utility from different densities of visitors. In the extreme case the visitor to Stonehenge, the Sistine Chapel or the Lascaux cave paintings may thus experience no diminution of the quality of their tourism experience while simultaneously their feet, body warmth and breath respectively are causing such long term damage to these sites that their use as preserved heritage is threatened.

A quite fundamental difficulty of applying a free market commodification model is the absence of an efficiently operating pricing mechanism. How can demand be kept in balance through price when many of the heritage resources are unpriced, inadequately priced or indirectly priced? In addition much of the economic impacts of heritage tourism are external to the tourism industry. Therefore high costs may be incurred by the resource base that are not reflected in the direct charges to visitors who in turn are not deterred from purchase.

It is not necessary to defend the assertion that heritage tourism imposes more costs than benefits upon its heritage resources. The point is only that there is an absence of a mechanism maintaining equilibrium. Markets are not working in a way that secures the long term existence of the heritage resource base because there is no effective automatic homeostatic adjustment. The creation of such a system would require many of the same measures as are currently being discussed in terms of the natural environment because the problem is in essence the same. Externalities must be internalised and costs borne by the user. The difficulties in applying this idea to heritage tourism lie in its detailed operationalization rather than its logic. Nevertheless as Krabbe and Heijman (1986) argue, agencies must respond to the entropy they create. The tourism industry must take more financial responsibility for the long term maintenance of the heritage resources upon which it depends, either through substantial direct and voluntary subsidies to the agencies, usually in the public sector, managing the historic resources or failing such sponsorship through the taxation system. This latter is less direct but could be place or user specific.

The main argument against this is not that it imposes a competitive disadvantage upon particular places, as the tourism operators usually argue, because this is, of course, one of the main objectives. The difficulty is that, as discussed earlier, both the 'tourism industry' and the 'tourist' are difficult to define and thus isolate and tax.

4.5 Towards sustainable development strategies

The use of these ideas in the devising of management strategies designed to create sustainable heritage tourism can be considered at three levels of government.

The most effective level at which to implement such strategies is the local, because it is at this level that the problems are most apparent, policies are likely to receive most popular political support, and in most countries, where cities have existing limited powers over land-use and transport which can be exercised to implement either hard constraints or soft promotional policies. In addition the quality and intensity of the impact of tourism will very largely depend upon the distinctive attributes of the places that accommodate it. Tourists however are particularly dependent upon the flow of information received about such local attributes as a result of their lack of local knowledge and personal mobility. This information is in part manageable by local agencies. Printed information, trails, and signposting can be effective instruments for the manipulation of the spatial behaviour within the city at the micro scale.

It is not difficult to cite examples of such local policies aimed at spreading visitors in time or space in order to reduce congestion costs or spread local economic benefits. However such local policies have a number of intrinsic disadvantages. They are able only in effect to manage the local consequences of the tourist flows rather than influence them more fundamentally and thus such strategies are at best short term local reactions and at worst may just shift the spatial impact of the problem.

It is in any event unrealistic to imagine that a single local policy for heritage tourism can be developed and implemented by a single unified authority in a specific city. Heritage tourism is managed by a wide variety of different organizations, in both private and public sectors each concerned with particular facilities or stages in the production process and each having its own goals and pay-offs. Historic conservation and museum collection agencies, local tourism intermediaries, public utility and service providers and many others are likely to have their own strategies which may reinforce or contradict each other. In addition various levels in the government hierarchy may well perceive the problem in quite different ways and will therefore implement quite different strategies.

The more general problem of the mismatch of costs and benefits can be treated most effectively through fiscal and subsidy strategies at the national scale. It is also clear that a single city usually only provides one part of the much wider tourism product consumed by the visitor which may include other cities offering similar experiences. Similarly the urban tourism market is fiercely competitive and any one urban product is easily substituted by another. Thus policies implemented at the local scale to any one element in a complementary network or competitive arena will have impacts upon the others. Strategies for capacity for example in any one city will have obvious impacts in the wider context of the network of complementary and competing cities.

It is possible to extend these arguments to the international level. Heritage tourism is for many reasons on both the supply and demand side intrinsically international. The mutually supporting or competing networks of heritage cities discussed above increasingly ignore national borders. Thus strategies applied in one city will have repercussions on others in quite different national jurisdictions. An additional international dimension results from the possibility of exporting some of the external costs mentioned earlier while not developing compensating international flows of benefits. If the visitors to heritage sites are foreign then the discrepancies noted earlier between the costs incurred for resource maintenance and the benefits accruing to commercial enterprises cannot be corrected through national taxes and subsidies. If, as frequently occurs there is also a difference in the level of economic development between tourist generating and receiving countries then the problem can be described as an exploitation by the relatively rich visitors, much of whose expenditure accrues to the home country, of the relatively poor residents, who bear many of the costs. This is not a problem specific to heritage tourism but the addition of the heritage element in which visitors are directly using local cultural resources adds an extra dimension. Concepts such as 'world heritage' or 'international tourism' remain abstractions in the sense that they are not reflected in international agencies or agreements which can devise and implement policies at this scale. The regulation or taxation of heritage tourism in the cities of any one country would place them at a competitive disadvantage.

Finally all such sustainability issues involve more general social attitudes. Sustainability is ultimately a normative idea which involves the valuation of, and rights over, resources (Opschoor and van der Straaten, 1991) and thus clearly over how such resources should be used. Sustainable development is not the absence of development and the practical choices are only very rarely between the unrestrained development of heritage tourism and its complete exclusion. A major difference between cultural and natural environmental resources is, as was argued above, that many cultural resources including heritage can be regarded as being demand derived. If heritage cannot by definition be considered other than in terms of the demand for it, then heritage sustainability is clearly a development rather than a preservation issue. Management strategies for sustainable heritage tourism involves a complex set of choices about the relationships of the tourism production system to a resource system that is in simultaneous use for a variety of functions. Answers to the questions about what forms of tourism, at what intensity, at which specific times and locations, and with what set of objectives in mind must be sought within that wider context.

References

Ashworth, G.J. (1988), Accommodation and the historic city, *Built Environment* 15(2), pp. 92-100.

Ashworth, G.J. (1991), *Heritage Planning*, Geopers, Groningen.

Ashworth, G.J. (1992), Sustainable tourism: slogan and reality, review article, *Town Planning Review*, 63(3), pp. 25-30.

Ashworth, G.J. and de Haan, T.Z. (1986), Uses and Users of the Tourist - Historic City, *Veldstudies*, 10, Groningen.

Ashworth, G.J. and Tunbridge, J.E. (1990), *The tourist-historic city*, Belhaven, London.

Boorstin, D.J. (1963), *The image: or what happened to the American dream*, Penguin, Harmondsworth.

Borg van der (1992), *Tourism and urban development: the case of Venice*, University of Rotterdam.

Burtenshaw, D., Bateman, M. and Ashworth, G.J. (1991), *The European city: western perspectives*, Fulton, London.

Cheng, J.R. (1990), Tourism, how much is too much? *Canadian Geographer*, 24(1).

Decker, P. de (1991), Stad op stelten, *Planologisch Nieuws*, 11(3), pp. 220 - 34.

English Tourist Board/Countryside Commission/Rural Development Commission (1992), *The green light: a guide to sustainable tourism*, London.

Government of Canada (1990), *Canada's Green Plan* Environment, Canada, Ottawa.

Graefe A.R., Vaske, J.J. and Kuss, F.R. (1984), Social carrying capacity: an integration and synthesis of 20 years research, *Leisure Science*, 6(4).

Hewison, R. (1987), *The heritage industry: Britain in a climate of decline*, Methuen, London.

Horne, D. (1984), *The great museum: the re-presentation of history*, Pluto, London.

Hughes, G. (1991), Conceiving of tourism, *Area*, 23(3) pp. 263-7.

Jansen-Verbeke, M.C. (1990), Toerisme in de binnenstad van Brugge: een planologsiche visie, *Nijmegse Planologische Cahiers* 35.

Krabbe, J and Heijman, W.J.M. (1986), *Economische theorie van het milieu*, Van Gorcum, Assen.

Mathieson, A. and Wall, G. (1982), *Tourism: economic, physical and social impacts*, Longmans, London.

Ministry of Housing, Planning and the Environment (1989), *National Environmental Policy Plan: to choose or to lose*, SDU, The Hague.

Mossetto, G. (1990), A cultural good called Venice, *Nota di lavoro* 90.14 Dept. of Economics University of Venice.

Mossetto, G. (1991), The economics of the cities of art; a tale of two cities, *Nota di lavoro* 91.10 Dept. of Economics, University of Venice.

Nijkamp, P. (ed.) (1990), *Sustainability of urban systems: a cross-national evolutionary analysis of urban innovation*, Avebury, Aldershot.

Opschoor, H. and van Straaten, J. (1991), Sustainable development: an industrial approach. Paper to European Association of environmental economists. Stockholm.

Pfafflin, G. (1987), Concern for Tourism, *Annals of Tourism Research* 9, pp. 576-88.

Sinclair T. and Stabler, M. (1991), *The tourism industry: an international analysis*, CAB International, London.

Smith, V.L. (ed.) (1977), *Hosts and guests: the anthropology of tourism*, Blackwell, Oxford.

Tourism and the Environment Task Force (1991), *Tourism and the environment maintaining the balance*, Vols:
Report of the countryside working group
Report of the historic towns working group
Report of the heritage sites working group
Visitor management: case studies
Maintaining the balance: a summary
London.

Turner, L.J. and Ash, J. (1976), *The Golden Horde: international tourism and the pleasure periphery*, Constable, London.

Wall, G. (1983), Tourism cycles and capacity, *Annals of Tourism Research* 10, pp. 268-70.

Westover J. and Collins, G. (1987), Perceived crowding in recreation settings, *Leisure Sciences* 9(2).

Wheeller B. (1991), Tourism's troubled times, *Tourism management*, 12(2)

5 Private and public development strategies for sustainable tourism development of island economies

H. Janssen, M. Kiers and P. Nijkamp

5.1 Introduction

One of the most important prerequisites for attracting tourists to an area is the beauty of the natural environment. But if such an attraction force becomes successful, it has to be recognized that too large a number of tourists will damage or even destroy the natural environment, thus eroding the very basis of tourist activity. Several examples clearly illustrate this observation, like the case of Venice: a further increase of tourists in Venice will negatively influence the tourist attractiveness. This provokes of course the question of *carrying capacity* (and related policy strategies) of tourist areas.

Is it possible to avoid a situation in which the natural environment is damaged as a result of severe negative external effects from tourism? As a first orientation regarding this question it seems meaningful to introduce the notion of **sustainable tourism development** (STD). With STD we mean that tourism development is both in volume and in direction of development evolving in such a way that the pressure on the natural environment remains below the level of the carrying capacity for both the present and the future generation (see also the Brundtland report). One way of analyzing this is by means of appropriate indicators. STD indicators can help determining whether or not the development of tourism is damaging the natural environment, and to what extent. Some examples are: quality of the surface water, the level of noise in a certain area, etc.

The problem of obtaining a sustainable tourism development is certainly a complex one. Many interested parties and organizations are involved in tourist activities and the sum of all their actions determine the possible success of STD. Each individual action in the tourist sector has its own environmental impact. To reach STD, it is important to streamline all such actions in order to reach a minimum of environmental stress. This means the selection of proper STD strategies. When the economic and/or environmental basis of an area is small, like on many islands, the need for the right STD strategies is even more important. Many island economies are economically dependent on revenues from tourism and need thus a careful implementation of STD strategies.

An important question is how different options for STD can be evaluated. Therefore, the main objective of this chapter is *identify for island economies breeding on tourism a set of development objectives and options with the aim to evaluate such strategies on the basis of STD (e.g. by using scenarios).*

As previously mentioned, the tourist sector comprises a multiplicity of actors. Because of the large number of actors involved, we may categorize them and for our research we categorized them in the following groups: tourists, local inhabitants, local business, governments (local, national and supranational) and non-local business (like tourist agencies).

The diversity of interests means that an evaluation of tourist strategies in a certain area has to be based on a broad spectrum of relevant (public and private) policy criteria. It is therefore difficult to present a standard answer to multiple problems that occur in many different situations. Therefore, we do not try to present a blueprint, but to offer a framework for analyzing these kinds of complex dilemmas.

The chapter is organized as follows. First, Section 5.2 will deal with some background remarks on the concept of sustainable development. Then, in Section 5.3, various actors will be dealt with, emphasis being on public and private sector responsibilities for development. Next, various STD strategies will be presented, while in Section 5.5 - by way of empirical illustration - a set of scenarios from the Greek island Lesvos will be discussed. The chapter will be concluded with some prospective remarks.

5.2 Drive to sustainable development

In developing a framework for judging the economic feasibility and environmental compatibility of new economic initiatives, it has to be recognized that economic development is not in the first place a matter of *quantity*, but also of *quality*. Despite the admirable progress of our economies in a quantitative respect, we observe increasingly a decline in quality of life and environmental conditions to such an extent that also the well-being of future generations is severely eroded.

Although we are witnessing nowadays a widespread concern about our quality of life (both global and local), it should be noted that environmental decay is not exclusively a phenomenon of our century. The Greek philosopher Plato already complains in his Critias about the landscape changes in Attica which had transformed the environment into: "... bones of wasted body... richer and softer parts of the soil having fallen away, and the mere skeleton being left" (cited in Clark, 1986, p. 6). Also in many other countries one observes many examples of earlier soil erosion which as a result of agricultural and forestry activities has affected the landscape in all time periods between nomadic cultures and modern high-tech agriculture (Wilkinson, 1973). Thus environmental problems seem to be intrinsically linked with human activities.

Despite the recognition of the long history of environmental problems, it should be noted that until the beginning of the twentieth century, in general, only relatively modest environmental changes were taking place, as the prevailing technological and economic system was unable to alter environmental conditions on earth dramatically. However, especially after World War II mankind's capacity to destroy our habitat has increased significantly, partly as a result of radical technological changes (generating huge amounts of air, water and soil pollutants including many toxic materials), partly as a result of the rise in world population (and its subsequent rise in consumption and mobility patterns). The strive for a concerted development of the economy and ecology based on a coherent and integrated viewpoint has stimulated many social scientists to adopt systemic notions and concepts for achieving a balance between natural and socioeconomic systems. The functioning of such natural and socioeconomic systems has, in their view, to be studied from the angle of material inputs of all production and consumption processes. In this context, new sub-disciplines such as human ecology and environmental economics have come to the fore, in which serious attempts have been made to ensure a merger between economics and ecology (see also Nijkamp, 1979). These efforts have been very intensive, especially in the past decade (see for a review Van den Berg, 1991). The awareness has grown that a balanced development is not only a matter of quantity in the present, but also of quality in the future.

Meanwhile, increasing political interest has developed regarding the depletion of the earth's natural resources and the environmental decay. Despite many efforts, local, national and international policy bodies have been unsuccessful in ensuring a viable economic development trajectory that was compatible with environmental quality. For instance, the UN Conference on Human Environment (Stockholm, 1972) has only very moderately achieved the high goals which were set for our planet.

The World Commission on Environment and Development, established by the General Assembly of the United Nations in 1983, was assigned the task of providing concrete recommendations for action on the interrelated issues of environment and development, seen from a strategic long-term viewpoint. The Commission Report (1987), 'Our Common Future' (often named the Brundtland Report after the President of the Commission), is a remarkable document in that it offers concrete hope for sustainable development.

The Commission believes that despite the potential catastrophes incorporated into our modern way of life, human resources, knowledge and capabilities are available to create a sustainable development. Sustainable development is defined here as pathways of human progress which meet the needs and aspirations of the present generation without compromising the ability of future generations to meet their needs. It hence requires a fairer distribution of wealth within and among countries and groups in society. In this context, economic growth is not by definition a threat to sustainability, but the only feasible weapon in the fight against poverty and disaster; with economic growth we can create the capacity to alleviate poverty and solve environmental threats. This requires that economy and ecology be merged from a local to a global perspective.

Environmental, resource, cultural heritage and coastal zone policies are fraught with many conflicts that threaten the idea of an *ecologically sustainable economic development*, advocated inter alia in the above-mentioned Brundtland report. The intertwined nature of all processes in an economic-environmental system call for due attention to be given to economic and ecological considerations or paradigms from the steady state and/or long-term perspective.

Despite the global nature of many environmental problems, it is noteworthy that a problem is caused by the *local scale* of environmental externalities, in terms of both cause and effect. For example, global problems such as acid rain, sedimentation, desertification, ozonization, eutrophication, ocean pollution and resource extraction are often the result of a large number of small-scale and local activities (without being controlled by an environment watchful constituency), while also the far-reaching environmental impacts can be observed most clearly at a local or regional scale. Consequently, the local/regional problems of land use (interpreted in a broad sense, including landscape, 'cityscape', soil quality, marine environments) are of central importance to environmental management.

In this context, we may also quote Clark (1986, p. 11), who stated:

"...we have learned just enough about the planet and its workings to see how far we are from having either the blueprints or the operators' manual that would let us turn that diffuse and stumbling management into the confident captaincy implied by the 'spaceship' school of thought."

Clearly, many attempts have been made in the past decade to model or replicate the complexity of dynamic economic-environmental systems, but strategic components were usually not adequately included, so that these models fail to provide effective and preventive environmental policies for co–evolution ensuring a balance between economic development (all quantitative and qualitative changes in the economy that lead to a positive contribution to welfare) and ecological sustainability (all quantitative and qualitative environmental changes that serve to improve the quality of an ecosystem and have hence also a positive influence on welfare). This applies to both the global level and the local level (like tourist development on the islands in Greece).

To clarify our thinking, the following scheme may be helpful (see Figure 5.1). The feedback from the externality (social costs) box to the resource box is especially important here, as it is becoming increasingly clear that environmental decay erodes the quality and quantity of the resource availability (as we witness nowadays in agriculture, forestry and fishing).

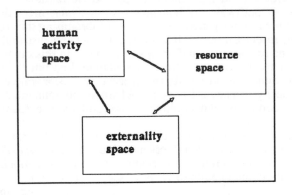

Figure 5.1 A system representation of human activities, resource use and externalities

Sustainable development would then normally require either a strict technical progress exceeding the degree of environmental decay per capita, or an application of strict economic pricing principles (e.g., based on the trustee principle where the government represents the unborn generation, or on the economics of altruism or solidarity).

In a recent article, Pearce (1988) adopts a specific position in the co-evolution debate by claiming that a further decline in natural resources beyond the point that we have already reached is actually injurious to economic development. Assuming that sustainability is a necessary condition for economic growth, he argues that the stock of 'natural capital' should at least be kept constant (and preferably increased), while the economy is allowed to develop only within this restricted space. Clearly, this viewpoint raises important questions concerning the measurability of environmental quality.

Unfortunately, our current economic apparatus has not yet managed to devise an operational methodology for analyzing all the complexities involved in ecologically sustainable economic development (see Opschoor, 1987). This is also witnessed in a statement in the World Bank Annual Report (1985):

"Degradation and destruction of environmental systems and natural resources are now assuming massive proportions in some developing countries, threatening continued, sustainable development. It is now generally recognized that economic development itself can be an important contributing factor to growing environmental problems in the absence of appropriate safeguards. A greatly improved understanding of the natural resource base and environment systems that support national economies is needed if patterns of development that are sustainable can be determined and recommended to governments."

In conclusion, planning for sustainability requires a shift in our thinking on the development of our economic system. There is an evident need for more strategic thinking, more cohesive thinking and more multidimensional thinking in order to ensure a compatibility of economic and environmental interests. This means that both the strategic significance of sustainable development and the implications for practical policy strategies have to be envisaged, not only at the global level but also at the local level. This also calls for more attention for sustainable regional and local planning and for a sustainable plan and project evaluation. The case of the Greek islands presents an interesting example here, as all ingredients of conflict planning and management seem to prevail here. Especially in this context the notion of STD is relevant, as it is a major challenge to seek development strategies which use tourism as a pivotal activity (as tourism shows a very clear feedback between the resource box and the externalities box) and which ensure co-evolutionary development reconciling economic growth interests, social distributive interests and environmental interests not only in the short run, but also in the long term. This idea leads of course to the question which actors and initiators play a key role in STD policy. This will be discussed in Section 5.3.

5.3   Actors and initiators in STD

In general, one may take for granted that people are interested in both prosperity and a high level of quality of their environment. In tourist areas prosperity can be generated by means of the tourist industry, but the development of the tourist industry may be at odds with the desired quality of environment. Policy-makers may try to avoid this possible conflict by developing tourist policy packages for STD.

A balanced co-evolutionary development will have to be based on the interests of all relevant parties involved. Tourism is an essentially 'normal' economic activity which requires private initiatives (building, developing, financing, etc.). Thus the private sector is a key force in the tourist sector. It is also important from the viewpoint of income generation of local inhabitants, the creation of social overhead facilities for favouring tourism, and the organization of the market. However, actions of the private sector may overlook social costs and distributive effects. Therefore, the government is also an important party in an STD policy.

Then the question is: what are the consequences when policy-makers or governments choose STD as a policy goal? One of the ways for the government to influence the tourist market is through the supply side. Only along these channels can they change the kind or the level of tourism facilities that are available. Clearly, this change in supply can only be profitable if it is met by an effective demand. This means that when a government wants to intervene, it has to be aware of the consequences for the supply of tourist facilities. Secondly, public decision-makers have to consider whether there is a demand for these tourist facilities. However, in this chapter we will not focus any further on the demand side, while also the equilibrium between supply and demand falls outside the scope of this chapter.

We have discussed above the reasons why the government might be interested in STD, viz. the interest of its voters in economic prosperity and the quality of the natural environment. But if a government chooses STD as its major orientation, what are the implications for government policy regarding tourism? Is there a clear role for a government policy in this sector?

In order to provide an answer to these questions, we will present and discuss possible arguments for government intervention in the tourist market. Traditional arguments for government intervention are (see Fokkema and Nijkamp, 1994):
. infant-industry argument
. market imperfections
. ethics and justice
These considerations will now be briefly discussed.

Infant industry argument
This argument is especially, but not only, valid for island economies.

The most typical characteristic of an island is its isolated situation which affects both the economy and the environment. Due to the isolated situation, there is a limited basis for both the economic structure and the ecological system. As a result, the government may be quite eager to protect the ecological and economic system against unbalanced development. So the argument here is that the government wishes to protect the environment and/or the economy, because of the weaknesses ('infant-industry') these two sectors have due to isolated location.

Market imperfections
Often governments wish to intervene when there are market failures. These failures can be: imperfect competition (this forms the reasons for providing public services), imperfect information (in order to protect less informed actors) and the absence of markets (in case of non-excluding goods or in case of third party externalities). The argument concerning the absence of markets and especially third party externalities refers also to environmental damage. Environmental damage is often insufficiently incorporated into market transactions, so that governments - from the viewpoint of sustainable development - wish to issue environmental regulations.

Motives of ethics and justice
If the government judge the market outcome as inequitable or unacceptable according to its ethical or political belief, then this too might be an argument for intervention. This often leads to policies which try to establish an adjustment in the distribution of incomes and wealth or where the government tries to (de)promote (de)merit goods.

Next to these arguments, there is the fact that besides market failures (which the government might use as an argument for intervention in the market system), there are also **government failures**. These failures might result from imperfect insight into the real demand for public services, insufficient recognition of (positive and negative) effects of policies (that occur in the long run), and bureaucracy and complicated and non-transparent legislation. So the government should always measure its own possible failures against the 'market failures' they try to prevent or correct. If the government decides that these arguments are, given their specific situation, sufficient reason to intervene, the question of how a government policy should be shaped is immediately at stake.

The policy can be designed as a **top-down activity**, which may be the best way in case the government knows exactly what the best thing to do in every (specific) situation and if this centralized model is accepted by the public as well. But due to the fact that this is practically impossible, it might be interesting to examine arguments for a bottom-up approach.

This carrying capacity of ecological systems and the pressure on these systems due to human activity, differs in each situation, especially in the case of islands which have their own isolated microcosm (see Coccossis, 1992). Because a policy should take all the relevant specific factors into account, a policy blueprint suitable for each specific situation is impossible to design.

Secondly, a sustainable development is difficult to reach, because in an interactive economy each action of all actors involved is relevant. The sum of all human actions together determines whether or not a development is sustainable. This means that the actions and goals of all actors have to be considered and preferably incorporated into a policy. Otherwise, a development can hardly ever be sustainable.

Consequently, due to the fact that the specific situation of the local ecology and the specific demands and actions of the actors involved have to be taken into consideration in a policy for sustainable development and due to the fact that (island) ecologies are vulnerable, a policy has to be in agreement with specific local situations. Therefore, a **bottom-up approach** may be recommended, as then the specific requirements for policies can be better incorporated.

It should also be noted that economic and ecological systems are dynamic and this provokes the nee for regular readjustment of STD policies. The only way to react effectively to changed situations are short communication lines between the people who notice the change and the policy-makers or decision-markers. These lines are in general shorter, when the geographical distance is lower, especially when there is hardly any distance. Thus, in the case of island economies, effective reaction to changes in situations is best guaranteed if the policy-maker or decision-makers reside on the island itself. For this reason, it seems plausible that the local business and local governments play a leading role in a sustainable tourism and island development.

We have seen in this section that the private sector in general and the local business and local governments in particular should play a critical role in the development of a sustainable tourism development. But how should such a policy come about? This question will be the central issue in the following section.

5.4 Strategies

As described in the introduction, STD as a general orientation for a development strategy means that the tourism development evolves in such a way that the pressure on the natural environment remains below the level of the carrying capacity. This can be made more explicit by means of several key indicators. The carrying capacity of an ecological system should be expressed in the maximum level that these key indicators are allowed to reach. This means that **specific goals** should be set by determining the maximum level of the key indicators, given the framework of STD.

Before a policy can be developed to reach these goals, it is necessary to know which problem will arise on the path towards these goals, and thus a **problem analysis** should be carried out. For example, given the present policy for the tourism development, what is the expected level of the key indicators in the long term? If this level exceeds the maximum level that has been predetermined, the problem(s) definition regarding an STD has to be explicitly stated. If the new situation leads to incomplete outcomes, a new strategy has to be chosen in order to reach the goals after all.

Which possibilities does the region have for a policy toward STD? This is determined both by the power structures and the resources of the region itself and in comparison with other regions. Relative strengths and weaknesses are important in determining the region's possibilities.

The **strengths and weaknesses** are usually easy to identify by looking backward. Looking forward is much more difficult. Apart from the use of common sense, a proper use of methods or tools can be of great help. One way of identifying strong and weak points is by distinguishing five critical success factors (or necessary conditions). Each of these five factors can undermine the success of policies if they have not been sufficiently taken into account. The five critical success factors are incorporated into the so-called Pentagon model (Maggi et al., 1992):

*Ecoware   (ecological aspects)
*Finware   (financial aspects)
*Orgware   (organizational aspects, including the government organization)
*Software   (human aspects, like education and labour market training)
*Hardware   (environmental technology for protection of the natural or the physical environment)

The relative strengths and weaknesses of each of these five factors have to be determined.

In order to take the possible future developments into consideration, the expected **opportunities and threats** both in the current situation and in the future need to be examined. This can be done by means of the same framework.

After a thorough investigation of all relevant STD aspects in the past, current and future situations (see also Figure 5.2), strategic choices have to be formulated. In our analysis (see also Section 5.5) we have distinguished two steps.

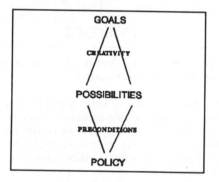

Figure 5.2 Scenario development

The first step is to broaden the view. With the use of **creativity** (and with the list of strengths, weaknesses, opportunities and threats) it is possible to invent many STD possibilities. This is a way to prevent the hazard of always using the same strategy for a problem, even if it might not be the best solution (the social costs of inertia). A straightforward way of using creativity is to draw up a list of possible options which can be used as goals. This can be done in several ways, for example:

*analogy (looking at similar problems in the past)
*brainstorming (active joint reflection on STD)
*lateral thinking (to break through the standard thinking)
*comparative advantages (compare the present state with (potential) competitors or competitive areas)

*morphological analysis

After inventing more ideas in the creative stage, it is important to screen them. A proper way of cutting down the number of possible options is by confronting them with preconditions. Therefore, the relevant **preconditions** have to be described, both in physical or material (e.g. money) and in non - physical terms (e.g. knowhow) as well as political and legal restraints. In order to reach STD, the ecological preconditions and constraints have to be given due and balanced attention. It is very useful - in coping with STD problems - to know how 'hard' certain preconditions (especially political) are in relation to the carrying capacity of a tourist area. It is also important to know how flexible politicians are in regard to economic demands or how exactly key indicators can be assessed.

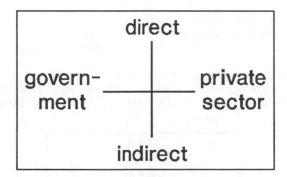

Figure 5.3 Balance between government and private sectors and between direct and indirect instruments

After having made the strategic choices, a policy can be developed and implemented. Depending on the specific local condition, more or less emphasis can be put on two key actors, viz. the **private** or on the **public** sector. For this purpose, the policy options can be measured on two axes: one for the initiator (or main actor) and one for the (in)directness of the intervention in the market system (see Figure 5.3).

Table 5.1
Pros and cons of market intervention

	pro	con
government	* coordination * unification	* less support for implementation * bureaucracy
private sector	* support for implementation * specialization * efficiency	* economy-driven instead of ecology-driven motives
direct	* result oriented	* very strict * decrease in flexibility
indirect	* freedom/flexibility * space for creative ideas	* not result-oriented

Policy-makers have to choose to what extent they wish to have an intervention in the market system or whether they prefer, for example, to let it be completely determined by the private sector. The same applies to the private sector.

In Table 5.1, a brief overview of the advantages and disadvantages of the four options from Figure 5.3 is given. This overview is useful when a choice for one or more of the policy instruments has to be made.

These pros and cons have to be kept in consideration when the policy instru - ments are to be chosen. An illustration of these instruments is shown in Table 5.2.

Table 5.2
Overview of main policy instruments

	government		←--------→	market forces
indirect	1) education/ information	4)	infrastructure	7) free market
¦	2) subsidies/ taxes/ pricing	5)	agreements	8) niches
direct	3) legal instruments	6)	permissions quota	9) investments

Here we will give a concise description of the instruments included in Table 5.2.

1 Information and education from the side of the government is mainly meant to make citizens, tourists and companies aware of the environmental problems and their role in it; it serves to show how they can contribute to the solution of environmental problems. It may also increase public support for government policy. An example is information on the amount of waste tourists produce (for the tourists) and the costs they impose on society (for the local inhabitants).

2   Subsidies belong to the group of economic instruments; it is a market-oriented instrument. This means, for instance, that it is not prohibited to pollute, but policy activities will be (relatively) more expensive. The government can in this way stimulate environment-friendly behaviour (for instance, by imposing lower prices on tourist facilities in ecologically less vulnerable areas). **Taxation** is a similar instrument and tries to discourage environment **un**friendly behaviour. The government can impose a tourist-tax ('tourist pricing') to discourage tourism in a specific area.

3   Legal instruments can have many forms. One of them is liability; this means that companies and citizens are liable (responsible) for damage they (or their products) cause to the environment. It is even possible to use this instrument in such a way, that companies have to prove that their products are **not** harmful to the environment. Hotels, for example, might have to prove that the tourists they receive (or their tourist facilities) do not cause any damage to the environment.

4   The government may, for example, supply public **infrastructure** like waste treatment facilities, but they can also supply an infrastructure to make it easier for the private sector or tourists to act more environment benign (e.g., supply public transport to tourist attractions). However, it is of course not certain that they will actually use it. This type of infrastructure can be supplied by the private or the public sector but also by public-private partnerships (PPPs) for efficiency reasons.

5   The government can also make **agreements** about e.g. the reduction of pollution. This instrument is more flexible than strict regulations or quota. It is however, important to point out that the government can always resort to laws if companies are not willing to act as agreed upon (to prevent the 'prisoners dilemma'). For example, the maximum number of hotel rooms or the maximum height of hotels can be agreed on. This instrument is especially useful in 'prisoners-dilemma' situations, which often occur in the tourism development.

6   **Permissions or quotas** for the amount that a company is permitted to pollute are instruments which give the government the opportunity to determine the exact amount of future pollution. With subsidies or taxation, this is not always possible. The problem of permissions is that it can lead to market imperfections and illegal actions. A way to decrease this problem is by making the permission tradable: the permission can be sold by means of an 'auction'. The maximum number of tourists can also be fixed in this way ('tourist quota').

7   **Free market** means here that there is no direct intervention in the market system by the government.

8   **Niches** are specific fractions of the total market. A group of suppliers of tourist facilities can, for example, decide to concentrate on a certain segment of the tourist market, like nature tourism or health tourism.

9   By **investments** are meant mainly large investments made by the private sector (e.g., large tourist organizations) which significantly determine the image of the tourism in a certain area.

After one or more policies have been implemented, they have to be evaluated. In this situation the central question to be answered is to which extent they lead to an STD. In other words, STD assessment focuses on the question wether it can be expected that in the long run the relevant key indicators will be below the maximum level of the carrying capacity.

We will show some of the above described methods in the following section. A subsequent section will offer examples of a study carried out on the island of Lesvos in Greece.

5.5   Scenarios

Various theoretical issues discussed above will be referred to in this section in the description of the **scenarios**. Scenarios can be a useful tool to clarify future implications of policy decisions. For that purpose scenarios very much simplify the reality and are not meant to predict the future.

The achievement of an overall STD objective is a central issue when activities for tourism scenarios have to be chosen. For example, in the case of Lesvos one may presume that mass tourism, large hotel complexes and beach clubs, sophisticated infrastructure etc. can be ingredients for strong economic growth and therefore for an economic growth scenario. A scenario incorporating all such activities has various implications in many fields (e.g., environmental impacts), and these implications can be determined using several indicators.

Before we discuss in more detail the case of Lesvos, some issues which play generally a role in a 'scenario discussion', will be pointed out:

A   the objectives and the possible combination of objectives
B   the importance of scenarios for the different actors
C   the evaluation of scenarios from a 'sustainability' point of view.

A *Objectives*

In policy analysis many objectives can be chosen; therefore have we categorized here the objectives in three main groups or three general objectives: efficiency, equity and conservation. In our research we have developed three different extreme contrast scenarios each based on only one of these **general objectives** (see Giaoutzi and Nijkamp, 1993).

This approach means that the *efficiency scenario* is completely based on activities, which will lead to a maximum of (quantitative) economic growth. Some examples of those activities are: hotels, airports, highways, many recreation areas, etc. Each activity in this scenario is allowed, as long as it will lead to further economic growth.

The second extreme scenario is the *equity scenario*. In such a scenario all activities must lead to a more equal socioeconomic distribution of wealth and knowledge and a higher level of well being. Education and health care are very important elements in this scenario.

The last extreme scenario is based on *conservation*. Protection and conser - vation of the environment and culture will form here the central criterion for all activities. Ecological farming and small scale fishing, for example, are first of all conservation-based activities.

As said before, these are three extreme scenarios. They can be used for thought experiments as they can clarify some implications of certain policy decisions. They are not used to predict the future. Clearly, in reality the objectives are usually more complex (and not of a mixed nature). For this reason, it is interesting to pay attention to combinations of these three contrast scenarios. This can be illustrated by using the Möbius triangle in Figure 5.4, which allows to make all combination of these extremes.

The combination of efficiency and equity objectives (no. 4), equity and conservation (no. 5) and conservation and efficiency (no. 6) form new and also interesting point of views. But in reality policies will tend to use a combination of all three (main) objectives, and therefore the seventh scenario is important. This scenario which makes a simultaneous connection between all three extreme scenarios, may then be seen as the result of a balanced mix of the three main objectives. Finding the right balance between these extremes will then be the main focus of STD policy assessment.

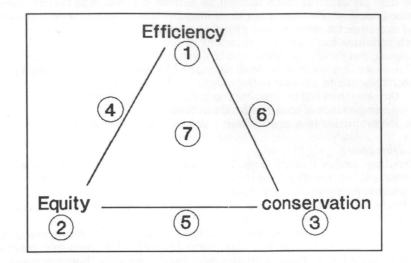

Figure 5.4 The balance between efficiency, equity and conservation

B Actors

In the first section of this chapter five groups of actors were distinguished. The role of each group in the scenario discussion can be very different. Each group will have its own objectives. And these objectives have to be considered if each group should be stimulated to cooperate in achieving STD. As the actions of all actors involved partly determine the success of an STD, a scenario which has incorporated most objectives of the different groups, will likely lead to the best results (i.e., with the strongest general support).

Policies may of course always have general objectives, which may not always be interesting for individual actors, but are of great importance to society as a whole. For this reason, policy makers find it often more appropriate to choose a more abstract objective, like 'sustainable development'. The basis for a scenario is the general objective and not the actor, but when creating and choosing proper policy instruments due attention to the different actors will have to be paid.

C Evaluation of scenarios

The third important issue here is the evaluation of scenarios. Scenarios are useless if they are not used to evaluate the various STD options. If several scenarios are created each based on a different STD strategy, the question of the best scenario has to be answered. Therefore, the determination of indicators - in relation to evaluation criteria - is crucial. If the general objective would be sustainable development, different indicators will be used compared to an objective like 'economic growth' (or at least the weight that is given to specific indicators is different).

In the case of the research on the island of Lesvos, we used the theoretical framework described above. In the following section some elements of the research undertaken are presented, to show some of the practical applications of this framework.

5.6   The case of Lesvos

In this section the empirical work undertaken for the island of Lesvos will be briefly described. It is not useful to describe here all research results and therefore only some main issues will be shown. Three scenarios will be presented here, two extreme scenarios and a mixed one, to illustrate the differences.

Scenario 1. Efficiency Scenario
Although Lesvos has good potential for **exclusive tourism** - a limited number of tourists but of a high quality and using expensive facilities - it is not possible to develop only the exclusive kind of tourism. Therefore, it is better to allow for and control the other types of tourism development. There will be always a group of other tourists like mass tourism. In this scenario first priority is given to exclusive tourism and secondly to a controlled development of other types of tourism, which may function as a side activity.
In this paper we describe just the main economic activities of this scenario.

Main economic activities
*a large number of small and luxury (high quality) **hotels, pensions;**
*8 - 10 **foreign villages**; these villages may count some 200 - 500 houses; people who live in these villages are foreigners; they stay here during the whole year (no seasonal problem), while in summer only some of them will stay (or otherwise they will let it to other tourists). These villages have their own (foreign) identity, shops, services, etc. Japanese tourist behaviour in Australia is a good example of the latter phenomenon;
*many **villas** and other high quality houses will be let
*a large number of specialized **restaurants**, high quality tavernas, etc.
*a few larger **tourist centres** for other types of tourism: sun, sea, sand; sports; it will be spread over about 3 locations with middle class hotels, beaches, bars and restaurants (not exclusive).

Next to these main economic activities, there are several side activities like large infrastructure projects and supporting services. Important indicators in this scenario are the gross regional product and the amount of employment.

Scenario 2. Conservation Scenario
Lesvos has a long history of economic activities like agriculture, stock breeding, fishing and some typical kinds of industry. Nowadays new economic development is not focused on these original activities, for example the production of olives, because there is world-wide competition on this market and profit margins are very low. There are many reasons to develop other activities.

On the other hand there will always be a demand for agricultural products, fish, etc. Conserving the cultural and physical environment and knowing there will be a market for these more traditional (but essential) products, the development of Lesvos can be concentrated on the **traditional economic activities**.

However, this is not as simple as it seems at first glance; first of all, the demand for agricultural products is not always the same. There are always new products, modernized production techniques, etc. The expectation for the next era is that specialization in high quality and nature based products may become very important (with an increasing demand) and competition in this field will be strong. Furthermore, the mentality of the people (the attitude of Lesvos inhabitants) is not very innovative; they are not very open to new developments. This means an extra handicap to specialization.

Nevertheless, this scenario will focus on conservation and from that point of view it is useful to think about development in the traditional sectors, albeit in a modernized way. One has to exploit what has been built up over thousands of years. This leads to the following set of activities.

Main economic activities
* **ecological farming**; this type of farming is not based on the idea of economies of scale but on the idea of producing in a natural way (high quality products, production on a continuity basis, without chemicals). In Western European countries this type of farming is becoming more popular; future expectations are favourable. So, for Lesvos most of the farms will change into ecological farms under scenario 2. This change in the agricultural sector will be difficult, but the current decline of this sector has to lead to a new modernized sector.
* **stock breeding**; Lesvos has always had many sheep and produces the famous Greek yoghurt. More specialization and better marketing will lead to good prospects.
* specialized fishing; the traditional way of fishing does not have good prospects due to depletion of the fishing grounds. On the other hand the fishing tradition can be used on a new, small scale on the basis of **specialized fishing**, for example, by setting up new fishing farms which use the natural thermal sources of the island. Specialized fishing is not only good from a conservation point of view, but it will lead to higher profit margins (efficiency).
* **culture tourism**; some events and activities for a limited number of tourists. This tourism can be based on the cultural history of Lesvos.

The basis of this conservation-oriented scenario leads to completely different indicators like the built up areas, the level and amount of cultural activities and the pollution level. Indicators like these can be used to assess the success of this scenario.

Scenario 3. Sustainable Tourism Development
The scenario with the STD orientation is built up from elements of all three extreme objectives. Although the balance of these objectives is open for discussion, the main lines of this scenario are as described below, based on a

compromise between tourism, environment, growth and distribution.

In this development a **network of conference centres** for national and international congress tourism may be very important. Favourable locations for high quality centres for conferences and seminars are often characterized by a quiet and inspirational environment. The location is an important issue when organizing conferences. But alongside an inspiring environment there must be a network of supporting facilities and activities (e.g., telecommunication services).

For various reasons it is attractive to develop such centres:
- they generate a large and direct inflow of money; there is a high profit margin in these activities
- such centres need a good network of services, infrastructure, etc. and most of these activities also support the development of the island in general
- commercial education and conferences will have their impact on the island's education level
- these activities are spread all over the year; only in summer there are less activities, so it is complementary to tourism activities. In particular, the importance of a development based on activities which are spread all over the year has to be stressed here; it is more efficient, the employment is more stable and there are better possibilities for a structural conservation policy.

The other main activity is agriculture; we have alluded already to the potential of more **specialized agriculture**. In this scenario, specialization is not based on the 'process' (like ecological farming) but on the 'product'. Although the production methods would have to change, the future of the current agriculture can be based on some *new specific products*. A network of services can support it.

The following activities can now be distinguished:

Main economic activities
* **conference centres**; the island of Lesvos is not the best place for mass conferences, but there are good possibilities for smaller and medium sized centres. In this scenario a plan of 2 medium sized centres (max. 500 people) and 10 smaller centres (50 - 100 people) seems to be ideal.
* 5 professional **education and research institutions**, especially in the field of tourism, agriculture, culture, etc.
* **archaeological centre** for research and education; one may think of a centre for traineeships for archaeology students.
* some bigger and medium sized **farms** which are specialized in some new products; there has to be a clear specialization in specific products, because Lesvos has natural/physical disadvantages for the production of mass goods.
* a number of **ecological farms**; although this scenario is not based on this process specialization, it is good to take part in this trend.

Indicators for success can be the evaluation indicators used for the measurement of success in the previous scenarios, but the main emphasis has to be put on the key indicators which are of vital importance for the sustainable tourism development (see Section 5.4).

It is in principle possible to design numerous STD scenarios, based on combinatorial combinational analysis of distinct choice options (see for details also Giaoutzi and Nijkamp, 1993). The evaluation of such scenarios will normally be based on multiple policy criteria, and hence multicriteria analysis (MCA) may be a proper analytical way to select the best possible alternative (see for further experiments with MCA for the development of islands; Giaoutzi and Nijkamp, 1993).

5.7   Final remarks

The concern for environmental decay is as such not recent, but especially in this century mankind has been able to turn it into a global in stead of a local or regional problem. The global problems are, however, mainly the result of the local scale of externalities in terms of both causes and effects. Therefore, solutions have to be found on a regional scale, but also because of the poor results so far of international bodies in dealing with global environmental problems.

There is not - and probably will not be - a blueprint for a STD policy. As described before, each situation is different and requires a different approach and solution, especially in the case of peripheral island economies. Our arguments have been based on the assumption that 'solutions' cannot be brought about top-down, but bottom-up; a shift in thinking might be necessary here. The local market with its own initiatives should in this view form the basis for sustainable development.

There is also a role for governments especially local authorities, as they can influence developments into a desired direction. They should not try to coordinate and influence the entire process of development, but rather assure that the growth of the economy and the ecology be a balanced growth.

For developing a policy for STD, in our study several aspects and phases have been described, as well as certain strategic choices that have to be made (e.g., the extent of government influence that is desired). We have also tried to put forward the consequences of our ideas in several scenarios for Lesvos. It should be emphasized that these scenarios are not meant as policy proposals, but as exercises to point out what the consequences of certain decisions may be, and how they can be systematically assessed and evaluated ('flight simulators').

With this chapter, we have tried to present a framework to identify a set of policy objectives and options in order to determine a strategy which can form the basis for a sustainable tourism development.

References

Bergh, J. van den (1991), *Sustainable Economic Development*, Thesis Publ., Amsterdam.

Clark, W.C. and Munn, R.E. (eds.) (1986), *Sustainable Development of the Biosphere*, Cambridge University Press, Cambridge.

Coccossis, H., Janssen, H., Kiers, M. and Nijkamp, P. (1991), Tourism and Strategic Development, *Series Research Memoranda*, Free University,

Amsterdam.

Coccossis, H. (1992), *Regional Science, Island Economies and Border Areas*, paper RSA World Congress, Palma de Mallorca.

Fokkema, T. and Nijkamp, P. (1994), The changing role of governments, *International Journal of Transport Economics*, (forthcoming).

Giaoutzi, M. and Nijkamp, P. (1993), *Evaluation Methods for Regional Sustainable Development*, Avebury, Aldershot.

Nijkamp, P. (1979), *Theory and Application of Environmental Economics*, North-Holland, Amsterdam.

Opschoor, J.B. (1987), *Duurzaamheid en Verandering*, Inaugural Address, Free University, Free University Press, Amsterdam.

Pearce, D.W. and Redclift, M. (eds.) (1988), Sustainable Development, *Futures, 20*, special issue, pp. 3-21.

WCED (1987), *Our Common Future*, World Commission on Environment and Development, Oxford University Press, Oxford/New York.

6 Planning for tourism at local level: Maintaining the balance with the environment

J. Westlake

6.1 The meaning and nature of planning

Planning implies the need for an orderly arrangement of activities and practices in order to minimize the uncertainty which arises in any future position. In addition because in any economic system there is the need for resources which are not always infinite to be allocated between different sectors and users. Tourism as an activity, being based on interactions of particular destinations and so requires coordination and the cooperation of the various providers both public and private, small and large; the tourist industry is diverse and fragmented and not one single identifiable sphere of activity, hence the need for specific attention be given to its organisation, format and future condition. Particular requirements for tourism are that potential conflicts between visitors and residents be minimized and that in an ideal world the concept of 'dual use' of facilities be practised; some man-made attractions depend on various forms of demand and customers for the facility to be viable and feasible. (Gunn, 1982) So called natural attractions are threatened by their misuse and mismanagement; sustainability is a relative concept based on the means by which management techniques may be used and are applied. (Cooper and Westlake, 1989)

If tourism planning is seen as a new conception it has been preceded historically by physical land-use planning and economic planning. There followed concepts of social planning related to, the possibility for example, to develop and revitalize urban areas. The history of planning during the twentieth century has seen a move, both towards and away from specific foci and approaches often not relevant to tourism as such; ideas of comprehensive and socially responsive planning for the community are approaches which at times have been in fashion with planners. Achieving such goals for the community are often seen as politically driven and hence their non acceptance by some. Tourism is only one sector of activity within a nation region or locality; but increasingly as an activity its importance has brought about the realisation that this industry and activity deserves special attention. In greenfield situations in developing countries the decision to use tourism as a tool for development has led to the concept of tourism masterplanning; whereas in more developed or congested contexts, like Britain, the notion of a physical strategy for tourism has emerged. The end result in the 1990s is that using the best approaches from past experience we may merge economic planning and the master plan approach in with the physical or land use approaches to plan for the total needs of the tourist sector in the form of strategies at scales from national to local level. (Inskeep, 1991)

6.2   Reasons for tourism planning

The many reasons which may be cited for tourism planning is to avoid the negative impacts that occur to the sociocultural and other environments. (Pearce, 1989) Through orderly change the benefits arising from the developmental process may be maximized. (Murphy, 1985) The life cycle concept of Plogg itemized groups of customers with different views of preferences for the destination, but Butler's work stresses the need to identify the threshold at which a destination may begin to lose its appeal and so for us to formulate and take remedial action; destinations without management may become overloaded spatially and temporarily. (Mathieson and Wall, 1982) Others cite the problem of loss of cultural identity. (Mill and Morrison 1985)

6.3   Destination and market foci

There have been barriers to the acceptance of a planned approach to tourism. In Britain the historical development of a unitary approach to planning, giving municipalities powers to zone land uses and to control the subsequent development of activities have given planning a somewhat negative connotation; planners are seen as reactive rather than proactive. Tourism itself, which is not a fully understood activity by people, politicians and even planners has led to the focus in the past, on supply based control mechanisms. Notions of absolute units or thresholds do not recognize the relative and movable limits to usage levels; ideas of capacity and measurability has not taken into account the means by which management, information provision and interpretative facilities allow for more flexible thresholds to be developed. (Copper, 1981) Carrying capacity is a relative concept especially in as far as conceptions of individual personal space are concerned. An appreciation of the characteristics of the market, the characteristics of the product as part of an approach of market orientation, leads to the possibility to channel, augment, substitute or reduce flows.

6.4   What is market orientation?

Market orientation implies that there are customer characteristics which if known and understood allow for a variety of positive and negative methods/techniques and powers to be implemented. Certain key questions may be posed to those engaging in the formulation of strategies for tourism:

• Do we have clear objectives; are they agreed or imposed; what form of consultation processes have been engaged?

• Do we have adequate data of visitor demand, types and flows. If this does not already exist do resources exist to collect this; are we able to monitor the position for the future and to carefully clarify problems which have been or are identified?

• Are there specific and clear legislative and organisational powers which allow for the tourist sector to be able to be developed and managed?

• What evidence is there of the possibility for, and the existence of public and private sector cooperation and liaison. Tourism as a key element in society and the economy depends on public infrastructure and to a large degree private superstructure or businesses.

• What evidence is there of market orientation? As well as detailed resource analysis, have we evidence of market research and the effective use of information services including signposting?

These are of course some of the key elements forming the basis of planning for tourism. Market orientation does not mean the same as depending on free market forces. Free enterprise cultures may help to create new business activity but can lead to the degeneration of tourist destination into unmanageable and undesirable mixes of activity at tourist destinations. Possibly the key issues are the extent of understanding of what constitutes a tourist strategy and the extent of legal and organisational support structures to allow for effective implementation and management.

6.5   The development of tourism strategies in the UK context

Without taking time to go into detail on the history and environment of British planning structures and procedures, some brief statements are necessary. There has been the rise of a municipality based administrative system of some strength alongside some central forces in government. Regional planning apart from the 1930s and 1960s which were reactions to regional economic decline has not been a feature of British life; land use planning at this level has also been divorced from economic planning.

Planning legislation based on the powers of municipalities originally evolving under public health provision and concern for the poor in the 1800s led to the development of controls on the spread of roads, housing and industry in the 1930s and ultimately in the 1947 Town and Country Planning Act. Revisions to former development planning of the 1980s and the 1960s led to the concept of structure planning in the 1970s, with substantial emphasis on the participation of the public in such plan making processes. Tourism did appear in some plans at local level, whereas others particularly local politicians thought their role was to plan for people (or residents) and not tourists; of course some resorts had always seen tourism as their livelihood. With the passing of the Development of Tourism Act in 1969 and the subsequent establishment of the

Country Boards (England, Scotland and Wales) followed by Regional Tourist Boards the notion of giving advice to municipalities by such bodies emerged. (English Tourist Board, 1981)

The notice given by the Department of the Environment to local authorities that tourism was a sector of activity worth considering (DOE Circular 13/79) was a significant and noticeable event; the service sector was recognized as a creator of jobs. Likewise the notion of a systems approach to planning within regions and municipalities in the 1970s led to the idea of a planning process being applied to tourism. (McLoughlin, 1969) This approach of collecting data and identifying assets and problems, to framing goals and objectives, to evaluating alternative strategies often involving the public to an eventual policy implementation; the final stage was the need to monitor and provide feedback to such initial goals.

6.6   The move towards tourism specific planning in the 1980s

Various initiatives were launched by central government in the 1980s, such as the Tourism Development Action Plans (TDAPs) established in 1984. Tourism Growth Points (Hansen, 1970) were set up in the 1970s as a function of regional economic development initiatives and based on economic theory applied to manufacturing industry in the past; TDAPs replaced such ideas and comprised 20 areas in seaside resort, urban areas, heritage towns and rural regions, earmarked for short term programmes. Public and private sector partnerships funded such activity. (Branwell and Broom, 1989)

There had been previous project assistance given to developers via the so called Section 4 part 2 of the 1969 Development of Tourism Act, but this for England was withdrawn in 1988 in the interests of cuts in Government expenditure. Despite the valuable advice given by the Country Boards to municipalities all through the 1980s there had been constant reviews of their effectiveness and use of so called public funds.

6.7   The 1990s: more initiatives for the environment but less public funding for tourism

During the last two years the concept of sustainable tourism has been introduced by government and its agencies such as the Tourist Boards to the municipalities. In 1991, 'Tourism and the Environment, Maintaining the Balance' has been published; guidelines on how to achieve sustainability are outlined in terms of how statutory plans at local level can bring about planning, gain via the interdependence of tourism and the environment. A 'Task Force' was set up to produce an advisory document backed up by visitor management case studies and studies on Historic towns, the Countryside, and Heritage Sites. The key message was that those who benefit from tourism in the private sector should also contribute towards the costs which are often met by the public. More recently in 1992 'The Green Light - A Guide to Sustainable Tourism' was produced by the English Tourist Board and the Countryside Commission and others; sponsorship was gained from industry partners such as British Airways.

More recently there have been significant initiatives following changes in planning legislation, such as the consolidation of previous legislation and a White Paper on the Environment. A draft guidance note on tourism produced by the government has appeared in the form of a Planning Policy Guidance Note. (DOE, 1992) Local Authorities have wider powers of regulation control and enforcement of decisions to maintain and sustain the environment within the context of tourism development.

6.8 Planning for the future

Visitor management schemes are now firmly embodied within planning for tourism in Britain; heritage sites, historic towns, the countryside and the seaside all appear to have adapted to the needs of market orientation in knowing the customer and managing the visitor in a considered and sensible way. Concepts of sustainability have been published and promoted. However the notion that private industry must pay the costs of their actions and contribute to the wellbeing of such initiatives and schemes is more open to discussion and doubt; should they and will they contribute? Alongside these measures, funding to local authorities from central government has been reduced and may well be reduced further with modified forms of local taxation being introduced for the future. The market system is intended to be firmly instituted for the future; Britain has evidence of market orientation in place in terms of well established approaches to visitor management. Progress made to date will no longer receive such public financial support as in the past, so the extent to which sustainable tourism can be maintained by the private sector is a key issue in Britain today. The lack of any formal statutory requirement for municipalities to raise local taxes specifically for tourism plus overall budgetary constraints may be the reason why we will find it difficult to sustain sustainable tourism.

References

Bramwell, R. and Broom, G. (1989), Tourism Development Action Programmes: An Approach to Local Tourism Initiatives, *Insights 1989*, ETB, London, pp. A6-11 to A6-17.

Cooper, C. (1981), Spatial and Temporal Patterns of Tourist Behaviour, *Regional Studies* 15 (5), pp. 359-371.

Cooper, C. and Westlake, J. (1989), Developing and Managing Tourism: An Enlightened Technique for Destination Planning, *Proceedings of Conference - Tourism and Environment in the Post Industrial Society*, FAST Milan.

English Tourist Board (1981), Planning for Tourism England - A Planning Advisory Note, London.

English Tourist Board (1991), Tourism and the Environment: Maintaining the Balance, London.

English Tourist Board (1992), The Green Light: A Guide to Sustainable Tourism, London.

Gunn, C.A. (1982), Destination Zone Fallacies and Half Truths, *Tourism*

Management 3(4), pp. 263-269.

Inskeep, E. (1991), *Tourism Planning*, Van Nostrand Reinhold, New York.

Hansen, N. (1970), Development Pole Theory in a Regional Context, *Regional Economics*, MacMillan, London.

Department of the Environment (1979), Local Government and the Development of Tourism Circular 13/79, London.

Department of the Environment (1992), *Planning Policy Guidance, Tourism*, London.

Mathieson, A. and Wall, G. (1982), *Tourism: Economic and Social Impacts*, Longman, London.

McLoughlin, J.B. (1969), *Urban and Regional Planning - A Systems Approach*, Faber, London.

Mill, R.C. and Morrison, A.M. (1985), *The Tourism System*, Prentice Hall, New Jersey.

Murphy, P.E. (1985), *Tourism: A Community Approach*, Routledge, London.

Pearce, D. (1989), *Tourist Development*, Longman, New York.

7 Specialization in tourism: The case of a small open economy

A. Lanza and F. Pigliaru

7.1 Introduction and non-technical summary

Let us suppose that at a certain moment in its history, a small country with important natural tourist attractions finds itself facing the following trade-off: to better exploit the opportunities offered by international markets, it must decide whether to concentrate its own limited resources on developing, above all, the tourist sector or to concentrate primarily on development of its industrial sector. Let us also suppose that in this economy there exists a 'social planner', meaning an institution interested in obtaining the maximum welfare from existing resources, and not open to influence by pressure groups lobbying for non-general interests. To decide, the planner will have to address certain questions. The first is obvious: which of the two sectors guarantees the most rapid growth rate, both for current and future generations? The second is: if it is decided to focus on tourism, what is the economically optimal way to use the natural resources which attract tourists?

Up until a few years ago, it would not have been easy for our planner to get clear answers. As for the first question, the existing literature is rather thin and mainly empirical (Ghali (1976) and McKee (1988), for instance), since growth theory was not suited, up to very recently, to analyze long-run growth effects in general, and trade-induced growth effect in particular. A significant step ahead was achieved with the development of endogenous growth theory, to which we refer in the first part of the chapter. In particular, we use a number of results developed in Lucas' model of endogenous growth in small open economies (Lucas (1988)) in order to define under what conditions specialization in tourism (as compared to manufacturing) is not detrimental to a country's economic growth.

Generally speaking, high rates of income growth are often associated with the development of the industrial sector, due to the latter's inexhaustible capacity to produce and adopt technological innovations. However, factor productivity growth is not the only source of income growth, especially for a trading economy. Indeed, when comparing the growth rates of the two possible specializations, is necessary to take into account the changes over time in the price of 'tourist goods' with respect to industrial goods. Everything else being equal, everyone would prefer to produce a good whose value increases

91

constantly, over time, with respect to that of other goods. Tourism (or at least tourism based on natural resources) is a good of this type specifically because its supply grows slowly, unlike that of industrial products.

To better assess the relative importance of this point, we consider consumers who live and work in an industrialized country undergoing rapid (endogenous) economic growth, and who spend a proportion of their income for their vacations, renting for instance holiday homes supplied in a fixed quantity in attractive locations. In general, their availability of funds for holidays grows together with total income. But by how much? This is the crucial point. If tourist preferences are such that they spend a non-diminishing proportion of income on rents then the economic profitability of the houses grows at least as fast as the tourists' income. In other words, the expenditure of tourists creates a linkage between industrialized and tourist countries, to the advantage of the latter. In this way, it is entirely possible that specialization in tourism would not be economically damaging in terms of growth, notwithstanding the (relative) technological 'inferiority' of the sector.

Thus far we have only confronted the first of the two initial questions. Nothing has been said about the management of the quality of the natural resources. There is no doubt that specialization in tourism carries risks of creating incentives for excessive use of natural resources by the private sector, and thus putting the economy on a dangerous course from both the economic and ecological points of view. In fact what applies to tourism applies to any other economic activity in the presence of public goods: since the market does not assign realistic prices to public goods, there is risk of their excessive and non-sustainable use. However, our work shows that economies that specialize in tourism have some well-defined economic motivations to favour (but not guarantee) the careful management of natural resources.

To justify this conclusion we consider the following issue: what is the economically optimal mode of maximizing revenues from the touristic use of natural resources? Our answer is based on a reasonable hypothesis that concerns consumer preferences. According to this hypothesis, the quality of the resources, as valued by the tourists, is inversely proportional to the degree of crowding (exploitation). In other words, tourism is a 'snob' good (Leibenstein 1950): the more crowded the resources, the less consumers are willing to pay to stay in the area under consideration. In this respect our model is similar to that developed in Tisdell (1991) (see also Butler (1980), McConnell (1983), Tisdell (1984)).

In this setting, our social planner has two good economic reasons to preserve the high quality of the resources, over time. The first motive relates to the income growth rates derived from tourists' exploitation of resources. Since a fairly uncrowded natural resource is, ceteris paribus, higher quality compared with one that is more crowded, then it is probable that consumers would be willing to pay ever greater proportions of their growing incomes to acquire 'luxury goods', and vice versa for the other good of inferior quality. For this reason, the proceeds obtained in a more 'exclusive' place tend to grow more rapidly than those from a crowded one.[1] Therefore, preserving resources can mean growing more quickly. But does it also mean being richer in the long run? To find out, we must put aside growth rates and concern ourselves instead with how the (steady-state) relative level of total income changes according to the degree of crowding.

In general, from a strictly economic point of view, it is worth 'crowding' until the fall in tourist expenditure per capita, due to the aversion to crowding, is greater than the rise in the total number of tourists. The optimal level of crowding (i.e. that which maximizes the proceeds obtainable from the resource) falls in line with rising consumer sensitivity to the problem of quality. Thus, in the case of high aversion to crowding, one easily reaches the conclusion that to 'crowd' a lot is economically less sensible than to 'crowd' a little. This is the second economic reason which favours nature conservation. But it is also clear that much depends on the degree to which real consumers react to variations in the quality of touristic resources. Unfortunately, until now, there have not been conclusive empirical studies of this issue, and in their absence it is not easy to reach a clear conclusion on the optimal policies. In this sense, our work may serve to underline the urgency for acquiring this information via a specific case study.

However, a rather general conclusion can be formulated on the basis of our analytical model, even without empirical data, if (i) we can hypothesize that the degree of consumer reaction to quality variations would be significantly higher today than yesterday, and suggest that in the future it will be even higher; and (ii) we take into account that tourist exploitation of resources often requires irreversible reductions in resource quality. In this setting, it is conceivable that, due to present consumer preferences, maximum proceeds can only be achieved by increasing current levels of natural resource exploitation. Can the planner permit further 'consumption' of resources? Only on the condition that it does not prejudice the right of future generations to obtain at least the same returns from their natural inheritance.[2] But this is not always possible because such a rate of exploitation, while optimal today will not be so anymore tomorrow - if preferences change in the direction just suggested, the quality of natural resources today may deliver future lower returns. In other words, responsibility towards future generations gives a further strong indication favouring extremely cautious management of natural resources. Less built-up coastlines today may imply sacrifices made by the current generation in favour of all future ones, while heavily developed coastlines could impose sacrifices on the latter, to the exclusive (and uncertain) advantage of the present.

The chapter is organized as follows. The growth effects of tourist specialization are described in the next Section, while the choice over quality-differentiated tourist goods is evaluated in the third one. In the Concluding Remarks we sum up the main results and suggest some directions for future research.

7.2   Economic growth and specialization in tourism

In this section we aim at identifying the conditions under which tourism specialization maximizes the long run rate of per capita economic growth.[3] An alternative to tourism specialization of course must be available - more precisely, we need both another sector and a technology allowing comparative advantage to be endogenous, so that policies can be designed to fill any accumulated competitive gap in the desired sector, whatever the initial condition of the economy. These requirements are met by the recently developed approach known as endogenous growth theory (see below; for a general and detailed introduction to this class of models, see Grossman and Helpman (1991)).

In the following, the alternative to tourism specialization is manufacturing. We make this choice because this alternative is by far the most attractive of all for real world economies - one reason being that manufacturing is generally regarded as the only sector capable of generating a process of endogenous technological change strong enough to make the whole economy grow at a non-diminishing rate in the long run (Romer (1990), Grossman and Helpman (1991)).

The model on trade and endogenous growth developed in Lucas (1988) fits our needs particularly well. In this model, the world economy is formed of a continuum of small countries producing two goods. Each sector is characterized by its own rate of endogenous accumulation of sector-specific (productivity enhancing) 'human capital' h. We call the high-learning sector 'manufacturing' and the low-learning 'tourism'. In each country h is accumulated through a learning-by-doing process, the benefits of which are in the form of 'pure external economies'. Production and accumulation functions (linear in h, the cumulable factor) are as follows:

$$Q_i = h_i L_i \qquad (i=M,T) \qquad (7.1)$$

$$\dot{h}_i = \lambda_i h_i L_i \qquad (7.2)$$

where M is manufacturing, T tourism, λ_i is the sectoral learning-by-doing parameter, and L_i is the sectoral labour force. The growth rate of sector i

$$\dot{h}_i/h_i = \lambda_i L_i \qquad (7.3)$$

Assume that the fixed stock of labour available to our economy is equal to one, and that, following the above characterization of the two sectors, $\lambda_M > \lambda_T$ - ie, human capital accumulation is faster in manufacturing than in tourism for similar allocation of the fixed factor.

International trade makes these economies specialize completely according to the comparative advantage they obtain at the point at which they enter the world market. In this setting, long-run growth rates are very easy to define in terms of the single good produced by a completely specialized economy, since they reduce to $\dot{Q}_i/Q_i = \lambda_i$. This result seems to suggest that specialization in manufacturing is always the growth-maximizing choice. This conclusion would be wrong, however - in fact, an economy with no manufacturing, and therefore deprived of the main 'engine of (productivity) growth', may grow even faster than (initially) similar economies specialized in manufacturing. Of course, everything depends on how the price of the tourist good changes over time relative to the price of the manufacturing good so as to partially or entirely offset the sectoral gap in productivity growth. In other words, in order to evaluate the two growth rates in terms of a common good we have to take into account the rate of change of the terms of trade $p \equiv p_T/p_M$. As shown by Lucas (1988), the latter, under CES international homothetic preferences, with all existing countries completely specialized in either manufacturing or tourism, turns out to be

$$\dot{p}/p = (\lambda_M - \lambda_T)\sigma^{-1} \qquad (7.4)$$

Where $\sigma = 1/(1+\rho)$, i.e. the elasticity of substitution. Clearly, $\dot{p}/p > 0$ since $\lambda_M > \lambda_T$ (the supply of the manufacturing good grows faster than that of tourist services). Then the growth rate of a country specialized in tourism (say ∂_T) in terms of the manufacturing good is simply $\lambda_T + (\lambda_M - \lambda_T)\sigma^{-1}$, so that

$$\gamma_M \gtreqless \gamma_T \text{ according to } \gamma \gtreqless 1$$

Therefore everything depends on the elasticity of substitution between manufacturing and tourism. If $\sigma = 1$, the time path of the terms of trade, that continuously favours the tourist good,[4] exactly offsets the sectoral difference in physical productivity growth. As is apparent by now, specialization in tourism is relatively harmful to growth only if $\sigma > 1$.

Since we are dealing with preferences regarding two very distinct bundles of goods such as 'manufacturing' and 'tourism', a low elasticity of substitution seems plausible, thus we cannot rule out the hypothesis that the higher growth path is associated with specialization in tourism. Clearly, an empirical investigation on the actual value of σ in international markets should yield very valuable information for the assessment of the growth effects of tourism specialization.

In the next section, we turn to our second topic - namely, the choice of the quality of the good supplied by an economy specialized in tourism in the case of an ever-increasing real expenditure on the services yielded by this sector.[5]

7.3 Tourist goods of different quality

In this section we describe how the growth rate and the income level of a small economy specialized in tourism may vary according to the quality of the tourist good it chooses to yield. To this aim, a crucial step is to describe how the prices of the quality differentiated tourist goods change over time in the world market, so that our small economy can identify the quality that maximizes its income growth and level. Before turning to the determination of international prices, however, we need to adopt a definition of quality.

Quality and preferences - The definition of quality we are thinking of is based on some negative relationship between quality and some index of exploitation of a natural resource. We start by defining our tourist goods as 'snob' goods (Leibenstein, 1950). We consider a resort attached to a natural attraction such

95

as a beach. The quality and the quantity of per capita services available to tourists are invariant to the resort's scale, so that the goods are differentiated only by the per capita availability of the natural resource, which in turn depends on the number of tourists allowed to stay there. Not surprisingly, preferences are such that more of the natural resource is preferred to less.[6] This setting yields a workable definition of *quality*: as perceived by all consumers, quality simply coincides with some index of per capita resource availability.[7] As a consequence, each resort faces a downward sloping relationship between 'quality' and its tourist population. Formally, we define the quality index α as a function of T, an index of crowding, given by the ratio of the tourist population to the size of the beach (say, $Q*/S$)[8]; for the time being assume that $\alpha(T)$ takes the following specific form

$$\bar{\alpha}(T) = \delta T^{-\beta} \qquad \beta, \delta > 0 \tag{7.5}$$

where $-\beta = \varepsilon_{\bar{\alpha}T}$, the elasticity of perceived quality with respect to crowding.

As for the functional form of the consumers' preferences at the world level, quality resorts are 'luxuries' and lower quality ones are 'necessities', and we can describe how the expenditure shares (and the relative price of the two tourist goods) change as economic growth in manufacturing continuously increases the consumers' real income.

Under this approach, each consumer is supposed to buy all kinds of tourist goods available in the marketplace, in proportions that depend on both prices and income (i.e., prices and income levels determine how she allocates her annual holidays between higher and lower quality resorts).

To keep the foregoing analysis as simple as possible, we make a number of assumptions. The main one is that two tourist 'goods' only are supposed to be supplied - 'crowded' and 'luxury' resorts of similar natural endowments. The advantage of this assumption is that it allows us to work with a simple quasi - homothetic utility function of the Stone-Geary type. The drawback is that the description of the relationship between quality and quantity becomes sketchy - the choice of tourist population for our hypothetical resorts is limited to two exogenous quantity indexes (say $\bar{T}_1$ and $\bar{T}_2$ for 'crowded' and 'luxury' resorts respectively). However, our main results do not depend on this assumption.

In this simplified setting, a small economy's total revenue from tourism is either $R_1 \equiv p_1 \bar{T}_1 S$ or $R_2 \equiv p_2 \bar{T}_2 S$, where S is the exogenous size of the natural resource; costs associated with the supply of the tourist good are assumed to be zero. Then, to evaluate how the growth rate and income level of this economy are affected by the quality of its tourist good, the main step is to describe how the international relative price p_2/p_1 is determined at the world level, and how changes in the (ever-increasing) real per capita income affect it.

The determination of the international prices - As already said, international preferences over the two tourist goods take the form of a Stone-Geary quasi–homothetic utility function:

$$U(Q_1, Q_2) = (Q_1 - \gamma_1)^{\alpha 2} \cdot Q_2^{\alpha 2} \quad 0 < \alpha_1 < \alpha_2 < 1, \quad \alpha_1 + \alpha_2 = 1, \quad \gamma_1 > 0 \quad (7.6)$$

where α_1 and α_2 are related to the above defined quality indexes (see equation 7.5). More precisely, $\alpha_i \equiv \bar{\alpha}_i / (\bar{\alpha}_i + \bar{\alpha}_j)$, so that $(\alpha_i + \alpha_j) = 1$, and both the constraints required by the utility function are satisfied; γ_1 characterizes good 1 as the 'necessity'. The budget constraint y is defined by the optimal overall expenditure on tourist services as defined in Section 7.1 (recall that endogenous growth makes this expenditure grow over time).[9] Now consider the FOCs for the solution of this problem:

$$\left\{ \begin{array}{l} \alpha_1 (Q_1 - \gamma_1)^{\alpha 1 - 1} Q_2^{\alpha 2} = \lambda p_1 \\ \alpha_2 (Q_1 - \gamma_1)^{\alpha 1} Q_2^{\alpha 2 - 1} = \lambda p_2 \\ y - p_1 Q_1 - p_2 Q_2 = 0. \end{array} \right. \quad (7.7)$$

The demands for the two goods are[10]

$$Q_1 = \gamma_1 + \alpha_1 (y/p_1 - \gamma_1) = \gamma_1 (1 - \alpha_1) + \alpha_1 y/p_1$$

$$Q_2 = \alpha_2 ((y - p_1 \gamma_1)/p_2) = -\alpha_2 \gamma_1 p_1/p_2 + \alpha_2 y/p_2 \quad (7.8)$$

To define how p_2/p_1 changes as real income increases, first consider the ratio of the expenditure share of good 2 to that of good 1:

$$\frac{p_2 Q_2}{p_1 Q_1} = \frac{(-\alpha_2 \gamma_1 p_1/y + \alpha_2)}{(\gamma_1 (1 - \alpha_1) p_1/y + \alpha_1)} \quad (7.9)$$

For finite values of y/p_1, $\partial(\cdot)/\partial(y/p_1) > 0$ where $(\cdot)$ stands for the share defined by equation (7.9). Increases in $p_2 Q_2/p_1 Q_1$ can be decomposed to show that

$$\dot{Q}_1/Q_1 - \dot{Q}_2/Q_2 \geq 0 \Rightarrow \dot{p}_2/p_2 - \dot{p}_1/p_1 > 0 \quad (7.10)$$

i.e., the relative value of the high quality good is increasing in real income as long as its supply does not grow faster than the supply of the low quality good. Now consider the limit of equation (7.9):

$$\lim_{y/p_1 \to \infty} (p_2 Q_2/p_1 Q_1) = \alpha_2/\alpha_1 \quad (7.11)$$

To sum up, (i) under reasonable assumptions regarding the relative growth rate of the two supplies,[11] the relative price of the high quality good is increasing in real income, for finite values of the latter; (ii) as y/p_1 grows over time, the ratio of the two shares approaches a constant value α_2/α_1).

Implications for a small economy specialized in tourism - Given this determination of the international prices, we can now turn to discuss the implications for a small economy specialized in tourism, endowed with a natural resource of size S. First, total revenue for a small economy specialized in tourism is $R_i \equiv p_i \bar{T}_i S$ (i=1,2), so that $\dot{R}_2 / R_2 - \dot{R}_1 / R_1) = (\dot{p}_2 / p_2 - \dot{p}_1 / p_1)$. Then point (i) above tells us that, for this economy, the growth rates achieved by specializing in the high quality good are generally higher than those associated with the low quality good, for finite values of y/p_1[12] (in the long run, the two growth rates may converge as $y/p_1 \to \infty$).

Does this outcome about relative growth rates suggest that specialization in the high quality good is always the best choice for a small economy? Of course not. Consider the system in the proximity of its limit as described by equation (7.11); assume further that the supply Q_1, Q_2 are now either fixed or share a common growth rate, so that the relative price is constant at $\alpha_2 Q_1 / \alpha_1 Q_2$. Then it is entirely possible that the faster growth path associated with good 2 actually leads to a steady-state relative income level favourable to specialization in good 1. So we need a more detailed analysis of the long run value of the annual relative total revenue accruing from tourism.

Using equation (7.11), the function for relative total revenue can be defined as

$$\frac{R_2}{R_1} \equiv \frac{p_2 \dot{T}_2}{p_1 \dot{T}_1} = \frac{\alpha_2 Q_1 \dot{T}_2}{\alpha_1 Q_2 \dot{T}_1}$$

(7.12)

Equation (7.12) simply says that if $(\bar{T}_1 / \bar{T}_2) > (\alpha_2 Q_1 / \alpha_2 Q_2)$, then the flow of total revenue is maximized by specialization in good 1. However, since the function $\alpha(T)$ is defined, we can be more precise than this. Substituting equation (7.5) into equation (7.12), we get:

$$\frac{R_2}{R_1} = \left(\frac{\dot{T}_2}{\bar{T}_1}\right)^{1-\beta} \frac{Q_1}{Q_2}$$

(7.13)

The value of β is therefore crucial. Since $\beta | \varepsilon_{\alpha T} |$ (see equation (7.5))[13], our results show that:

If $| \varepsilon_{\alpha T} | \geq 1$ in the relevant range, then $Q_1 > Q_2$ represents a sufficient condition for the total revenue associated with specialization in good 2 to be larger than that associated with specialization in good 1.

Then everything hinges on the elasticity of the perceived quality with respect to increases in the intensity of use of the natural resource. *Ceteris paribus*, the annual income accruing from the tourist exploitation of the resource is the more likely to be maximized by a 'luxury' resort the more consumers are sensitive to quality variations (a flat $\bar{\alpha}(T)$ curve would make specialization in the low quality good more remunerative).[14]

with a small country case, each country could sell, by definition, any desired amount of its services for a given international price (i.e., each country faces a horizontal demand curve for any good of a given quality). However, the presence of a quality crowding trade-off does introduce a negative relationship between quantities and prices from the viewpoint of small countries. In other words, these countries face downsloping demand curves exclusively because of the consumers' reaction to the worsening of quality due to crowding (see Tisdell, 1991) for the definition of a similar demand curve). As soon as such a demand curve is in place, it turns out that each resort or country faces the simple monopolist's profit maximizing problem.[15] So our result fits the general case - if the price elasticity is less than one,[16] total revenue as well as profits are maximized by reducing supply.

Finally, notice that in equation (7.13) R_2/R_1 is increasing in β, as shown in Figure 7.1 (drawn for the simplified in which $Q_1 = Q_2$). Therefore, changes in the preferences over T_1 and T_2 might make tomorrow's maximizing quality level different from today's (for a brief comment on this point, see the Concluding Remarks below).

R_2/R_1

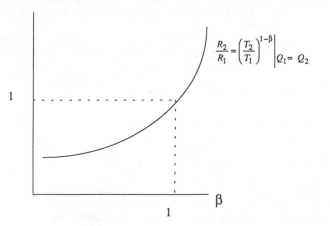

$$\frac{R_2}{R_1} = \left(\frac{T_2}{T_1}\right)^{1-\beta}\Big|_{Q_1 = Q_2}$$

Figure 7.1 Ratio of revenues as function of quality elasticity

7.4 Concluding remarks

Our analysis of the economic effects of specialization in tourist services based on natural resources can be summed up as follows.

First, we used the endogenous growth model developed by Lucas (1988) to show that the possibility exists for a small country to specialize in tourism and still retain a growth rate comparable to that of countries who allocate their resources in sectors where productivity grows faster. Adopting Lucas' characterization of the growth process in small open economies, tourism turns out to be 'harmful' to long run growth only if the elasticity of substitution between manufacturing goods and tourist services is high. A thorough empirical investigation on this point therefore represents an interesting task for future research.

Second, we wanted to describe how the ever-increasing real expenditure accruing to the tourist sector is subdivided between quality-differentiated tourist goods. A simple characterization of quality-differentiation was achieved by defining the tourist good based on a natural resource as a 'snob' good. To further emphasize the role played by differences in quality, preferences over tourist goods of different qualities have been assumed to be quasi-homothetic, as in the Stone-Geary utility function. Then the value of the high quality good relative to the low quality one is increasing in real expenditure on tourism, as long as its world supply does not grow faster than the supply of the low quality good. From the point of view of the small country with given quantities of tourist goods to offer, this means that the growth rate is maximized by specializing in the high quality good.

Third, we addressed the problem of what tourist specialization maximizes the level of long run income accruing from the natural resource. As in the first result mentioned above, here too an elasticity plays the key role: if the elasticity of quality (as perceived by consumers) with respect to some index of crowding is higher than or equal to one, then specialization in the high quality good does maximize the income level under very reasonable assumptions concerning the relative world supply of the two goods.

Taken together, these results point out the need for a careful management of the natural resource that attracts tourists. Crowding decreases its market value because it lowers its quality. Because of this, excessive exploitation of the natural resource may lower both the growth rate of the economy (if preferences are non-homothetic) and the level of the total revenue accruing from the tourists.

This conclusion may be supported by some further considerations. The trade–off between quality and crowding may become more 'rigid' over time (future generations might value quality more than the present one), as suggested for instance in Fisher, Krutilla and Cicchetti (1972)), so that specialization in high quality might become (more) convenient tomorrow. This possibility deserves careful scrutiny especially if crowding causes irreversible damage to the natural resource. Moreover, in the absence of public restrictions, most resorts are likely to become overcrowded, since individual investors may ignore their own contribution to the depletion of the natural resource. Therefore, careful planning might allow a country to sustain a stable supply of a good for which relative scarcity increases (perhaps irreversibly) over time in the world market. Finally, by depleting its natural resource, a country may end up competing against man-made tourist attractions - a kind of tourist good for which cumulable factors such as human capital is what matters most. In this market segment, countries endowed with natural resources of lower quality are likely to have acted as first movers, and therefore to have developed a competitive advantage not easy to overcome.

These considerations, together with the testable implications of our results, suggest some directions for future research - both theoretical and empirical - on the economics of tourism based on a natural resource.

References

Abala, D. (1987), A theoretical and empirical investigation of the willingness to pay for recreational services: a case study of Nairobi National Park, *Eastern Africa Economic Review*, 3, pp. 111-119.

Bakkal, I. (1987), *Analysis of demand for international tourism in North Mediterranean counties*, Northern Illinois University, unpublished dissertation.

Bakkal, I. and Scaperlanda, A. (1991), Characteristics of US demand for European tourism: a translog approach, *Weltwirtschaftliches Archiv*, 127, pp. 119-137.

Barbier, E.B. and Markandya, A. (1989), The condition for achieving environmental sustainable development, London Environmental Economics Centre Discussion Paper, 5.

Barten, A.P. and Turnovsky, S.J. (1966), Some aspects of the aggregation problem for composite demand equations, *International Economic Review*, 7, pp. 231-259.

Butler, R.W. (1980), The concept of a tourist area cycle of evolution: implications for management of reserves, *Canadian Geographer*, 24 pp. 5 - 12.

Copeland, B.R. (1991), Tourism, welfare and de-industrialization in a small open economy, *Economica*, 58, pp. 515-529.

Edwards, A. (1992), *The international tourist forecasts to 2005*, The Economist Intelligence Unit, London.

Fisher, A.C., Krutilla, J.V. and C.J. Cicchetti (1972), The economics of environmental preservation: a theoretical and empirical analysis, *American Economic Review*, 62, pp. 605-619.

Ghali, M.A. (1976), Tourism and economic growth: an empirical study, *Economic Development and Cultural Change*, 24, pp. 527-538.

Gorman, W.M. (1959), Separable utility and aggregation, *Econometrica*, 27, pp. 469-481.

Gorman, W.M. (1970), *Quasi separable preferences, costs and technologies*, University of North Carolina, mimeo.

Grossman, G. and E. Helpman (1991), *Innovation and growth in the global economy*, MIT Press, Cambridge, Massachusetts.

Lanza, A. and F. Pigliaru (1994), The tourist sector in the open economy, *Rivista Intenazionale di Scienze Economiche e Commerciali*, January 1 and ERRATUM, March 3.

Leibenstein, J. (1950), Bandwagon, snob and Veblen effects in the theory of consumers' demand, *Quarterly Journal of Economics*, LXIV, pp. 183-207.

Lucas, R.E. (1988), On the mechanics of economic development, *Journal of Monetary Economics*, 22, pp. 3-42.

McConnell, K.E. (1983), The economics of outdoor recreation, in Kneese, A. and J. Sweeney (eds.), *Handbook of Natural Resources and Energy Economics*, North-Holland, Amsterdam.

McKee, D.L. (1988), *Growth, development and the service economy*, Praeger, London.

O'Hagan, J. and M.J. Harrison (1984), Market shares of US tourism expenditure in Europe: an econometric analysis, *Applied Economics*, 16, pp.

919-931.

Romer, P. (1990), Endogenous technological change, *Journal of Political Economy*, 98, S71-S102.

Tisdell, C.A. (1984), The provision of wilderness by Clubs, *Rivista Intenazionale di Scienze Economiche e Commerciali*, 31, pp. 758-761.

Tisdell, C.A. (1991), *Economics of environmental conservation*, Elsevier, Amsterdam.

Notes

1. Technically speaking, this result holds under the additional assumption that preferences regarding the two quality-differentiated tourist goods are quasi-homothetic, as defined in the Stone-Geary utility function. Non-homotheticity is strongly supported by a number of empirical studies (for instance, O'Hagan and Harrison (1984), Bakkal (1987) and Bakkal and Scaperlanda (1991)).

2. We assume here that the planner is committed to the implied simple definition of sustainable growth.

3. The main results of this Section are presented in a rather informal fashion. For more analytical detail, see Lanza and Pigliaru (1994).

4. Whether local residents in countries specialized in tourism actually reap the gains from this continuous improvement in p depends on several aspects (such as factor mobility and land ownership) not included in our model. On the role of these aspects in a static framework, see Copeland (1991).

5. To identify what conditions support this case, consider the rate of change of the purchasing power in terms of the tourist good of a person living in a country specialized in manufacturing. From the analysis developed above we know that the growth rate of Q_M in terms of the tourist good is

    $$\dot{\gamma}_M \equiv \lambda_M - (\lambda_M - \lambda_T)\sigma^{-1}.$$

    So $\gamma_M > 0$ as long as $\sigma > \sigma^*$ $(1 - \lambda_T/\lambda_M)$ (notice that λ_T/λ_M lies between zero and one for $(1 - \lambda_T \leq \lambda_M)$. Therefore, real expenditure on tourism grows over time as long as $\sigma > \sigma^*$. In the next section this condition is assumed to be fulfilled.

6. To quote from an empirical study on a similar matter, "human congestion in the (Nairobi National) Park has a significantly negative impact on the users' willingness to pay for park services" (Abala, 1987).

7. A more complex approach should allow for a less simplistic definition of quality. For instance, by introducing some forms of increasing returns in

the supply of tourist services, the decline in the resource quality might be (partially or entirely) offset by increases in the per capita availability of tourist services.

8. Our equation (7.5) is consistent with some examples in the literature on sustainable development (Barbier and Markandya, 1989). In this literature, a link between dS/dt, the rate of environmental degradation and dX/dt, the rate at which environmental quality is changing, is usually established - the basic relation being dX/dt = -a(dS/dt).

9. Since preferences are non-homothetic, y enters the determination of the international relative price (see equation 7.9) below). Since income levels differ among countries, we may think of y as some world average of per capita expenditure on tourism.

10. It is easy to show that, for finite values of y, the income elasticity ε_{iy} is >1 for Q_2 and <1 for Q_1. However, notice also that in the limit

$$\lim_{y\to\infty} \varepsilon_{1y} = \lim_{y\to\infty} \varepsilon_{2y} = 1.$$

In other words, for $y\to\infty$ the Stone-Geary function approaches a homothetic function.

11. For instance, individual investors' incentives might be such that a significant number of (initially) high quality resorts end up as low quality ones - see the section on Concluding Remarks for a brief discussion about this possibility.

12. We are comparing the growth rates under complete specialization, i.e., we ignore the trajectories describing changes of specialization.

13. Notice that $\varepsilon_{\alpha T} = \varepsilon_{\alpha T}$ since $\alpha_i \equiv \alpha_i /(\alpha_i + \alpha_j)$.

14. Notice that this conclusion applies to any two values of T, so that we can easily identify the value that maximizes total revenue globally.

15. Note that the small country context adopted here allows us to abstract from strategic considerations concerning other countries' reaction to our country's choices.

16. Suppose that $Q_1=Q_2$, so that the price elasticity is simply $1/\varepsilon_{\alpha T} = -1/\beta$. Then $\beta>1$ implies that our demand curve is 'inelastic'.

Part B
POLICY CASE STUDIES IN SUSTAINABLE TOURISM

8 Assessing the interaction between heritage, environment and tourism: Mykonos

H. Coccossis and A. Parpairis

8.1 Introduction

The continuing growth of international tourism (Table 8.1), expected to become even stronger in the next decade (Table 8.2), suggests increasing pressures on tourism destination areas. Furthermore, important changes in the structure of tourist supply and demand appear to lead to the emergence of a new 'profile', in which tourism is intricately interlinked with the quality of the environment. It is now generally agreed that uncontrolled growth in tourism as a source of development, which in less than a century of existence, often involves substantial risks leading not only to environmental deterioration of the host areas but also to their long term decline as tourist centres. Furthermore it seems that such deterioration is pervading, with alarming consistency, other, broader, facets of the environment. Fortunately there are signs that this process is now changing directions.

The great socioeconomic and geopolitical transformations experienced recently, particularly in Europe but also in other parts of the world, are expected to influence the development and characteristics of international tourism to a great extent. These changes in the scale and quality of demand in parallel with the expected responses of supply (infra/superstructure) of tourism must be carefully considered in a new approach to planning for tourism in which heritage and the quality of the environment is a priority issue within a broader strategy towards sustainable development.

The aim of this contribution is to outline how the structure of tourism is affected by the current global changes and to explore an approach to the practice of planning for tourism. In this respect it is very important to develop methods and tools which take into consideration the interrelationships of tourist activity with the historical-cultural and natural environment. This intricate relationship becomes more pronounced in the case of an island context, with rich cultural and natural resources, due to the sensitivity and particularity of its socioeconomic and environmental systems.

Table 8.1
Development of international tourism
Arrivals and receipts in Europe, 1950-1990

YEARS	TOURIST ARRIVALS (Thousands)	ANNUAL % CHANGE	TOURISM RECEIPTS (Million US$)	ANNUAL % CHANGE
1950	16839	-	890	-
1960	50351	199.01	3918	340.22
1970	113000	124.42	11200	185.86
1975	153859	36.16	26363	135.38
1980	196000	27.39	61654	133.87
1981	195289	-0.36	57240	-7.16
1982	197759	1.26	55544	-2.96
1983	192828	-2.49	55367	-0.32
1984	207628	7.68	57319	3.53
1985	214263	3.2	61181	6.74
1986	215396	0.53	77024	25.90
1987	230752	7.13	96341	25.08
1988	239347	3.72	106746	10.80
1989	266946	11.53	109007	2.12
1990	275500	3.2	136300	25.04

Attention is drawn to some of the special issues faced in areas/islands with rich historical/cultural resources in regard to the development of tourism and presents a methodological framework for this assessment through qualitative and quantitative methods. The concept of carrying capacity, for example, attracts considerable attention in this context particularly because of its potential for identifying an optimal use level of an area/island. To test the applicability of this concept several methodological and operational tools have been examined and applied to the case study of a tourist pole: the island of Mykonos. The emphasis of the analysis lies in the interaction between the natural heritage, social and physical components of carrying capacity.

Table 8.2
International tourism forecasts and shares by region 1995 - 2000

	FORECASTS		SHARE OF WORLD TOTAL	
	1995	2000	1995	2000
WORLD				
Arrivals (mn)	515	637	100	100
Receipts ($bn)	343	527	100	100
AFRICA				
Arrivals (mn)	23	32	4.4	5
Receipts ($bn)	10	14	2.9	2.7
AMERICAS				
Arrivals (mn)	103	128	20.1	20.1
Receipts ($bn)	95	146	26.9	27.8
EUROPE				
Arrivals (mn)	294	338	57.2	53
Receipts ($bn)	152	206	43	39
ASIA/ OCEANIA				
Arrivals (mn)	95	140	4	21.9
Receipts ($bn)	86	161	24.4	30.5

Source: WTO

8.2   The background of tourist development

Tourism has been one of the economic success stories of the last 40 years. It has grown into a major component of the world economy and one of the most highly developed and dynamic industries with an important contribution to incomes and employment. Part of it being in less developed regions it helps to an extent - etceteris paribus - to spread economic development and reduce inequalities in the geographical distribution of income.

Tourism at the same time is increasingly becoming an important subject in environmental and social sciences as the result of many socioeconomic and environmental factors influencing the movements of people (Nijkamp, 1974). The major factors which have contributed to the rapid growth of this activity are the rise in incomes, increase in the time available for leisure, the advent of declining costs of travel, etc. Tourism grew at such a scale that, within a short period of time it almost tripled from 160 million international arrivals in 1970 to 430 million in 1990 (WTO, 1991) - a rapid increase unquestionably. International tourism recorded its highest growth rate of arrivals and receipts during the period 1960-1980. The early 1980s were hit by a recession of international travel, a recovery began in 1984 but was interrupted by terrorist events in 1986. In the late eighties and early nineties, tourism experienced record levels in terms of both arrivals and receipts.

The importance of tourism in the emerging 'European economy' is increasingly recognized as a positive development strategy providing opportunities for improving the local environment and regenerating the local economy (Breakell, 1991). The contribution of the tourist sector in the EEC of 12 countries - just to present a few indicators of the significance of tourism - represents 5% of the GNP in 1990 (Figure 8.3) with Spain 9.4%, France 9% and Greece 7.4% surpassing the average of the Community. The comparable figures for employment structure in relation to tourism in the EEC show that the average represents 6.0% of the total working force with Spain at 9.3%, Portugal, 8.8% and Greece 7.2% (above the average). This picture shows clearly not only the importance of tourism in many countries in Europe, but also worldwide (WTO,1991) due not only to the intensification of intraregional travel, but also to an increasing number of arrivals from other mainly industrialized regions.

The continuation of tourist growth largely reflects the overwhelming importance of the sector for many countries, like Greece, but it also emphasizes the need to give critical attention to the role of tourism in stimulating and sustaining economic growth. The peculiarity of tourism is that it is dependent on the availability and quality of tourist resources. Among these, environmental quality becomes increasingly important since tourism uses environmental resources as primary inputs in the production of the tourist product and as sinks for the residuals generated during the production and consumption of this product (Briassoulis, 1991).

Although technology can to some extent alleviate certain types of negative impacts on the built heritage and natural environment there are still important aspects of impacts which largely escape the conventional policy means of modern societies. In the last twenty years or so such externalities have come to the forefront of policy priorities in the developed and the developing world as well. In spite of the tremendous growth of tourism little effort has been invested in anticipating and controlling the externalities of tourist development on the natural, manmade, social, economic and heritage - cultural environment (deterioration, stress, congestion, pollution, depletion of resources, etc.). Yet, tourism is definitely attracted by environmental assets (in the widest sense).

In an increasingly competitive world countries must constantly improve coordinated measures to ensure the safety and protection of the environment and improve the quality and attractiveness of their tourist product (WTO, 1987). It is also necessary to adopt effective strategic planning to meet the fast growing tourist demand, taking into account the long-term preservation of heritage and of natural resources in order to effectively face the negative impacts associated with the expected increase in environmental, economic and social pressures.

8.3   The new tourism profile

The phenomenon of 'mass' tourism, which has existed for less than a century, has often led not only to catastrophic use of the host environment resources but also to the destruction of tourist expectations. It is patently clear that most visitors during their tourist experience search among other things for a refreshment of mind, body and spirit (England, 1991) and look forward to fulfilling a dream of a personal utopia. The process of tourism which developed until the nineties has now changed towards new and different directions (Coccossis and Parpairis, 1991). From the dominant post war model of 'mass' and 'package' tourism there has been a shift to energetic, selective, exclusive, cultural and environmental (eco, soft) oriented tourism, which is expressed in the protection-conservation of the natural, historical-cultural and social environment, the preference of quality over quantity of services, and the safeguarding of the stay: a process which leads to sustainable tourist development.

Parallel to that, changes in the behaviour pattern of tourists - a result of many factors such as higher standards of living, accumulation of experience, sensitivity to the value of the natural, social and cultural environment, the internationalization of environmental awareness - have also led to a gradual restructuring of the tourist industry. The above shifts have been complemented by shifts in public policy in support of environmental issues. The focus for environmental control has shifted away from regional or national centres to international bodies, such as large multinationals, non governmental agencies and intergovernmental organizations (EEC). This has provoked a number of radical changes at the level of demand and supply in tourism. On the part of demand, sample investigations (Parpairis, 1993) have concluded that the majority of tourists prefer those tourist destinations which present important and unspoiled particularities and at the same time attract low volumes and sizes of tourist flow.

Similarly on the supply side there is an increasing tendency to plan at the micro and macro scales and offer high quality environments, exploiting the comparative advantages and diversity of local resources and setting higher standards for infra/superstructural resources. Tourist, local and sector-related bodies are all well aware that tourism depends for its success on the host environmental quality. Accordingly, developers for their part are led to improve their environmental performance and prepare convincing 'planning obligations' (Fyson, 1991), - packages covering infrastructure, landscaping and environmental costs. The degree of protection offered to special 'environments' (island, designated areas, national parks, green belts, historical-cultural areas, traditional settlements, etc.) is bound to remain a matter of dispute, but there is little case for extending exceptionally favourable treatment in general planning terms to an 'industry' which is itself dependent on environmental quality to attract its customers.

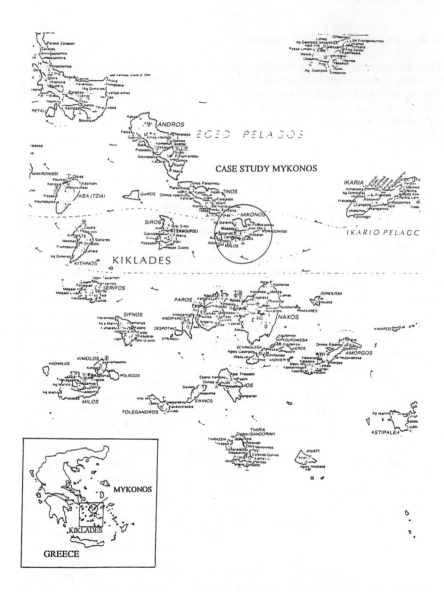

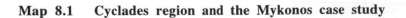

Map 8.1 Cyclades region and the Mykonos case study

It is evident, that the combination of a series of factors which determine tourist preferences and the corresponding demand for a specific tourist destination, push tourism to a new profile where quality and quantity presuppose a different relationship between demand and supply, based on the sustainable use of environmental resources in the future. In this new process of tourism one important concept dealing with the protection of the environment is that of carrying capacity. This concept has been developed earlier in other disciplines but is also increasingly applied to tourism (Parpairis 1993). Carrying capacity has already been employed in several outdoor recreation projects and, although it has received considerable criticism in the recreational literature, this concept can serve a useful purpose especially when it encourages tourism planners and others to give greater consideration to heritage and natural environmental matters.

8.4   Tourism in the island context: case study of Mykonos

There is no doubt that tourism has already attracted considerable attention in issues related to an island environment and particularly the development of small islands. The growing demand for tourism opens up new opportunities even for small and isolated places, contributing to income and employment for island inhabitants, but at the same time it has direct effects on their sensitive and unique environmental resources (Coccossis, 1987). This situation has already influenced local awareness of environmental issues especially in some cases where the expansion of tourism was rapid and intensive.

The development of tourism is basically attracted by the area's natural features - landscape, plant and animal life - complemented by cultural and social attractions. Although these features and attractions should be protected, tourist development unfortunately is often in sharp conflict with the protection of uniqueness since it is associated with modernization, change in culture, urbanization and extensive exploitation of resources, (from boom-bust agricultural and fishery activity to the monopoly of tourism where landscapes and coastlines are being visibly affected by widespread urbanization and the intrusive impacts of hotel, marina, airport and road construction (Towle, 1985)).

The potential effects of environmental degradation due to uncontrolled and intensive tourist development, inevitably affects tourism itself and the sensitive island ecosystem on which tourism is based. However there seems to be wide agreement to place emphasis on the management of at least some key island resources (coasts, freshwater, agricultural land, marine resources) in an attempt to highlight the interdependence of socioeconomic phenomena and environmental processes. In this respect the carrying capacity is becoming a critical tool in creating an efficient management (static component) and allocation (dynamic) of environmental resources.

Mykonos is an internationally well-known tourist island with an environment of high quality which has experienced rapid tourist development during the last 30 years (Figure 8.1 and Table 8.3). It offers a good case for the examination of tourism impacts on the island's environment and the accompanying dangers of adopting inappropriate tourism policies during the different stages of tourist development subject to little or no control. Mykonos is part of the Cyclades archipelago and belongs to a sub-group composed of three islands (Mykonos, Dilos and Rinia) with a total surface area of 103,5 square kilometres and 81.5 kilometres seashore (Map 8.1).

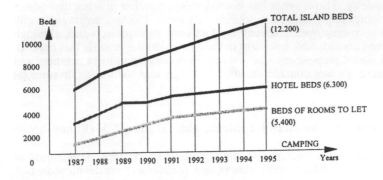

Figure 8.1 Trends in growth of tourist supply

Table 8.3
Development of tourist supply (composition indicator)

a/a	TYPE OF ACCOMODATION		1951	1961	1971	1981	1991	PARTICIPATION %	AVERAGE CHANGE	CHANGE 5 61/71	71/81	81/91	61/91
1	HOTELS	U	-	2	11	40	121	6,9	14,9	450	263,6	202,5	5950
		R	-	54	384	895	2492	31,2	1129,6	611	133	311,4	4519
		B	-	98	720	1934	4724	29,8	1180	634,7	168,6	144,3	4720
2	ROOMS (N.T.O.)	U	-	-	-	-	460	26,2	-	-	-	-	.-
		R	-	-	-	-	1861	23,3	-	-	-	-	-
		B	-	-	-	-	4026	24,8	-	-	-	-	-
3	CAMPING	U	-	-	-	1	2	0,2	100	-	-	100	-
		R	-	-	-	56	168	2,1	200	-	-	200	-
		B	-	-	-	168	504	3,1	200	-	-	200	-
4	VILLAGES	U	-	-	-	100	172	9,8	72	-	-	72	-
		R	-	-	-	200	480	6	60	-	-	60	-
		B	-	-	-	800	960	5,9	20	-	-	20	-
5	SUMMER HOUSES	U	-	-	-	-	1000	56,9	-	-	-	-	-
		R	-	-	-	-	3000	37,4	-	-	-	-	-
		B	-	-	-	-	6000	37,1	-	-	-	-	-
6	TOTAL	U	-	2	11	141	1755	100	29233	450	263,6	1145	5950
		R	-	54	384	1251	8003	100	4906,7	611	133	593,7	4519
		B	-	98	720	2902	16214	100	5481,6	634,7	168,6	558,7	4720

Source: OUTSIDE OFFICIAL CONTROL
U = UNITS, R = ROOMS, B = BEDS

The natural environment of the island, typical of the Cyclades, is characterized by low vegetation due to the dry climate, lack of fresh water and poor soil conditions. Rural activities have adapted over the centuries to the low capacity of the terrestrial ecosystem to provide few agricultural products. The marine environment is of unique beauty and still largely undisturbed. The stronger attraction of the island though, is its unique architectural heritage in the built environment. However, the rapid tourist development and its expansion to a scale which can be considered large in relation to the size and population of the island (Figure 8.2), threatens not only its rich built environment heritage and the natural environment but also its socioeconomic structure and local culture.

This situation - common to many other islands in Greece as well as in other parts of the world, where tourism is rapidly developing - leads to the question of whether the present development in this island is sustainable. Mykonos contributes to the Greek economy and of the Cyclades region in particular, from which it also reaps the fruits of various spillover effects. Because of its size and its traditional activities, this small island never became a commercial, administrative or political centre nor reached a state of economic influence as happened to the nearest island of Syros or other Aegean islands like Rhodes, Samos, Lesvos and Chios, but it became a universal cultural centre mainly because of its historical/cultural and natural resources. For this reason Mykonos is strongly dependent on its indigenous natural and manmade resources (Coccossis and Parpairis, 1993).

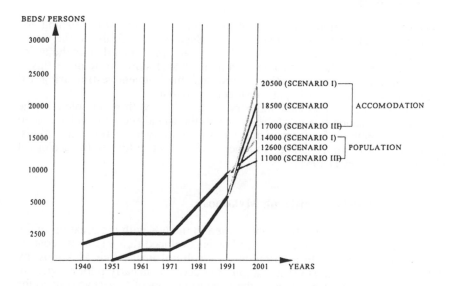

Figure 8.2 Comparative growth of population and tourist supply
(carrying capacity indicator)

115

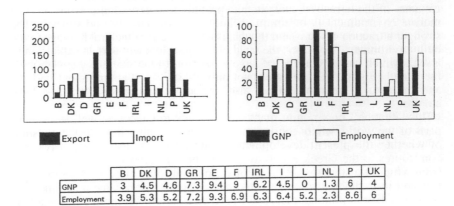

	B	DK	D	GR	E	F	IRL	I	L	NL	P	UK
GNP	3	4.5	4.6	7.3	9.4	9	6.2	4.5	0	1.3	6	4
Employment	3.9	5.3	5.2	7.2	9.3	6.9	6.3	6.4	5.2	2.3	8.6	6

**Figure 8.3 Development of international tourism
export - import, GNP, employment in EEC**

Source: EUROSTAT (1991)

The traditional economic activities of the island were agriculture, fishing and sea trade but during the last 30 years it has changed dramatically to the visitor industry (tourist and service sectors). Today tourism is regarded as the major export industry of the island although there is still some agriculture this is limited because of harsh weather conditions, employment restructuring and scarcity of water which is largely absorbed by tourism.

Although tourism is a major industry of the island with great potential, the one-sided orientation towards tourism makes the island economy vulnerable to regional competition for tourism and the ups and downs of the world tourist industry. Furthermore such 'monoculture' is at odds with ecological sustainability (OECD 1981).

8.5   The tourist profile of Mykonos

The first tourist phase of the island started in the 60s with the creation of the first hotel (Xenia) - one of a series of hotels developed throughout the country especially in places with a strong historic/cultural image like Mykonos, by NTOG (National Tourist Organization of Greece) in an early pilot program to introduce tourism to accommodate the increasing flow of tourist arrivals to the island (Figures 8.1, 8.4 and Table 8.3). This pioneer effort soon stimulated the development of new hotels and other types of private sector accommodation. Accommodation capacity jumped from 98 hotel beds in 1961, to 680 in 1971 and more than 1,796 in 1981. In the last decade, however, more hotel beds have been added to the island's capacity.

It is estimated that in 1991 there were 4,700 hotel beds, more than 4,000 beds in rooms (provided mainly in houses), another 2,000 beds in single houses and another 960 beds in single houses, villas and apartments. To this capacity one must add two organized tourist villages of 120 apartments for tourist and summer holiday makers, about 3,000 single units of summer houses (6,000 beds) and one campsite with 168 places. The total accommodation capacity on the island for the visitor industry is estimated to be over 16,000 beds of all types and is believed to be conservative, based on information from local realtors and tour operators (Parpairis, 1993). The number of arrivals also jumped from 5,150 in 1965, to 28,115 in 1971 and from 53,982 in 1981 to more than 259,012 in 1991. Similarly, bed nights in hotel beds only, increased from 34,350 in 1965 to 132,881 in 1971 and from 353,621 in 1981 to more than 1,549,555 in 1991.

Parallel to the expansion of the tourist industry there has also been an increase in the island's population size. In 1951 there were only 2,690 inhabitants, in 1961 2,872 and 3,863 in 1971. During the last two decades - in which tourism developed more rapidly - the island's population increased even more to reach 5,530 in 1981 and over 8,500 in 1991 (according to preliminary unofficial estimates). In the sector of tourism it is estimated (Parpairis, 1993) that more than 6,000 persons are directly or indirectly involved, a ratio of one employee for every five beds. Growing population and aspirations dictate that the productivity of these activities increase but in the long-run small-scale, diversified, and closely managed forms of resource-based enterprises owned by local residents may provide more benefits to the island population than those promised by mass tourism organizations (McElroy, 1987). In the case of Mykonos one can already observe such a situation in the structure of the tourist sector.

The island already presents some evidence of saturation and emerging undesirable effects on the island's sensitive environment (natural, cultural and social) such as congestion, safety, pollution of water and soil, especially during the peak summer season. The two existing traditional settlements of the island - Hora and Ano Mera - as well as the other newly developed villages throughout the island, on which tourist industry was mainly based during the pioneer phase of development have already been transformed in scale, volume of built-up area, character, and environmental quality conditions (natural, social, cultural) because of the uncontrolled and rapid development of tourism (Table 8.4). Effective conservation measures were not considered necessary at the peak of tourist development during the last decade. Such measures are urgently required to be based on land development, monitoring and enforcement mechanisms, environmental education and public participation. Realistic identification of community needs, careful resource and technology assessment and option analyses may indicate multiple benefits for locals and tourists. Priority in all measures should be directed to increasing the island's cultural tourism (by means of appropriate guidance, incentives and training) and escaping from the production-consumption cycle and the model of mass tourism development. Emphasis should be given to the distribution of tourist demand and supply in space and time, on preservation policies of natural, cultural and social environment and on the effective planning and management of growth of both local and visitor population.

This case study is a good example for analyzing the issue of sustainable development in the process of tourist development of vulnerable areas. In this context the achievement of ecologically sustainable economic development not only requires strategic research on a variety of environmental research problems (Nijkamp and Giaoutzi, 1991) such as multi-functionality, user's conflicts, carrying capacity, sustainable economic yield, risk analysis etc., but also the adoption of effective environmental management strategies as part of a broader-based development policy.

The evidence of Mykonos suggests that there is a definite relationship between the notable increases in tourists and the gradual conflict over the island's scarce resources (productive land, underground water reservoir, marine resources, cultural resources etc.) as recent empirical evidence from many other countries also suggests (Dinell, 1987).

8.6   The concept of carrying capacity

The concept of carrying capacity has attracted considerable attention during the last decade, particularly in its potential role to control the optimal use - level of an area with regard to the development of any human activity - such as tourism. This particular concept has often been proposed for islands due to their characteristics of well defined size and resource, isolation and identity, uniqueness in many aspects and the quality of the relationship which has been established between the island and the outside world (Hache, 1987).

Table 8.4
Comparison of population - arrivals - bednights
From 1940 to 1991 and projection of 2001 for the
island of Mykonos

a/a		1940	1951	1961	1971	1981	1991	2001
1	POPULATION	2150	3546	3718	3863	5530	* 8500	12600
2	ARRIVALS	-	-	-	28115	53982	259012	1107432
3	BEDNIGHTS	-	-	-	132881	353629	1549555	6916078
4	ACCOMODATION (BEDS)	-	-	98	720	2902	16214	18500

* Temporary facts

118

Table 8.5
Land use distribution of the coastal zone of the island of Mykonos

Length of coast in km. - surface in acres

a/a	COASTAL USE BASIC	1961		1971		1981		1991		CHANGE %	
	GROUPS	SURFACE	LENGTH	SURFACE	LENGTH	SURFACE	LENGTH	SURFACE	LENGTH	SURFACE	LENGTH
1	SANDY*	360	24	335	22,5	330	22	312	20,8	-8,3	-5,4
2	ROCKY*	965	51	965	51	965	51	965	51	-	-
3	MIXED	437	12,9	413	12,9	401	12,9	367	12,1	-	-6,7
4	CHANGE OF USE (PORT, SETTLEMENT)	12	0,8	35	2,3	42	2,8	72	4,8	230	71,4
5	TOTAL	1774	88,7	1748	88,7	1738	88,7	1716	88,7	-2	-1,3

* Medium width of surface of coast 15 m.

However, in operational terms carrying capacity presents inherent difficulties, particularly if applied in a broad sense, that is, including social and cultural dimensions. In spite of the fact that the quantification and qualification of the concept requires complex models, carrying capacity is still useful in policy making since it provides a conceptual tool which can serve as a basis and as an indicator of the man-environment system. In addition, it can be employed as a vehicle to quantify specific policy options (Coccossis and Parpairis, 1990).

The realization of the existing relationships between natural and human environment in terms of responses to stimulate of a temporal and spatial nature, will be useful and the concept can be integrated into a single operational definition, under the carrying capacity umbrella which includes ecological, (Ricci, 1976) socioeconomic, institutional and policy aspects (Vries, 1989). The concept of carrying capacity is well defined in ecology/anthropology, resource economics and in the man-made environment tradition. Biologists, forest specialists and soil scientists have made the greatest contributions in biophysical carrying capacity studies while geographers have contributed in exploring the behavioural aspects. Continuing progress will undoubtedly require combined research efforts from a variety of disciplines since the dynamic and complex phenomenon of tourism requires a comprehensive approach. In that respect, one suitable definition of the concept could be as follows:

"the number of user unit use periods that a tourist area (island) can provide each year, without permanent biological/physical deterioration of the site's ability to support recreation and tourism and without appreciable impairment of the recreational experience".

In theory the concept of carrying capacity of a tourist island could be defined as reaching a crucial stage when the minimum infra/superstructural requirements, as well as the natural resources which create demand, have become insufficient to meet the needs of both the island population and the visiting tourists, whereupon the threat of environmental hazards appears (Coccossis and Parpairis, 1990). The problem therefore is related to the question of what levels of change of the 'environment' can be permitted in the island under consideration. A similar definition of the concept could also be one referring to life cycle products (Dragicevic, 1990 and Parpairis, 1992) where the product can be quickly adapted or replaced and completely removed from the market by a new technological solution. This cannot be so easily done with the tourist site as a market product if the phase of its saturation is not objectively recognized - particularly in a case of exaggerated commercialization. It might lose its attractiveness for both mass market and new products or market innovations.

The optimal land-use for an island can be assessed in a similar way to range management, on the basis of four factors - physical extent of the island, ecological characteristics, human behaviour/psychology and economics - in combination or alone, acting to limit the intensity of tourist use. Different definitions of carrying capacity have been developed, based on one or more of these elements, although to combine these into a functional general definition is a very difficult exercise mainly because each factor involves the use of different units. Moreover these definitions do not seem to take into account the ways in which tourist activities interact with the island ecosystem. The island's natural environment is not only affected by the volume of people (locals and tourists) and their activities, but also by the length of time this level of use is maintained, the way in which it is distributed through time and space and also the way it is (or isn't) managed.

From a sociological point of view the carrying capacity concept is strongly related to visitors' satisfaction. It is often an issue of quality versus quantity (Nielsen, 1977) and raises such questions as: at what point is crowding perceived to be incompatible with a particular resource; or at what point does crowding destroy the experience of that resource. Assuming that user satisfaction is an appropriate and measurable concept this model has some serious problems when put into operational use.

Finally from a physical environment point of view the concept is one of determining the spatial ability of an island to accommodate people (tourists and locals). This simplifying definition is concerned with the size and the volume of suitable places for tourism and it also includes the urban technical infrastructure.

The above definitions of the concept of carrying capacity are only a sample of those already developed from a wide range of perspectives which obviously vary depending on the type of area, type of ecosystem and differences among societies in terms of the perception of the outdoor experience.

Regarding the measurement of the concept, it becomes obvious that an overall carrying capacity model can also be constructed on the basis of a multidimensional profile approach. For that reason, it is considered that a qualitative and quantitative model also can be constructed, which could reflect the structure of the complex system (physical and social environment variables). One possible model, similar to that of impact analysis (Nijkamp, 1988) can be developed in the form of an impact structure matrix which combines the environmental elements of the system at hand and the range of possible impacts on these elements from the development of tourism at a certain level (Parpairis, 1993).

Among the tools which seem promising in the context of a structured matrix are: comparative studies, user satisfaction surveys, natural resource parameters, ecological indicators, field studies, social surveys, behavioural inquiries, norms and standards (WTO, 1983), multiple measurement techniques, environmental impact studies, stochastical and system processes etc. In this context carrying capacity should be seen in the majority of cases as a result and not a value which has been assigned ad hoc in advance (Parpairis, 1993). It must also not be considered as an absolutely definite limit that is unalterable for each area of discussion, but rather as a means to an end, a rational management tool for sustainable development.

8.7 Testing the concept of carrying capacity

In the case study of Mykonos island the concept of carrying capacity has been examined in relation to environmental changes and to negative effects that have been observed during the peak period (1970-1990) of the island tourist development. It has been suggested that the expansion of the existing island's traditional villages - Hora the capital and Ano Mera the municipality - moves from a 'pretourist stage' or 'pioneer phase' (Miossec, 1976) or 'stage A' (Young, 1991) or 'traditional stage' (Rostow, 1960) to the third phase of tourist development, that of 'mature' or 'touristization phase' or the 'beginning of hierarchy and specialization phase' (according to Miossec's model of tourist space).

The urbanization of the island is significantly and solely propelled by tourism. The main findings of case studies is that while international tourists are mostly dissatisfied with the way development is proceeding, local people and especially people involved directly in the tourist industry, are very satisfied and expect more tourist development in the next decade.

These conflicting views and feelings are quite reasonable and exist among the 'actors' in the context of tourism. In view of the lack of specific case studies for comparison, this particular study has concentrated on trying to clarify the concept of carrying capacity in a way that would be helpful to those involved at different stages of tourist development.

In this context two broad categories of criteria controlling the concept were used, those affecting the indigenous environment and those affecting the tourist image/product. These criteria include: ecological aspects (acceptable level of visual impact; point at which ecological damage occurs; the need for conservation of wildlife and marine life), economic benefits (level of employment providing optimum economic benefits, level of employment suited to the local community), social (the volume of tourism that can be absorbed in the social life of the island), cultural (the level of tourism that will help maintain heritage, monuments and cultural traditions without detrimental effects), and resource availability (public utilities, water, transport facilities, other essential community facilities like hospitals, trained tourism personnel etc.). The second group of criteria that of tourism image/product include physical characteristics and issues (climate, pollution, attractiveness, quality of accommodation), group of criteria - that of tourism image/product includes physical characteristics and issues (climate, pollution, attractiveness, quality of accommodation), economic (the cost of holiday), social/cultural (the quality of local attractions, community culture etc.), resource availability (standards for transport, infrastructure and tourist services). The above criteria inevitably vary between those that are measurable (accommodation) to those where accurate measurement is not practical (psychological impact on visitors). The overall carrying capacity of the case study appears to be the result of the combination of both types of criteria.

One part of the methodological framework of the case study of Mykonos was based on the findings of a public perception study of tourism. It was hypothesized, in this study, that the monitoring of public opinion on the various effects of tourism, as a means of incorporating community reaction into the planning of tourist development, is valuable information for the measurement of the concept of carrying capacity as well as for the planning of tourism, because of the significance of public attitudes in creating a hospitable environment for tourists in general (Davis, Allen and Cosenza, 1988).

In this study the main investigation instrument was a group of 8-item questionnaires for tourists, local residents and those involved in tourist activities. Significant differences were observed in the attitudes of the three groups on tourist issues like: attraction characteristics, cost of holiday, satisfactory-dissatisfactory features, saturation characteristics etc. As in some other cases of recent research (Var and Lee, 1991) the above case study has generally concluded that those people who benefit from tourism perceive in a lesser degree the negative social and environmental impacts of tourism and have more favourable attitudes towards tourism development (Pizam, 1978). Those who have higher levels of education and skills and those who are engaged in the tourism and travel industry, when compared with those who have not (unskilled labour force, local population), perceive the impacts of tourism more favourably.

Different views were observed regarding the saturation characteristics of the island between different 'actors', opinions and time-periods (from May to September). Similar findings can be illustrated with respect to their perceptions, attitudes and views toward satisfactory-dissatisfactory features of the existing tourist development of the island.

There were also differences between the 'actors' views regarding the attraction characteristics of the island. Among the main factors were: for tourists, the natural and cultural environment; for local people, the quality of services (drinking water, transport, food, etc); and for people working in tourist activities the cost and the quality of services.

In this respect three sub-groups can be clearly identified:
i   Those supporting further expansion of tourism (local people, working in the tourist industry)
ii Those considering the restructure of the tourist product towards better quality of services (visitors and summer holiday makers).
iii Those who hold neutral attitudes (mostly domestic tourists).

8.8   Conclusions

The above suggests certain policy implications for tourism planning and management. In the case of Mykonos there is evidence that it has approached a crucial stage of tourism development. Local authorities should carefully formulate more detailed policies oriented to development control through planning and management with the aim of achieving the optimum capacity. Such policies should define and exercise acceptable maximum social and natural environment capacity, overcome bottlenecks and restraints (development corridors, transport centres, distribution in time and space etc.) and reduce demand in sites where capacity restraining cannot be overcome.

From the above short presentation it must be recognized that heritage and the quality of the natural environment are key tourism resources. No matter what the short or medium term economic benefits of tourism development appear to be, tourism can not be sustained at the optimal level if the natural and cultural environmental resources are degraded beyond a threshold capacity. Understanding the potentially very complex relationship between tourist activity and the maintenance of the heritage, as well as of the natural environment, is crucial to the success of tourist programmes and policies.

What we can propose is actually a set of policy instruments which is capable of sustaining tourist success and avoiding negative affects especially on the fragile environment. Accordingly a comprehensive plan for tourist development must be elaborated taking into consideration the capacity of infrastructure and superstructure resources at acceptable standards and norms, incentives and disincentives, a more coherent framework for the private sector (Roe, 1991) and measures to increase the attractiveness of the island while at the same time to securing the financial means to support the island's system. Finally in order to protect the island's heritage and natural environment - which is approaching the stage where Mykonos will be at risk - in the interests of its tourist long term success, future research should address the need for a more holistic and systematic approach to the identification of critical areas and the assessment of potential environmental impacts from the restructuring of the tourist product and from the expansion of summer holiday houses, a trend which in the long run will cause unforeseen and unacceptable environmental degradation.

References

Briassoulis, H. (1991), Tourism and the Environment: Planning issues and Approaches, International Symposium on Architecture and Tourism in the Mediterranean, Istanbul, Vol. 2, pp. 31-41.

Breakell, M.C. (1991), Learning from Europe: Britain beyond Bruges, *The Planner*, Volume 77, No. 40.

Coccossis, H. (1987), Planning for Islands, *Ekistics*, Volume 54, No. 323/324.

Coccossis, H. and Parpairis, A. (1990), Tourism and the Environment: some observations on the concept of carrying capacity, in Van de Straaten, J. and Briassoulis, H. (eds.), *Tourism and the Environment: Regional, Economic and Policy Issues*, Kluwer Academic Publishers, pp. 23-33.

Coccossis, H. and Parpairis, A. (1991), The relationship between historical/cultural environment and tourism development: some lessons of the impact of saturation in two Greek case studies, International Symposium on Architecture and Tourism in the Mediterranean, Istanbul, Vol. 2, pp. 331-352.

Coccossis, H. and Parpairis, A. (1993), Environment and Tourism Issues: Preservation of Local Identity and Growth Management, in D. Konsola (ed.), *Culture and Regional Development*, I.R.D.: Athens pp. 79-100.

Davis, Allen, and Cozenza, (1988), *A geographical analysis*, Longman, London.

Dinell, T. (1987), Hawaii: planning for Paradise, *Ekistics*, Volume 54, No. 323-324.

Dragicevic, M. (1990), Methodological framework for assessing tourism carrying capacity in Mediterranean coastal zones, UNEP Priority Actions Programme/Regional Activity Centre, Split.

England, R. (1991), Cultural Identity and Consumerism the Phenomenon of Mass Tourism, International Symposium of Architecture and Tourism in the Mediterranean, Istanbul, Vol. 2, pp. 15-29.

Fyson, A. (1991), The planning agenda, *The Planner*, Vol. 78, No. 7.

Hache, J. (1987), The island question: Problems and prospects, *Ekistics*, Vol. 54, No. 323-324.

McElroy, J and others (1987), Old problems and new directions for planning sustainable development in small islands, *Ekistics*, Vol. 54, No. 323/324, pp. 93-100.

McElroy, J. (1990), Challenges for Sustainable Development in small Caribbean Islands, *Man and the Biosphere Series*, UNESCO, Paris, pp. 299-316.

Miossec, J.M. (1976), Un modele de l'espace touristique, *L'espace Geographique*, Vol. 1, pp. 41-8.

Nielsen, J. (1977), Sociological Carrying Capacity and the Settler, *Syndrome*, Pacific Sociological Review, Vol. 20, No 4.

Nijkamp, P. and Giaoutzi, M. (1991), A strategic environmental information system and planning model for marine park development: case study for the Northern Sporades (mimeo).

Nijkamp, P. (1974), Environmental Attraction factors and Regional Tourist Effects, Paper 14, Free University of Amsterdam.

Nijkamp, P. (1977), Operational methods in studying tourist and recreational behaviour, paper 47, Free University of Amsterdam.

Nijkamp, P. (1988), *Environmental Policy Analysis*, John Wiley and Sons, New York.

Parpairis, A. (1991), The concept of carrying capacity: case study Mykonos, University of the Aegean.

Parpairis, A. (1992), The life cycle of the Tourist Product, paper presented at the International Conference on Tourism and the Environment, Molyvos, Lesvos.

Parpairis, A. (1993), Ph.D research paper, Methodological framework assessing the carrying capacity for tourist development, Department of Environmental Studies, University of the Aegean, Mytilini.

Roe, B. (1991), How to solve conflicts between private industry development

124

and cultural landscape qualities: Example from the Psarou/Platy Gialos area of Mykonos, Greece, International Symposium of Architecture of tourism in the Mediterranean, Istanbul, Vol. 2, pp. 271-282.

OECD (1981), The Impact of Tourism on the Environment, OECD, Paris.

Pizam, A. (1978), Tourist Impacts: The Social Costs to the Destination Community as Perceived by its Residents, *Journal of Travel Research*, Vol. 16, No. 4, pp. 8-12.

Ricci, P.F. (1976), Social Stability Analysis: Can Carrying Capacity provide answer to Public Policy in Canada, *Social Stability Analysis*, Ontario, Canada.

Rostow, W.W. (1960), *The Stages of Economic Growth*, Cambridge University Press, Cambridge.

Towle, E.L. (1985), The island microcosm, *Costal Resources Management: Development Case Studies*, Washington, pp. 589-749.

Var, J. and Lee, T.H. (1991), Pros and cons in tourism in perception: an exploratory approach of clustering the different views, paper presented at the International Symposium on Architecture of Tourism in the Mediterranean, Istanbul, Vol. 3, pp. 143-163.

Vries, H.S.H. (1989), Sustainable resource use: an enquiry into modelling and planning, Rijksuniversiteit, Groningen.

Young, B. (1991), At risk - the Mediterranean, The Mediterranean way, and Mediterranean tourism: perspectives on change, International Symposium on Architecture of Tourism in the Mediterranean, Istanbul, Vol. 2, pp. 43-48.

WTO (1991), *Tourism Trends worldwide and in Europe 1950-1990*, WTO: Madrid.

WTO (1987) Seminar on the development of International tourism in Europe by the year 2000, Madrid.

WTO (1983) Risks of Saturation of tourist carrying capacity overload in holiday destinations, Report B.4.2.2, Madrid.

9 Sustainable tourism development: A case study of Lesbos

P. Nijkamp and S. Verdonkschot

9.1 Introduction

Over the past forty years tourism has become a major activity in our society and an increasingly important sector in terms of economic development. It forms an increasing share in discretionary income and often provides new opportunities for upgrading local environments. Tourism is increasingly regarded as one of the development vehicles of a region, while it is an important growth sector in a country's economy. However, much empirical evidence has also shown the negative effects of tourism, in particular on the environment. Questions arise as to whether it is possible to keep on developing tourism in a certain area without negative or irreversible influences on the environment. A new concept which has begun to dominate the tourism debate in recent years is that of 'sustainable development'.

The idea of *sustainable tourism development* is now a popular concept and refers to allowing tourism growth while at the same time preventing degradation of the environment, as this may have important consequences for future quality of life. In this context, Buhalis and Fletcher (1992) quote Goodall who has suggested that sustainable tourism requires that "the demand of increasing numbers of tourists is satisfied in a manner which continues to attract them whilst meeting the needs of the host population with improved standards of living, yet safeguarding the destination environment and cultural heritage" (p.10).

This chapter will focus on the concept of sustainable tourism development. Various sustainable tourism development options resulting in a mix of policy instruments which can be used as a tool for achieving sustainable (regional) tourist development, will be assessed and evaluated. This framework will be applied to the Greek island of Lesbos. First, some general background observations will be made.

In a short period of time, international tourist demand in Europe increased from 113 million arrivals in 1970 to 196 million in 1980 and to 275.5 million in 1990. It is forecasted that the growth of tourism will continue to rise to about 340 million tourist arrivals in Europe in the year 2000.[1] This rapid increase in demand has created - and will create - several positive and negative impacts on the economy, society and environment of tourist countries and regions.

Tourism may have positive economic impacts on the balance of payments, on employment, on gross income and production. Also, tourism development may be seen as a main instrument for regional development, as it stimulates new economic activities (e.g. construction activities, retail shopping) in a certain area. Nevertheless, because of its complexity and connection with other economic activities, the direct impact of tourism development on a national or regional economy is difficult to assess. Clearly, a careful assessment of the environmental impacts of tourism is very important, because tourists tend to be attracted to the more fragile environments, for example, small islands, centres of high historical and cultural value, and coastal zones. Tourist development thus poses special problems for environmental resources which are 'exploited' by tourism. The use of such environmental resources for tourism has two consequences. The quantity of available resources diminishes and this, in turn, limits a further increase of tourism. Besides, the quality of resources deteriorates, which has a negative influence on the tourist product.

Tourism and the environment are thus interdependent. The environment is one of the most important factors in the tourist product, as the quality of this product depends on the quality of the environment, which is the basis for attracting visitors and hence has to be conserved. Tourist development depends then on a proper handling of this close relationship between tourism and the environment. Therefore, it is necessary to examine the various environmental impacts of tourism. In general, the major environmental impacts of tourism are:

a   **Permanent (sometimes irreversible) transformation of the environment.** Valuable natural areas have to make space needed for the construction of accommodation, infrastructure and other tourist facilities.

b   **Various kinds of pollution.** Tourists tend to increase the amount of *waste* beyond a level that traditional treatment methods can cope with. Litter left behind in vulnerable places like coastal waters or dunes, and uncontrolled dumping of waste can have dangerous and/or negative effects on the environment, such as fire, stench, pollution of ground water and degradation of landscape. Another widespread problem in tourist places is *water pollution*, through the discharge of inadequately treated effluent. Especially coastal waters suffer from this kind of pollution, because most of the population and economic activities are concentrated near the coast. *Air pollution* in the case of tourism is especially caused by transportation and motor traffic. The issue of traffic congestion plays also an important role here. Risk for human health and deterioration of buildings with a high cultural value are some of the consequences. *Noise disturbance* is another factor, caused by airplanes, motor vehicles, mopeds and industry. Also nightclubs and discos in tourist places may be a source of noise annoyance.

c   **Direct destruction of flora and fauna.** Threats to many rare species, to biological diversity and to the equilibrium of natural reserves arise from different kinds of pollution, the incompatibility of various economic activities, and the lack of integrated policies. Uncontrolled horse-riding, recreational walks, wild camping and other kinds of open air recreation

128

cause much damage to vegetation and wildlife. The effects of these activities include an increase in soil density, erosion and habitat changes.

d **Use of water resources.** During the tourist season an extra amount of drinking water is needed, but local supply is often limited. Ground water is used to supply drinking water, which leads to a lowering of the ground water table and hence to indirect ecological effects.

It is thus obvious that tourism can and does negatively affect valuable natural resources. Large natural areas have already disappeared or have been severely damaged. It is difficult to control this development, because tourism is of major economic importance and is likely to continue to be so. However, it must be realized that a clean environment is essential for the development of the tourist sector. The above observation will now be illustrated for the case of the Greek island of Lesbos.

9.2 Tourism on Lesbos, Greece

Up to the early seventies, Greek policy aimed at a rapid development of the Greater Athens Area. Later on, the emphasis of policy makers shifted to the mainland of Greece with the construction of surface transportation networks, electricity and communication lines. At the end of the seventies, the policy shifted more to a decentralization policy. By means of five year plans, policy has also aimed at the development of the backward regions of the country. Tourism development played an important role in these plans.

Tourism represents a major economic activity in Greece. In 1988 tourist revenues represented more than 7 percent of the Gross Domestic Product. Tourism also created a large number of direct, indirect or induced jobs. In 1990 about 480,000 people were estimated to be employed in the tourist sector of Greece. The number of tourist arrivals in Greece has grown by about 420 percent in the period 1971-1992.[2] This development is clearly reflected in many islands, e.g. on Lesbos.

The island of Lesbos is still one of the economically deprived and sensitive areas of Greece. The primary sector is the most important one of Lesbos' economy, because of the enormous olive oil and ouzo production.

While foreign tourism has existed on Lesbos since the 1960s, over the past 10-15 years it has had a significant impact on the island with the development of constrcuted holiday resorts and the expansion of facilities for tourism development. Because most of the tourists arrive on the island by air, the growth of tourist arrivals on the island can be assessed by the number of flights and passengers arriving at the airport over the past 15 years. Of particular importance for assessing the growth of tourist arrivals on Lesbos is the number of charter flights. In 1980, 17 charter flights arrived on Lesbos. This number has increased to 688 charter flights in 1993.[3] On Lesbos, tourism is a geographically concentrated activity at a few places, which are main destinations for 'sun, sea and sand' holidays (in general, 'cheap and mass tourism').

The number of hotels has grown in the period 1975-1992 by 163.3 percent. Molyvos, the main tourist place, maintains the market share in quality units, as each hotel is attaining a grade B from the Hellenic National Tourist Organization. In other areas the quality of accommodation tends to be more diversified, while also more lower class accommodation can be found. In the past few years, the upgrading of existing accommodation is noteworthy. The average utilization rate of accommodation is low for the island due to the short effective tourist season (June - September).

Support services such as tourist agencies, tour guides, vehicle rental shops and souvenir shops are not yet very well developed on the island. Tourist facilities, like hospitals, banks, sports and transport (bus) facilities play a role as complementary services. Most of the support services have little experience and organization in order to handle and promote different types of tourism on a professional basis.

The attractions of the island will of course play an important role in future tourist arrivals. Its Mediterranean climate, many beaches and bays, beautiful landscape, and the size of the island offer the advantage of diversified tourism with many options. Other natural features of the island are the petrified trees, thermal springs, olive gardens and the variety of the landscape. Archaeological sites, folk and art museums, Byzantine castles and cathedrals, ancient theatres, and Roman aqueducts can be visited. The island is also rich in religious buildings. There are many monasteries, which exhibit various icons. Of special importance are the old picturesque villages, e.g. Molyvos, and the traditional industries, like olive oil production, ouzo production, leather, wood carving and pottery industries.

The road network of Lesbos is not yet fully developed and contains many secondary unpaved roads which would be insufficient to accommodate future tourist growth. The road system focuses upon the main places on the island. The physical geography of the mountainous area makes development of new roads expensive and difficult, although upgrading and maintenance of existing roads is of critical importance.

Furthermore, more ports are needed on Lesbos, dependent on the types of tourism. Building of ports at different places may improve the island's socioeconomic situation, but requires costly infrastructure.

9.3   Environmental problems on Lesbos

The most severe environmental impacts of tourism concern waste disposal and the resulting pollution. The pollution of the gulfs of Kalloni and Ghera is widespread: the amount and quality of fish is decreasing and water is no longer usable for drinking or irrigation. Waste disposal (solid and liquid) is also a problem on the island. No effective garbage treatment exists; rubbish is just dumped into the sea or along the roadside without any control. Also waste of materials caused by the production of energy, and discharge of waste from boats into the sea takes place. Hence, the beaches on the island face several problems of pollution. Water shortage is also a problem on the island. Sewage facilities are poor and sewage is often directly dumped into the sea and the rivers.

Scenery is increasingly affected by the construction of new hotels and apartments. Furthermore, an increase in the number of tourists on the island means that transportation improvements and accommodation facilities are required with negative visual impacts.

Seen from a future perspective, different kinds of development scenarios for the island of Lesbos can be envisaged. In general, three main global development alternatives can be distinguished:

1   A '*growth*' strategy, which is stimulating the present growth trend of the economically profitable tourist sector, regardless of negative environmental consequences in the future.

2   A '*planning for decline*' strategy, in which any growth of the tourist sector will be opposed and restricted. This alternative is aimed at the protection of the environmental, traditional and cultural resources.

3   A '*sustainable development*' alternative, in which policy is supporting the tourist sector, because of its growth potential (as the other Greek islands have shown). However, the growth of tourist activities would have to be controlled, as protection of the environment is a main policy aim.

In our study we will mainly focus on the sustainable development option. Given the rising number of passengers arriving on Lesbos and the overall growth in European tourism (predicted to rise by 44 million tourists by the turn of the century),[4] it is essential that a sustainable tourism development plan for the island be accepted and designed. This plan should identify the areas that are suitable for economic growth without deterioration of the environment. In this context, it should be recognised that tourism on Lesbos consists predominantly of 'beach' (mass) type holidays. The consequence is that large numbers of tourists arrive on the island. In the short term this seems very attractive for the economy, but in the long term this may turn out to be environmentally negative. Furthermore, an economy which is only dependent on activities of the tourist sector, is vulnerable regarding external factors, such as tourist agencies, preferences of tourists, and international events (e.g., wars or political unrest). Replacement of traditional economic activities by tourist activities only may hence be risky. It is therefore important to develop a diversified base of tourist attractions.

It seems to be wise policy that tourism development should not aim primarily at an increase of the number of tourists visiting the island, but rather at the *increase of the benefits* for the island, e.g. measured in tourist expenditures per day. This would mean that the island needs to have high quality tourist facilities to attract high income tourists.

Another risk-avoidance strategy may be to extend the relatively short effective tourist season. This can be achieved by the development of new tourism options which are not only associated with beach facilities and not only concentrated in the summer months.

Besides, types of tourism which can take place at a distance from the coastal zone may be developed. The hinterland villages may then benefit, and the pressure on the vulnerable coast will be lower.

Use (and improvement) of existing accommodation and facilities would have to be encouraged. In any case, prevention of exclusively economic dependency on (mass) tourist revenues seems to be an important policy orientation for sustainable development.

In the next section various options for sustainable tourism development on Lesbos will be described in more detail. These options are based on the typical attractions of Lesbos described above.

9.4   Sustainable tourism development options for Lesbos

The previous section has demonstrated that it makes sense to focus in particular on the sustainable development alternative for the island. Therefore, in this paper various sustainable tourism development options will be identified, which support especially the latter alternative. The background is formed by the aim to diversify tourism with the development of the following options: exclusive tourism; agro-tourism; health tourism; adventure/sports tourism; sea tourism; cultural tourism; winter tourism; educational tourism. These options will now concisely be discussed below.

a   Exclusive tourism
Exclusive or top-class tourism is aimed at the arrival of high income tourists. A limited, rather exclusive market, which will not require a further extension of the present built up area, is needed. Exclusive tourism should first be implemented in the main tourist places, which have most 'B' level hotels. These existing hotels may first be upgraded to a higher category, 'A' or 'first class', through the improvement and addition of more (luxury) facilities, better service provision and higher standards of cleanliness. These improved standards of quality should also be applied to restaurants and other supporting facilities.

b   Agro-tourism
Agro-tourism is a kind of tourism which favours the economic activities in the agricultural sector at the same time. An important aim is stimulate these activities in relation to the agricultural potential so that the economy of the island will not become solely dependent on tourist activities. Agro-tourism contains, for instance, the construction of tourist accommodations and facilities at farmers' places. Besides, tourists may watch the processing of farm products. Olive oil, ouzo production and leather industry are popular traditional activities to which agro-tourism may also be applied. Agro-tourism can be implemented on the whole island.

c   Health tourism
The island may also develop facilities for curative tourism. For example, thermal waters (which are characteristic for the island) are recommended for people with rheumatic problems, bronchitis, back aches, skin diseases etc. Bath facilities, accommodations around the spa's and access roads may then be improved or established.

d Adventure/sports tourism
Lesbos is ideal for trekking thanks to its nature and culture. The National Tourist Organization has already established four different trekking routes on the whole island. An information guide with the different trails is also published by this organization. Such pathways need to be better cleaned, mapped, marked and developed. Another possibility is the organization of wildlife/discovery tours, so that organized tourist groups can make panoramic trips and see the countryside by walking, climbing and hiking. Other examples are bird watching, camping, horse-riding, cycling, golf or tennis. Proper facilities may be developed and constructed.

e Sea tourism
Lesbos has a strong comparative advantage in sea tourism, because it has an abundance of surrounding waters. The sea lends itself to wind surfing, water - skiing, snorkling and sailing. Establishment of modern water sports facilities may be established at some tourist resorts. Avoidance of already saturated places would be better. For yachting, the construction of a modern marina would be a prerequisite.

f Cultural tourism
Lesbos has a great variety of typical cultural, historic and natural attractions. By upgrading the level of and access to these attractions, the island will gain cultural prestige and may offer more interesting places to visit. The level of service and quality of museums might be improved. Organization of art exhibitions or other cultural manifestations may also be an interesting possibility. The typical traditional villages also require protection. The materials used and the design of buildings in such places may be based on local traditions. The exercise of cultural handicrafts might be encouraged.

g Winter tourism
Winter tourism may be encouraged to realize a year round tourist product. This is also related to targeting winter migration to the island by offering facilities to elderly people. An easily attainable island in the winter months and the presence of qualified tourist services are a prerequisite. An advantage of winter tourism is the creation of jobs in winter time, so that seasonal unemployment is reduced.

h Educational tourism
Tourism may also be developed on the basis of meetings, conferences, congresses or symposia. The construction of a congress centre would then offer a new opportunity. Extension of the university with more departments may make Lesbos more important as a scientific centre. Organization of language or cultural courses may also be considered.

These various tourism options seem to be the most feasible ones and do not exclude each other. The development of a mix of different options is thus possible. In the next section we will further evaluate these options.

133

9.5   Evaluation of the sustainable tourism development options

An operational assessment of the socioeconomic and environmental impacts of these options is fraught with some difficulties, because of the lack of hard quantitative data and uncertainty. A methodology which can be used is a *system's impact analysis*, derived from systems theory. One of the interpretations of systems theory is Passet's environmental approach (see Passet, 1979). This approach distinguishes three subsystems: an economic, human (or social) and natural (or environmental) system. Feasible impact indicators may be derived from the elements of these three subsystems. On the basis of these indicators a system's impact analysis on a qualitative basis can then be used to investigate the effects caused by decisions concerning different options for tourism development (see for an application Bithas and Nijkamp, 1995; Coccossis et al., 1991; Janssen et al., 1993). In the context of our chapter, the main feasible impact indicators are:

Economic indicators

* income tourist sector
* income other sectors (agriculture, construction)
* employment tourist sector
* employment other sectors (agriculture, construction)

Social indicators

* cultural identity

Environmental indicators

* cultural attractions
* restructuring of the environment and the landscape
* different kinds of pollution
* direct destruction of flora and fauna
* use of water resources

Clearly, it is very complicated to present all possible effects and relationships of the above mentioned options, due to lack of information, especially quantitative data and models. The most obvious effects of the options can be presented in a so-called qualitative impact matrix.[5] The above mentioned options a to h are presented in a matrix, which is shown below as a kind of qualitative survey table (see Table 9.1).

The precise impacts cannot be indicated for several options, because of lack of quantitative information. If this is the case, the places are left empty. The + or - symbols can only be meaningfully interpreted row-wise. Thus such an impact matrix may in principle be used to rank the different alternatives, by comparing their scores on the criteria. The options may now be compared in terms of their impacts on each separate indicator. Clearly, those alternatives may be chosen, which offer in the first instance promising options for future development of the tourist sector on Lesbos.

Table 9.1
Qualitative survey table with impacts

Alternatives	A	B	C	D	E	F	G	H
Economic criteria								
income tourist sector (tertiary sector)	+						+	
income distribution								
* agriculture (primary sector)	+	++			+			
* construction (secondary sector)	++	++	++	++	+	++		+
employment								
* tourist sector	+						+	
* agriculture		++						
* construction	++	++	++	++	+	++		+
Social criteria								
cultural identity		+			++			
Environmental criteria								
cultural attractions		+	+		++			
restructuring environment/landscape	--			-	++	+	+	
different kinds of pollution				-		+	-	
direct destruction flora/fauna					+			
use of water resources	-							

+ positive impact
- negative impact

It is thus possible that more than one option will be feasible for future tourism on Lesbos, as there is not a single option which outranks all other options. Of course, those options should be chosen which have a high score on the indicators concerned. However, it is conceivable that some key indicators are of more importance than others. The weighting of the three key indicators is dependent on the present policy framework. This implies that one also has to consider the regional policy objectives of the Greek government. In this context multicriteria analysis may play an important role (see Nijkamp et al., 1991; Giaoutzi and Nijkamp, 1993).

The above table shows that most of the proposed tourism options are feasible for sustainable development of the island of Lesbos. A further comparison also shows that in particular options A, B, C, E and F offer favourable sustainability opportunities. Options D and G may then act as complementary strategies.

9.6 Environmental policy instruments

Is it possible to develop a mix of policy instruments, which can be used for achieving the selected tourism development options favouring sustainability on Lesbos?

In general, three different categories of environmental policy instruments may be distinguished: regulatory instruments, economic instruments and communication instruments.

Regulatory instruments

Regulatory instruments can be described as institutional measures aimed at directly influencing the environmental behaviour of polluters by regulating processes or products used, by abandoning or limiting the discharge of certain pollutants, and/or by restricting activities (see OECD, 1989). These instruments include systems of monitoring and sanctioning in case of noncompliance. The most common form of regulation is setting *environmental quality standards*. Other forms are *licensing* and *zoning*.

Economic instruments

These instruments impact via costs and benefits of alternative actions open to economic agents, with the effect of influencing decision-making and behaviour in such a way that alternatives will be chosen which are favourable to the environment (see OECD, 1989). A basic feature of economic instruments is that the price of goods and services should truly reflect the associated environmental costs.

Economic instruments can be subdivided into *charges*, *subsidies*, *deposit–refund systems*, *market creation*, and *financial enforcement*.

Charges have an incentive impact and a redistributive impact in that the government collects tax revenues and can use them for stimulating projects or for paying subsidies. It is important to carefully consider the level of the tax for achieving the desired effect (dependent on substitution and price elasticities). Furthermore, it is important to inform people about the purposes for which the revenues will be used, in order to ensure a minimum acceptance level.

Subsidies act as an incentive for polluters to alter their behaviour or are given to firms facing problems in complying with environmental rules.

In deposit-refund systems a surcharge is put on the price of potentially polluting products. Pollution will be avoided by returning these products and the surcharge will be refunded.

136

Market creation takes place if actors can buy 'rights' for actual or potential pollution or can sell their 'pollution rights' on artificially created markets.

Financial enforcement can be used if non-compliance is a significant choice alternative for polluters.

Communication instruments
The third type of instruments in environmental policy-making is made up by instruments which internalize environmental awareness and responsibility into individual decision making, by *information provision*. These instruments are often brought about directly or indirectly in negotiations.

In practice, various combinations of economic instruments, direct regulation and communication instruments are designed.

Tourism concerns many important activities in which environmental policy instruments have not played a major role in the past. However, it seems reasonable to develop a framework for the application of environmental policy instruments to the field of sustainable tourism development. Therefore, we will now identify and discuss the most appropriate instruments.

Regulatory instruments
Standards may be used for:
* control of the number of tourist arrivals;
* control of the number of beds per hectare;
* guidelines to construct or rebuild buildings (maximum building heights, suitable architectural design standards);
* protection of the quality of the environmental resources;
* restrictions on land use;
* contracts between tour operators, tourists, hotel owners etc.

Permits may be used for:
* locational permits to construct or rebuild accommodations;
* development of tourist resorts.

Regulation at the source may concern:
* light vehicles and pleasure boats;
* siting of roads, airport, and marina's.

Economic instruments
Charges can be used to cover some of the costs tourism imposes on the environment, by raising tourist prices. Charges can be imposed:
* for controlling the number of tourist arrivals (e.g., a tourist tax may be included in the price of flights);
* as user charges on the prices of several beach facilities (entrance, restaurants, shops, etc.);
* for protection of the landscape.

Subsidies in the form of grants, soft and long-term loans, and tax facilities may be useful in the following forms:
* investment subsidies for partial reconstruction and maintenance of existing buildings;

* investment in proper systems of waste treatment, water provision systems, sewage systems, and the improvement and extension of the existing infrastructure;
* investment in high density accommodation in vulnerable areas;
* attractive investment conditions by providing, for example, tax reductions, low interest and amortization rates, for the development of special tourist attractions like a marina, recreation and sport facilities;
* cleaning up of sites;
* stimulation of typical local products;
* research and development projects;
* cultural events.

Deposit-refund systems may be used to reduce waste and keep the beach clean. This system can take place at different levels (e.g., municipality, hotel owners, tourists). The refunds should be high enough to encourage environmentally - friendly behaviour, but not so high as to discourage tourism.

Financial enforcement is possible in the case of imposing a non-compliance fee on the owner, for instance, if the architecture of the new building is not compatible with the traditional style.

Communication instruments
Different policy incentives in terms of information can be used to make people (tourists, tour operators, hotel owners, and other people involved in the tourist industry) aware of environmental problems. Examples are advertisements and exhibitions abroad; information, maps and education of people (higher quality, better service); public awareness campaigns; participation of local population in policy programmes; development of software (information about different kinds of tourist activities at several resorts for tourists, and information about bookings in transport and hotels).

It is evident, that different policy instruments may differentiate between the various tourism options discussed above. For example, exclusive tourism can be introduced by charging the tourist products and facilities. The revenues can be used for investment in the upgrading of the tourist facilities. Also agro - tourism, health, sea and adventure/sports tourism can be encouraged by investments and subsidies. Cultural tourism can be developed by an increase in admission fees, so that special attractions can be upgraded and protected. For winter tourism, it is only necessary that the tourist facilities can be used for the entire year. All forms of tourism need investments in the (re)construction of roads and the upgrading of public transport facilities.

9.7   Concluding remarks

Environmental instruments should be designed to facilitate the integration of environmental policy with other policies, such as regional development policies. Removal and correction of administrative and governmental intervention failures are therefore of importance for a proper integration of environmental policy with sectoral policies. This may end up in a better synergy and coordination of tourist activities with other socioeconomic activities.

A problem in achieving sustainable tourism development is the lack of experience, knowledge and financial resources, and the limited involvement of local authorities (see also Briassoulis and Van der Straaten, 1992). It is important that decisions which influence life at the local level will be taken at the lowest possible level of governance. Knowledge of the area involved and its problems increases local support in the development of a suitable action plan for sustainable tourism. The role of the local authorities should therefore be strengthened. This is particularly important, as environmental awareness is not yet highly developed in Greece. Education, information, promotion and training are therefore important measures in this context. Sustainable tourism is by no means a non-viable option. As this paper has argued: tourism development may certainly be compatible with environmental concerns.

References

Bithas, K. and Nijkamp, P. (1995), Sustainable Cultural Heritage Planning: A Case Study on Olympia, Research Paper, Free University, Amsterdam.

Briassoulis, H. and Van der Straaten, J. (1992), *Tourism and the Environment; Regional, Economic and Policy Issues*, Kluwer Academic Publishers, Dordrecht.

Buhalis, D. and Fletcher, J. (1992), *Environmental Impacts on Tourist Destinations: an Economic Analysis*, University of the Aegean, Mytilini, October.

Coccossis, H., Janssen, H., Kiers, M. and Nijkamp, P. (1991), Tourism and Strategic Development, Research Memorandum, Free University, Amsterdam.

Giaoutzi, M. and Nijkamp, P. (1993), *Decision Support Models for Regional Sustainable Development*, Avebury, Aldershot.

Janssen, H., Kiers, M. and Nijkamp, P. (1993), Private and Public Development Strategies for Sustainable Tourism Development of Island Economies, Research Memorandum 1993-68, Free University Amsterdam, December.

Nijkamp, P., Rietveld, P. and Voogd, H. (1991) *Multicriteria Analysis in Physical Planning*, Elsevier, Amsterdam.

OECD (1989), *Economic Instruments for Environmental Protection*, Paris.

Passet, R. (1979), *l'Economique et le Vivant*, Payot, Paris.

Verdonkschot, S. (1994), *Sustainable Tourism Development; a Case Study of Lesbos*, MA. Thesis, Free University, Amsterdam, August.

Notes

1. Source: World Tourist Organization (1991)

2. In absolute terms, this means a rise from 1,875,000 tourists in 1971 to 9,756,000 in 1992. Source: World Tourist Organization (1992)

3. Source: Civil Aviation Service, Yearly Statistics

4. Source: World Tourist Organization (1991)

5. A detailed analysis of the different effects of each option can be found in Verdonkschot (1994).

140

10 The environments of coastal marinas

J. A. Edwards

10.1 Yachting and marina growth

10.1.1 A growing demand for yachting

Since the early 1960s the growth of tourism has been related to two key elements. The first is the growth of cheap air transport to countries with ingredients of 'sun, sand and sea' (plus some sangria and sex). The second is the increased affluence of general populations as 'the age of high mass consumption' (Rostow, 1960) is attained. But two additional elements have emerged in more recent years. These are the desire for more individual choice, involving a greater plurality in living, recreation and leisure opportunities and the desire of many people to develop a life-style that incorporates home-living with leisure and recreation. Both trends were pioneered in the USA but have spread to western Europe in the past three decades and especially since the later 1970s.

In the United Kingdom, the popularity of beach-based holidays in such resorts as Blackpool and Bournemouth has declined in the face of competition from Mediterranean countries. Yet not all water-related activities have suffered: aqua-parks, surfing, board-sailing, canoeing and, in particular, yachting have grown in popularity. Indeed, 'yachting has proved to be one of the boom sports of the post-war period' (Sports Council, 1991, p. 196). General Household Surveys of 1997, 1980, 1983 and 1987 record that 0.6, 0.8, 0.9 and 1 per cent of the respective samples of the adult population of Great Britain took part in sailing (excluding powered craft and windsurfing) during the four weeks prior to interview. The one per cent sample represents about 450,000 people. However, a far higher figure of two million active sailors and windsurfers was suggested in a consultant report of 1989 (Martin, Mason and Smith). Equally uncertain is the lack of precise knowledge of numbers of yachts in the United Kingdom since there is no compulsory registration requirement. A recent report noted that a 1985 survey estimated that the population of pleasure craft was somewhere in the range 26,000 to 260,000 vessels (British Ports Federation, 1990). Notwithstanding the lack of accuracy of these different sets of figures, what **is** evident is that numbers of participants in water sports and yachting are growing and they are demand more varied and better facilities. Nowhere is this more true than for marinas in the United

Kingdom.

10.1.2 Marina growth

Marinas have become an established feature of waterside locations in many parts of the western industrialized world, especially since the early 1970s (Adie 1984; Blain and Webber 1989). There had been marinas in existence before that time but most were small in scale and had limited service facilities. However, the post 1960s growth and its impacts are a product not only of the more general trends noted above but also of an additional influence, viz. of marinas as 'vehicles' for two kinds of development. Many marinas have acted as a catalyst for the redevelopment of old, abandoned 19th century waterfronts and docklands beginning with the San Francisco and Baltimore developments in the USA. Here, central and local governments, in cooperation with private business, have played the leading roles. The success of these projects was followed by the second type of development, largely pioneered by private developers and with its origin in Port Grimaud in France. In this case, the marina acted as the focal point for larger multifunctional 'marina village' developments incorporating residential, commercial, leisure and entertainment uses.

All three types of development, basic waterfront/dock conversion and multifunctional, are evident in the United Kingdom and this chapter draws upon a range of research studies carried out since 1985 to illustrate the main changes and impacts of marinas upon coastal environments.

a Marina numbers

The number of marinas steadily increased by 75 per cent during the decade 1981-1991 (Table 10.1).

Table 10.1
UK - Numbers of marinas 1981, 1984, 1987, 1991

Country	Number of marinas			
	1981	1984	1987	1991
England	42	53	62	72
Channel Islands	3	3	3	3
Scotland	6	7	9	10
Wales	0	1	2	4
TOTAL	51	64	76	89

b Marina locations

Their geographical distribution is not only extremely uneven between these four countries but also within them. In this respect, marina development has corresponded to the general pattern of tourist growth. Most tourist attractions are firmly anchored to fixed locations: historic sites, beautiful sandy beaches, glorious scenic views or an attractive climate. They are immovable, act as 'honeypots' and it can prove extremely difficult to diversify these attractions so as to spread the load of tourism in space and time. Likewise for yachting and marinas which, traditionally, have been concentrated in the United Kingdom along the south coast of England and especially the river-estuarine areas of Hampshire and Sussex. These two counties alone accounted for 46 per cent of all marina moorings in the UK in 1981 (Figure 10.2).

c   Marina sizes

The size of marinas, a measured by pontoon berths, also increased rapidly during the second half of the 1980s (Table 10.2).

Table 10.2
UK - Size of marinas by berths 1981, 1984, 1987, 1991

	1981	1984	1987	1991
Number of berths	12868	16189	20842	26411
Number of marinas	51	64	76	89
Average number of pontoon berths/marinas	252	253	274	297

The most obvious reason for this is the growing demand for yachting and hence for marina berths. Secondly, there is some evidence that some marinas have been built to fill in a 'space' of water rather than to satisfy strictly commercial market-led demand. This is most noticeable in the marinas created in old Victorian inner-city docks. Their developers are usually local authority councils or Urban Development Corporations who may see it as equally important to provide a facility with a pleasant environmental impact for the general public as to be self-supporting financially in the long-term. Third, notwithstanding the previous comments, there is a need to maximize returns from capital investment by both public and private sectors. Few marinas are now constructed in the United Kingdom solely to provide serviced pontoon berths for resident or visiting yachters. Rather, they will form part of large multifunctional developments with a wide range of uses and facilities. The size of these land-based developments frequently means that while the water-area for yachts is large, the cost of providing serviced pontoons is minor in relation to total site and development costs.

d   Marinas in multifunctional developments

So the fourth dimension of marinas is that some are becoming focal points of large, multifunctional developments. As an example, Arlington Securities PLC will eventually invest 200 million pounds in the Port Solent complex near Portsmouth (Figure 10.3). Begun in 1986, this will eventually contain:
*   an 850 berth locked basin, divided between 470 non-residential and perhaps 380 residential berths
*   414 one/two/three bedroom houses

* 168 apartments
* the Boardwalk with 22 retail units, 5 restaurants, a wine bar, public house, 9 office suites and 7 apartments
* the Slipway complex of 36,000 square feet of commercial office space
* a second office complex of 60,000 square feet
* a hotel
* a multiplex cinema, and
* the Port House with marina administration, brokerage, chandlery, flotilla holiday company and the Waterside Club.

10.1.3 Planning and policy implications

There are a number of planning and policy implications that follow on from the above. Clearly, the demand for yachting and marina facilities is growing rapidly, needs to be anticipated and planned for. Demand cannot only surge rapidly but, as is evident from the current economic recession in western Europe, can also contract and so the speed, intensity and scale of developments need to be considered carefully and with flexibility. Thirdly, there is a tendency for yachters to concentrate upon well known 'honeypot' locations and marinas. If the above are recognized, then planners can anticipate such trends.

One policy response is to adopt a long-term strategic framework for yachting/marina growth into which investment and development can be fitted. This has been done over the past decade in Wales. In 1982, when there were no marinas but the latent demand was recognized, the Wales Tourist Board commissioned consultants to identify the potential for marina developments around the entire coastline. They were then categorized into three groups (Figure 10.4):

1 **prime sites** for marina development
   a already under development
   b with the potential for future development
2 **secondary sites** for marina development
3 **smaller** established **sailing centres** with some facilities.

The idea was that a 'necklace' of coastal sites could be identified and an adequate infrastructure built up so that yachtsmen could be attracted to the region. As a result a 'trickle-down/spread' effect from existing yacht harbours in Wales and marinas in England has evolved as a result of a combination of public and private investments. Four marinas were in operation in early 1991 (Table 10.4) and a further two were added by the end of 1992. The 'necklace' now includes full marinas at Conwy, Pwllheli, Neyland, Milford, Swansea and Penarth which are within easy sailing distance of other marinas in England (Liverpool, Bristol) and in Ireland. Harbour improvements have also been undertaken in Aberystwyth in mid Cardigan Bay. It is believed that this strategic marina development plan is unique in the United Kingdom.

The 1980s also saw extensive marina investment elsewhere in the United Kingdom (Figures 10.1 and 10.2). One consequence is that by 1991, Hampshire and Sussex accounted for only 36 per cent of all marina berths in the UK, a drop of 10 per cent over the decade. This decline occurred because Hampshire local planning authority began to oppose any new marina developments because of environmental and public pressures, because opportunities for marina development were recognized elsewhere in the United Kingdom as the 'culture' of yachting began to spread more widely and finally, because the cost of marina charges in these southern countries escalated so rapidly that alternative and cheaper marinas and moorings in different locations were sought.

10.2   Marinas, the environment and tourism

The environmental impact of marinas as tourist focii can be grouped under three headings: natural/physical, economic, and human (Table 10.3).

Table 10.3
Marina impacts

A Natural/physical	B Economic	C Social
1 Water	1 Employment	1 Water-borne
2 Land	2 Businesses	2 Land-based
	3 Income	3 Residents

A   Natural/Physical

a   Water
The three water areas, surface, sub-surface and over-surface, provide the visual and functional heart of the marina. Largely neglected except as a medium for accommodating yachts, it has not been realized that they should offer as diverse a product-mix and income generating potential as their surrounding land areas (Edwards 1990a, p. 15). For this reason, the concept of the **WATER STRATEGY** is emerging as a major area of interest. A water strategy should include six distinctive, yet interrelated, elements:

1   Water space use
Surface water users include recreational activities, commercial operators and tourist attractions (historic ships, floating restaurants. Sub-Surface uses would be exclusively tourist oriented, such as walk-through aquaria, underwater sightseeing vessels such as submarines, Jacques Cousteau type submersibles. Over-surface usage would include piled structures to accommodate bars, hotels, office, etc. over low-height vessels such as motor boats.

2   Water flexibility
Water surfaces are not static but form part of a dynamic area that must be adaptable to changing market demands and fashions.

3   Water economics
A number of key issues here include:
  i   calculations of the 'grid-square economics' of water space
 ii   the potential for berth-leasing/dockominiums
iii   shared-time use
 iv   increased boat densities

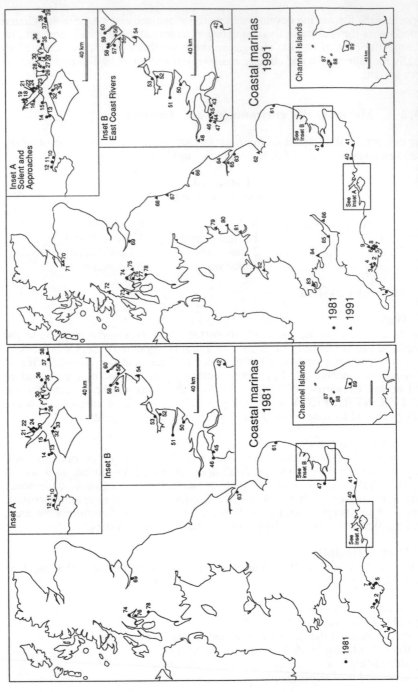

Figure 10.1.a United Kingdom coastal marinas 1981   Figure 10.1bUnited Kingdom coastal marinas 1991

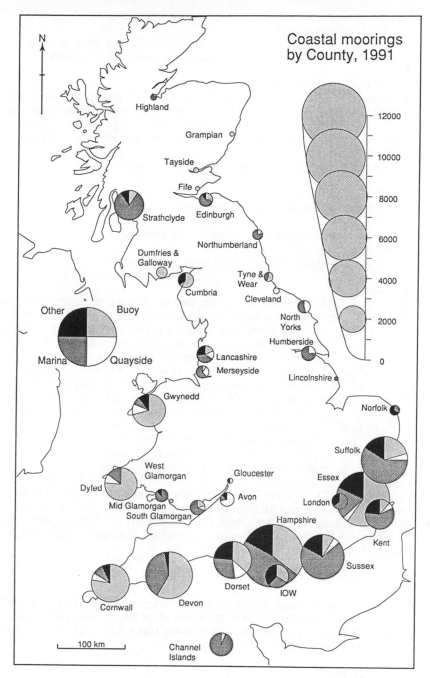

Figure 10.2 United Kingdom coastal marinas 1991

4 Water accessibility

Public accessibility to shorelines and marina water spaces needs to be considered, as do the needs of particular groups such as the disabled.

5 Water environment

Water quality is of the essence. In future, it is likely that marina developments will need to show that provision has been made for regular water sampling and testing, system hydrodynamics, dissolved oxygen, light levels and stratification to be measured and incorporated within a computer-based mathematical model.

Sewage discharge from yachts will need to be curtailed.

6 Water services

The key services being demanded and provided in many marinas include:

* water   * power
* sewage pump out   * emergency equipment
* telephone   * TV
* electronic metering * individual boat security

b Land

The land around the marina reflects the two key phases of marina development and their differing tourist orientations. Phase 1 marinas are little more than boat and car parks that often developed around a natural harbour with a traditional fishing fleet and pleasure/recreation yachting facilities. Around the quayside there may be long-established and informally arranged houses, bars/tavernas, fish storage/processing facilities. The marina accoutrements of pontoons and service provision have to fit into and around historic structures and activities. Phase 2 marinas are purpose-built of various stages and types of development. The most basic provide no more than pontoons, services, and land-based support facilities. The most advanced represent a 'total' development in the form of a Marina Village or Maritime Village. Port Grimaud in southern France was the progenitor of this concept which seeks to create a marina lifestyle and ambiance, as described earlier for Port Solent, Hampshire.

The positive aspects of such developments can include the physical rejuvenation of large areas of formerly derelict land and waterscapes to create attractive, dynamic and vibrant areas. Examples of this abound - in Swansea, the London Docklands, the Albert Dock in Liverpool. The **negative** aspects noted in the Economic Section below, include the loss of many traditional businesses.

B Economic

Marinas can play a major role in the economic environment of a region and are, perhaps, of particular interest to regional planners and politicians. The economic impacts can be classified under three headings of employment, business and finance.

Employment

The employment impacts of marinas vary greatly according to location, length

148

of establishment and range of facilities available, as is evident from Table 10.4. Thus Swansea marina has a number of advantages over the other three marinas: it is the longest established, it is located in an old Victorian dock in close proximity to the city centre, it has a wide range of attractions around and near the marina including a leisure centre, two museums, art galleries, theatre, shops, bars, restaurants, and it has a large residential population. The most recently developed marina of Pwllheli, in contrast, is located in a snall urban centre and has failed to benefit from residential development following a decision by the District Council not to allow such development around the marina. One encouraging aspect about the employment data is that, in overall figures, two-thirds of the employment generated has been permanent. However, in Penarth, Pwllheli and Swansea more part-time than full-time female employment has been created, much of this being in bars, restaurants, shops and offices.

Table 10.4
The employment impacts of four Welsh marinas, 1991

Marina	Year opened	Employment				Total
		Male full time	Male part time	Fem full time	Fem part time	
Neyland	1985	96	15	30	12	153
Penarth	1987	28	2	5	6	41
Pwllheli	1990	21	2	13	41	77
Swansea	1982	156	72	61	87	376
Total		301	91	109	146	647

Businesses
Marinas can be important generators of businesses, as revealed in a survey of four Welsh marinas (Table 10.5). This fourfold classification again shows that Swansea marina has generated the greatest number and widest range of businesses. As would be expected, each marina has only one business involved directly in its marina operations (Column 1) and having overall responsibility for the overall management and day-to-day running procedures. Although only one business is recorded, it actually encompasses a wide range of operations, including management staff, office personnel, marketing staff, and lock-staff who have responsibility for boat control and movements. The second column of businesses which depend for more than one-half of their turnover upon marina boats, includes such activities as boat sales, boat insurance, hull repairs, engine servicing, sail and rigging sales and maintenance, electrical and electronic sales, repair and servicing, etc. Their presence and the quality of their service are essential for the smooth running and success of a marina. A number of activities have a lesser dependence on the marina, including, for example, sport-fishing vessels, upholsterers and wood cabinet makers, nearby restaurants and bars. Finally, there are businesses which have direct links to and so benefit from the presence of a

marina. Most evident here will be estate agents who sell residential and commercial properties, bars, restaurants, art and card galleries, souvenir shops, etc. A typological classification of the wide range of marina businesses is provided in Table 10.6.

Table 10.5
Marina-related businesses in four Welsh marinas, 1991

Marina	Number of new businesses			
	Directly involved in marina operation	Very strong dependence on marina (>50%)	Lesser dependence on marina presence (<50%)	Direct links to marina presence
Neyland	1	8	8	6
Penarth	1	2	2	1
Pwllheli	1	6	4	-
Swansea	1	8	1	27

Table 10.6
Classification of marina businesses

Category of business
1 Boat related businesses
2 Marina service businesses
3 Commercial marine leisure
4 Marine eventing centre
5 Manufacturing activities
6 Waterside businesses: Retail
                                            Leisure/entertainment
                                            Food/drink
                                            Personal services
                                            Commercial services

It must be stressed that negative as well as positive business impacts can result from land development. For example, in 1974 at the beginning of the redevelopment of the Dockland Zone of Swansea Maritime Quarter, for example, there were 35 businesses in operation which employed 1101 people (Edwards 1988, p. 138). However, at the height of land clearance in 1981, there were only six businesses and these employed only 319 people. The total job loss, especially of fulltime male employment was very great and has not been replaced.

c   Finance
Infrastructure investment, income generation and expenditure impacts need to be determined in cost-benefit exercises of marina impacts. A study of Swansea marina (Edwards 1985, Edwards 1987) noted that the City Council had spent 9.2 million pounds on infrastructure investment 1974-1992 but that this had

generated a further 62.35 million pounds investment from private and (42.5) and public finance sources. The study also determined the taxation income (rates) from domestic and commercial properties in the developed Maritime Quarter in comparison with the pre-development period. For example in 1974, the Maritime Zone contributed to 1.23 per cent of Swansea City Council's total taxation income but by 1986 this had increased to 2.89 per cent. The expenditure impact of marina users was also calculated as a result of questionnaire surveys. In 1985, annual expenditure by boat owners in to the local economy on fuel, food and chandlery items exceeded 400,000 pounds per annum of which 62 per cent came from visitors from outside the local district. In addition, there was income from boat sales, insurance commission charges, vessel refurbishment.

C   Social

Marinas depend upon the presence of people to be successful. Two groups of tourists to marinas can be identified: water-borne and land-based while local residents provide a third group. A successful marina strategy must recognize and incorporate the differing requirements of each. Key aspects of their socioeconomic profiles are noted in Table 10.7.

Table 10.7
Age and socioeconomic groups at Port Solent

Group	Ages (%)					Socioeconomic group (%)						
	16-24	25-34	35-44	45-ret	ret+	1	2	3N	3M	4	5	R
Water-borne	2	27	29	37	5	14	37	32	4	7	0	5
Land-based	17	23	26	29	5	0	46	15	15	11	6	8
Residents	3	18	26	48	5	21	63	10	4	1	0	11

Socioeconomic groups
1   :   Professional/Upper middle class
2   :   Semi-professional/Middle class
3N :   Skill non-manual/Lower middle class
3M :   Skilled manual
4   :   Semi-skilled
5   :   Unskilled
R   :   Retired

Source: Port Solent Study (1990), Vol. 2.

a   Water-borne tourists
These are the visiting yachtsmen and women who visit a marina either as individuals or in a flotilla group. Their requirements are focused on two geographical levels, within-marina and extra-marina.

Within-marina requirements
To attract and maintain water-based tourists, a marina has to consider two

principal elements: yacht facilities and people services. A well-run marina should have a minimum of seventeen types of facility which can be subdivided into:

Boat servicing		People servicing
Drinking water	Chandlery	Laundry
Gas	Boat hoist	Toilet block
Electricity	Boat mover	Telephone
Sewage tank	Boat tractor	Trolleys
Waste disposal	Boat repair	Car parking
Petrol	Security	

Table 10.8
The 'old' and 'new' approaches to tourism

Old approach
* tourism as a residual fact
* supply distinct and not professionalized
* tourism assisted or controlled
* sporadic and partial promotion
* single-thread tourism (e.g. exclusively seaside)
* closed circuit
* economic fact
* separation between quality and quantity
* tourism 'wild' and aggressive

New approach
* tourism in a position to produce development
* tailored according to various segments of demand
* autonomously managed tourism (local management with legally binding budget and collective entrepreneurship)
* deregionalized and organized promotion
* multi-stranded tourism
* 'open-air' phenomenon
* also cultural and social facts
* integration of quality and quantity, and
* respect for the environment

Extra-marina/environmental attractions
Surveys of boat tourists to Swansea and Port Solent marinas show that visits are not related solely to the marina and its facilities and services. Rather, the availability of additional attractions in and around the marina is important. These are generally of three types: immediately adjacent manmade features such as the commercial retail/food/entertainment facilities described for Port Solent: land-based heritage and landscape attractions such as historic sites, ancient towns, beautiful scenery; and water-related attractions, such as scuba-diving, windsurfing or boardsailing. They provide multi-stranded tourism which has strong environmental dimensions using numerous open-air attractions of public events (boats shows, boat races, festival markets, shows, etc) and such

cultural attractions as music festivals/performances, heritage pageants). As such, they integrate into the 'new' approach to tourism identified by Barucci and Becheri (Table 10.9) (1990, p. 235). Further, using Port Solent as a case study, the marina has stimulated additional tourist development attractions in the form of a multiplex 10-screen cinema, numerous high quality retail outlets, food-drink establishments and office complexes.

b   Land-based tourists to marinas

At the minimum, marinas provide a visual and activity focal point for land–based tourists; but if the marina has a wide range of attractive land-based facilities and services there will be additional reasons for visits. Such is the case in many marinas constructed during the 1980s and studies of Swansea and Port Solent marina visitors confirm this. Visitors take great pleasure in simply looking at the water-surface: at the wide variety of yachts, in commenting and assessing the range of equipment evident, and in day-dreaming about owning such a vessel, probably in the sun-drenched Mediterranean or the Caribbean. If there are repairs being undertaken, or there are fishing boats busily engaged in offloading or preparing to go to sea, the range of interest increases. Secondly, visitors are attracted by facilities and services on the adjacent land-area. The example of Port Solent has already been referred to while the following types of attractions are found around the marina: leisure centre, museums (2), art galleries (3), theatre, historic ships (3), charter sea fishing (3), pubs/bars/restaurants/cafes (9), shops (4), personal services (2). The marina office also contains publicity brochures for tourist attractions in the neighbouring City and surrounding rural areas.

10.4 Planning and policy implications

It is evident that the developmental and environmental impacts of marinas are wide-ranging. The first major policy implication is that no development should proceed without an Overall Environmental Impact Assessment (OEIA) of the three key elements noted above. Duffield and Long (1979) indicate a relevant conceptual schema (Figure 10.4).

> "...which attempts to provide a general framework for assessing tourism impact in the context of the specific situations and the social and economic forces that characterise them.
>
> They argue for an interactive model which relates the impact of tourism, not only to the nature of the area concerned, but also to the planning environment which conditions the character of the associated physical, social and economic response. The keynote of this conceptual framework is to emphasise the impossibility of abstracting questions relating to tourism from the physical, spatial, economic and cultural environment within which they are set."

Duffield and Walker 1984, p. 482-283)

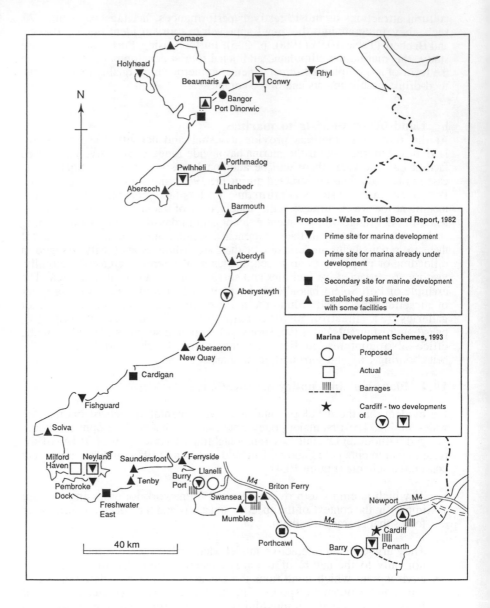

Figure 10.3 Wales - marina proposals (1992) and developments 1993)

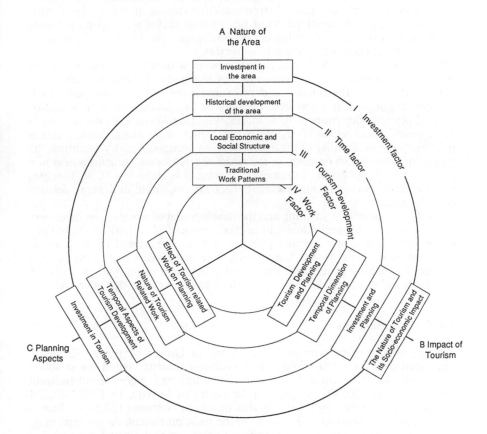

A Nature of
the Area

Investment in
the area

Historical development
of the area

Local Economic and
Social Structure

Traditional
Work Patterns

I Investment factor

II Time factor

III Tourism Development Factor

IV Work Factor

Effect of Tourism related
Work on Planning

Nature of Tourism
Related Work

Temporal Aspects of
Tourism Development

Investment in Tourism

Tourism Development
and Planning

Temporal Dimension
of Planning

Investment and
Planning

The Nature of Tourism and
its Socio-economic Impact

C Planning
Aspects

B Impact of
Tourism

Source: Duffield and Long 1979 (p. 7)

Figure 10.4 Tourism - a conceptual schema

Secondly, the growing importance of yachting and marina developments in tourism, leisure and recreation are making this an increasingly competitive market segment between countries. Therefore, quality of environment, quality of product and quality of service assume a premium. A 'Development and Monitoring Standards Authority' (DaMSA) for the yachting and marina sectors should be considered. While having some regulatory functions, its main role should be seen as positive, seeking to encourage the raising of standards especially through designated financial/investment powers. However, successful long–term development of this tourism sector will depend not only upon a good working relationship but especially on a good financial/investment relationship between public and private sectors.

Apart from the truly dedicated yachter who is willing to sail irrespective of weather and facilities, the expansion of this segment of the tourist market will depend also upon the interest and pleasure of the more casual participant. His/her response, it is suggested, operates at two levels: the first is that of general pleasure determined by a 'marina/yachting ambience'; the second is more specific and relates to the daily mechanics of yachting. Simple issues relating to the availability of clean showers and toilets, laundry facilities, the quality of water for swimming, or the range of sightseeing attractions near to a port/marina - these become extremely important. It is at this level that strategies for the three environmental elements become important and need detailed consideration.

Finally, the growth of yachting and the development of marinas can have very positive benefits for individuals, localities, regions and countries. These need to be identified, evaluated and publicized within processes of widespread consultation so that a general consensus can be achieved as part of the planing and policy making procedure. But development and change are not always beneficial and it is sensible to recognize this and to give them due attention.

10.5 Conclusions

The importance of tourism in the economy of Greece cannot be disputed. Published data for 1990 show that 9.3 million tourists visited the country, generated 4,275 million US dollars income, and gave direct/indirect employment to 350,000 people. On the island of Lesvos, in 1991, 47,334 tourists were received by charter flights of whom Germans (13,600), British (8,900) and Scandinavians (7,500) were the most prominent. As an expanding sector of tourism, yachting and marina activities can play a small but growing part in this. Participants tend to be older, from high socioeconomic groups and have higher disposable incomes. They form an ideal tourist 'target' group, but their needs and expectations must be fulfilled.

To do so, it is suggested that there is a need to work within the framework of a three-sided schema (Figure 10.5) that incorporates:

* the 'new' approach to tourism
* a strategic framework to marina/yachting development
* the three environmental elements.

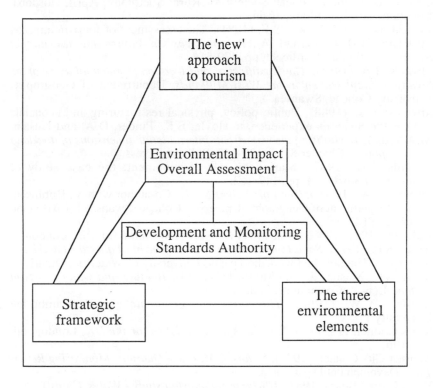

Figure 10.5   Marinas - a conceptual schema

References

Adie, D.W. (1984), *Marinas - a working guide to their development and design*, Architectural Press, London.

Blain, W.R. and Webber, N.B. (1989), *Marinas: planning and feasibility*, Computational Mechanics Publication, Southampton.

British Ports Federation (1990), *Light dues on pleasure craft*, London.

Duffield, B.S. and Long, J.A. (1979), *Reward and conflict associated with tourism in the highlands and islands of Scotland*, Paper given to the 10th Conference of the European Society for Rural Sociology, April, Cordoba, Department of Agriculture, Spain.

Duffield, B.S. and Walker, S.E. (1984), The assessment of tourism impacts, in: Clark, B.D. and Gilad, A., *Perspectives on environmental impact assessment*, Reidel, Dordrecht, pp. 479-516.

Edwards, J.A. (1985), *The identification and location of potential users of the Swansea Yacht Haven in the West Midlands*, Department of Geography, University College, Swansea.

Edwards, J.A. (1988), Public policy, physical restructuring and economic change: the Swansea experience, in Hoyle, B.S., Pinder, D.A. and Husain, M.A. (eds.), *Revitalising the waterfront: international dimensions of dockland redevelopment*, Chapter 8, pp. 129-145, Belhaven Press.

Edwards, J.A. (1987), Marina quarter development: the case study of Swansea, *Cambria*, 14, pp. 147-162.

Edwards, J.A. (1990a), *The Port Solent Study*, Co-author with V. Robinson, 3 vols. Department of Geography, University College, Swansea for Arlington Securities PLC.

H.M.S.O. (1977, 1980, 1983, 1987) *General Household Surveys*, London.

Lerner, S.C. (1977), *Social impact assessment; some hard questions and basic techniques*, Unpublished workshop paper, University of Waterloo, Ontario.

Martin, W., Mason, S. and Smith, D. (1989), *Boating and water sports in Britain*, Leisure Consultants, Sudbury.

Rostow, W.W. (1960), *The stages of economic growth*, Cambridge University Press.

Sports Council (1991), *A digest of sports statistics for the UK*, London, pp. 193-196.

Swansea City Council (1988), *Swansea Maritime Quarter - Monitoring Report 1988*, Development Department.

Wales Tourist Board (1982), *Harbour and marina study - Wales*, Cardiff.

11 Environmental impacts in the Loch Lomond area of Scotland

G. Dickinson

11.1 Introduction

The Loch Lomond area is located about 50 km to the north-west of Scotland's largest city, Glasgow. More than half of Scotland's 5 million population live no more than 2 hours' journey by car from the area. A significant proportion of this population makes at least on visit to the area every year. In addition to this large pool of domestic visitors, the Loch Lomond area is an important tourist destination for visitors from other parts of Britain and abroad. Development of the tourist and outdoor recreational industries of the area thus have rightly a high priority. This development has had the objective of boosting the economic benefits obtained from leisure activities, to a level which is long term sustainable. Sustainability means that the resource base on which tourism and recreation depends, must be conserved. The resource base for tourism and recreation comprises the diverse and beautiful physical landscape of the area, which is underpinned by a rich cultural heritage. Leisure infrastructure is more limited, but thus is target for development. To achieve both sustainable development, and resource conservation, a clear understanding of the nature of the impacts of recreation on the resource base is required. This knowledge can then be used to develop an effective resource management strategy, given an appropriate institutional framework for integrated resource management. This study examines the nature of recreational impacts, their role in overall environmental change in the area, and resource management strategies for the Loch Lomond region.

11.2 Recreation and tourism in the Loch Lomond area

As has been identified by the Countryside Commission for Scotland, this is one of the most scenically attractive areas in the country, with a high potential for tourism and recreation. (CCS, 1990). However, its accessibility, the spatial and temporal patterns of recreational pressures on the area, and the current arrangements for resource management cause concern that serious environmental impacts are resulting from the use of this area for outdoor recreation and tourism. This has been recognised in the local planning strategy for the area, along with the area's importance for tourism and recreation.The planning framework for the area, the local subject plan, is designated "for recreation, tourism and landscape conservation" (Loch Lomond Planning Group, 1982). Recently a number of studies on the patterns of tourism and recreation in the area have been carried out. These have been reviewed by Dickinson (1991a). The available evidence shows that there are four significant characteristics. These are; the majority of visitors come from central Scotland; the average length of each visit is short, typically about two hours in duration; passive pursuits, such as short walks or enjoying the scenery are the main recreational activities; and there are very significant concentrations of recreational activity in both time and space. It is estimated that about 90% of total use is by day visitors. This has considerable significance, both for environmental management, and development of a quality tourist industry.

A survey of 20000 visitors to the region was carried out for the central government supported local enterprise company (LEC), Dunbartonshire Enterprise, in 1991. About 80% of respondents fell into the category of day visitors whose means of travel was private car. Due to the sample structure of the survey, this is probably a low estimate. Nearly all of these visitors spent less than half a day in the area, and their expenditure on tourist services was low. The proportion of visitors involved in active recreational pursuit, such as hill walking or water sports, is less than 15%. Though a small relative figure, the absolute numbers of visitors involved in active recreation are quite significant, given the large total number of visits made to the Loch Lomond area annually. It is difficult to be precise about the annual total of visits, but this survey suggests a figure of 2 million.

In many respects the general pattern of recreational activity in the Loch Lomond area is similar to that for Scotland as a whole. (Dickinson 1988). Within the Loch Lomond area, which is defined as the catchment basin of the loch and the water body itself, there is a wide range of attractive physical environments, with a high resource value for passive and active recreational activities. (Dickinson, 1994). Variety of environments is one of the major attractions of the area for tourism and recreation, but also is a reason for the national and international importance of the Loch Lomond region for biological and landscape conservation.

Given the large number of visits to the Loch Lomond area it is scarcely surprising that there are environmental impact problems associated with recreation. Such problems are considerably exacerbated by two factors. First, the ecological and environmental conditions of sites used by visitors are fragile. Secondly the specific time and space patterns associated with tourist activity produce concentrations which make impacts much more serious. These two factors, and their consequences for environmental impacts resulting from recreational activities are now examined in more detail.

The range of environmental conditions which occur in the area include a number of ecologically sensitive habitats, particularly along the shores of the loch, and in the hill and mountain areas which surround the northern part of the basin. These are also amongst the most valuable scenically, and are the most heavily used recreational locations. Vulnerability, particularly in response to the physical impact of recreationalists, their cars and boats is related to the floristically simple, but ecologically specialised nature of the plant communities, and to the erodability of soils which are poorly drained, thin and humic.(Dickinson, 1991a). A very humid, cool climate increases the problem through slow plant growth rates and soil development, whilst promoting rapid natural erosion.

Access to the loch shore is restricted. Though the Highlands of Scotland have a reputation for open access to visitors, the reality is somewhat different. Most of the area is held in private land ownership with restricted public access. The only significant exceptions are tracts of state-owned forest land, particularly on the east side of the loch, and a few public visitor sites which are owned and managed by local government agencies. There are also some privately owned recreational sites which generally charge an admission price for use of their facilities. Consequently, there are relatively few locations that the loch shore can be reached from the roads around the loch. The result is that recreational activity is concentrated on a limited number of quite small sites. Impact pressures at these sites is much greater than the overall figures for visitor use of the area might suggest.

The spatial concentration is compounded by the temporal patterns of visitor use. In Scotland as a whole 75% of outdoor recreational day trips occur on Sundays, with most of the remainder taking place on Saturday. As well as this weekend bias, weather plays an important role. The majority of day visitors will make their decision to visit the area at the time of travel. Thus good weather will stimulate a much higher level of usage than at other times. Warm, sunny weather is not predictable beyond 2 or 3 days in Scotland, and as such conditions might only occur on about 6 weekends per year, the volume of visitor use at such periods can increase exponentially. Indeed the narrow east shore road, deserted in the winter, has become so congested on certain Sundays in summer in recent years, that it has had to be closed by the police for reasons of public safety.

11.3 The characteristics of environmental impacts

From the wide range of impacts which actually occur two are selected as examples. This is a function of their specific importance, and the fact that they have a wider significance in Scotland as a whole. The two examples are; impacts on the beaches and shores of the loch; and impacts on footpaths in the mountainous part of the area. In the first case impacts result from a number of agencies. These include direct foot pressures of visitors, damage related to picnicking, particularly fires, erosion related to car parking on the shore and damage caused by boat launching. The general characteristics of these impacts and their effects on loch shores have been reviewed by Tivy (1980).

Impact on vegetation from such pressure results in progressive physical damage to, and ultimately elimination of, species. Species elimination is in descending order of their vulnerability to such damage, so that as pressures increase, the floristic composition changes. Resistant species, typically grasses and mosses, become more dominant and with increasing areas of bare ground occurring. Amongst the most vulnerable of species, and thus those which are most readily destroyed are flowering herbaceous plants. In the wetland habitat at the shore line several of these fragile species are of biological conservation value. Though severe impacts are restricted to a relatively small number of sites at present, it is important for both biological and landscape conservation that further damage to plant cover is minimised. Furthermore loss of vegetation contributes to deterioration in soil conditions and thus to erosion.

Soil is damaged by pedestrian and vehicle pressures. Compaction is the main direct effect. In the case of foot pressures, compaction is confined to the uppermost soil layers, rarely more than 5 cm below the surface, whilst cars produce effects to a greater depth. The general characteristics of pedestrian impacts on both soil and vegetation conditions in Britain have been summarised by Liddle (1975), and the case study of a damaged footpath on the east shores of Loch Lomond has been analysed by Dickinson (1982). Local soils are highly susceptible to damage since the typically humic surface horizons have low consistence, and when compressed become waterlogged. This increases the already high natural risk of erosion by running water whenever there is any degree of slope.

If damaged soils are exposed to attack by the action of loch waves very rapid and substantial erosion damage will result. This will occur when the loch level is high and strong winds blow. Both observations and calculations show that waves up to 2.5 m in amplitude can be generated by the force of wind which would be expected on a number of days annually. In severe weather condi tions during March 1990, such wave action caused loch shore erosion which necessitated remedial work costing more than £1 million. (Dickinson and Pender, 1991, Dickinson, 1993). Current research has the objective of quantifying the contributory roles of human impact and natural environmental processes in continuing shore erosion.

Much of what has already been said applies to the hill and mountain land. Aitken (1988) has produced a summary of the impact of hill walkers on mountain vegetation and soils in Scotland. In the Loch Lomond area the hill sections of the heavily used West Highland way long distance footpath, and the track to the summit of Ben Lomond have been quite severely eroded in places. This has necessitated substantial restorative work. The strategy employed has been to prevent path waterlogging, to limit path widening and to maintain a stable substrate. In badly damaged and steeply sloping sites, this has involved engineered solutions, in which artificial drainage is installed, path foundations are constructed or steps are built.

11.4 Recreation and other factors causing environmental degradation

Two general categories of factor which are responsible for overall environmental change in the study area can be identified. These are changes in patterns of land use and changes in natural environmental conditions. It is clear that these are not mutually exclusive, and that there is interaction between the two. For example though recreational pressures may lead to soil compaction, it is runoff water which is the actual agency of erosion. Thus though high recreational pressures may predispose vulnerable areas to serious impact problems, changes in local hydrology, associated with variations in precipitation and runoff are equally important. Such changes may be caused by changes in land use or may be the result of long term variations in local climatic conditions. This is one area of environmental change which has been identified, though the underlying causes of the change cannot yet be specified (Dickinson and Pender, 1991).

Land use changes have been accelerating over the past 50 years. These have been analysed more fully by Dickinson (1994). One significant change over the past fifty years has been an increase in the area of land under intensive sylviculture. Most of the plantings pre-date 1960, and the main species is Sitka spruce *(Picea sitchensis)*. More recent plantings have been largely on privately owned land, though replacement after clear felling in the large areas of state forest land has continued. In this latter case, current forest management plans give a high priority to the maintenance of landscape amenity, and to sustaining conservation and recreation resources. It is likely that the extensive afforestation has had an effect on surface hydrology. Normally tree planting would be expected to slow surface runoff and thus to act as a check on erosion. However there are indications that in this instance the opposite is true and that erosion has accelerated. This appears to be related to inappropriate ground preparation, notably down-slope deep ploughing, and to the exposure of large areas of steeply sloping ground following clear felling.

Woodland in general is an important element in the landscape and ecology of the area, and a significant contributor to the recreational resource base of the area. Therefore it is encouraging to see that current management practices accord considerable priority to this. The oak woods along the loch shores, which are a relict of 18th and 19th century commercial plantings are a particularly important feature of Loch Lomond landscapes. Under legislation for Environmentally Sensitive Areas (E.S.A.'s) such as Loch Lomondside an element of Government grant to support conservative and amenity-orientated management of this valuable landscape and conservation resource is a welcome recent innovation.

Farming, both on the low ground in the southern part of the catchment and on the northern hills, is undergoing fundamental change. In the south, there has been a recent substantial switch from the established mixed and dairy farming to intensive rearing of sheep on improved land. Considerable land improvement in areas such as the Endrick Valley which drains into the south east corner of the Loch, have been undertaken since the 1960's. Field drainage schemes has been the most important action, and this has been accompanied by greatly increased use of fertilisers to boost output of sown grass. These actions have had an effect on water quality and local hydrology. Added to this, an expansion in the population of the settlements of the valley, with a consequent increase in sewage byproduct output, has also had an impact on the quality of the river water. As is discussed below, though not serious issues at present water quality may be a future problem.

Hill farming is facing a period of continuing decline. Hill sheep, the main hill land product, cannot compete with low ground sheep production. This latter has grown rapidly in recent years as a replacement for the contracting dairy industry in the south of the region. The reduction in dairying in turn, is a consequence of EC quotas and competition from more environmentally favoured areas in Europe. The resultant knock-on effects on hill land are likely to be profound. Regular, controlled burning which is the basis of moorland management is becoming uneconomic, and vegetation changes will occur if burning ceases. For example, this may mean some regrowth of scrub birch woodland on the lower slopes. Whether or not this will be beneficial for either biolog ical or landscape conservation is debatable.

Some hill farming areas may be given over to commercial afforestation, particularly on the lower hill ground. This has serious implications. The likely concentration of new forestry on the lower slopes (below 500 m), will mean that the higher ground, where there is a very short growing season, will have little value for animal production, when separated from the ecologically complementary lower zone. Wildlife and landscape conservation interests will also be harmed by this change. The full impact of the decline of hill farming on the area is not yet clear, but will have implications for sustaining the recreational resource base of the Loch Lomond region.

In spite of the pressures discussed above, as yet there has been no significant overall change in water quality within Loch Lomond. Loch water is abstracted for water supply purposes, currently at a rate of 221 megalitres/day. This is about 50% of the present potential. Monitoring reveals that the water taken is of generally excellent quality. However there have been concerns about localised areas, particularly around the mouth of the Endrick where algal blooms have developed in the last two summers. The marshes at the mouth of the river Endrick are a National Nature Reserve of European importance. Recreational impact on quality has not been detected in appreciable amounts, but, given the spatial concentration of recreation and the limited circulation of water in certain popular locations within the loch this situation requires continuing monitoring.

Recent changes in the pattern of recreational activities themselves have caused new environmental impacts. There are many examples, and two of the most significant illustrate this issue. Fast water craft, such as powerful speed boats and jet-skis now use the loch in appreciable numbers. Growth in this activity is related to road improvements over the past two decades which has increased the geographical sphere of access to the loch, and to restrictions on such boat use in other areas, notably the Lake District National Park in north-west England. On the one hand there is no evidence that wash from such craft is causing shore erosion. However on the other there are clear indications that the noise from these is unacceptable to the vast majority of other recreationalists, and that these water activities are causing disturbance and safety hazards to other recreationalists, such as sailors and anglers. Currently legal controls are being developed to control the high speeds of some users. However given the present management status of the Loch it is difficult to see how such controls, even if enacted, can be made effective.

Angling provides a particularly interesting example of the impact of a recreational activity on its own resource base. Loch Lomond has had a long established reputation for game fishing (fishing for salmonid species). During the mid-1970's it became popular for coarse fishing, especially pike (*Esox lucius*). This was based on the hitherto largely unexploited fish stock, and the previously mentioned improved access to the area for the large community of coarse anglers in northern England. Furthermore there is no closed season for coarse angling in Scotland, in contrast to England. The popularity of this new type of angling was such that, by the mid-1980's the target fish stocks were overfished, and coarse angling has substantially decreased in recent years.

However during this period the fish species ruffe (*Gymnocephalus cernus*) was first recorded in the loch. This was almost certainly the outcome of a release of live bait by a coarse angler. Numbers of this species expanded rapidly, to the extent that it is now the most common species in the loch. This has implications for other fish species, including the powan (*Coregonus clupeoides*), a species found only in Loch Lomond in western Europe, and thus of particularly high conservation interest. The dominance of ruffe may also have implications for animals further up the food chain such as herons (*Ardea cinerea*) or otters (*Lutra lutra*). This study of a environmental impact by a species accidentally introduced as a result of recreational activity, is dis cussed more fully by Adams and Tippett (1990).

11.5 Recreation and conservation management strategies and systems

At present the pattern of resource management is extremely complex. It is reckoned that at least 27 bodies have an interest in recreational land management, and impacts of recreational activities on the Loch Lomond area. No single body has overall responsibility for recreation and conservation, though some have strong interests in both. Responsibilities and authority are divided amongst various bodies and individuals and there is no overall strategic policy for the area. That this is an unsatisfactory state of affairs is self-evident. However the main problems and future challenges are identified in the following examination of three of the major bodies involved in management strategies and systems.

Local government has been involved in developing a strategic local plan for the catchment area. There are four local authorities involved in the area. The two top tier units of Strathclyde and Central Regions, and the two second tier districts, whose territories lie within the previously specified regions. These are Dunbartonshire and Stirling Districts. The plan is, as stated in the introduction to this paper "for recreation, tourism and conservation". It is commendable not only in objectives, but for the most part in the detail of its proposals. It seeks to balance the economic needs of local communities with the demands of recreationalists from outwith the area, within a framework of long-term resource conservation.

However the plan has limitations imposed on it, because of its relationship to central government policy. A land use development proposal requiring planning assent, which is refused by a local authority because it does not accord with the local plan may be overturned by central government. Furthermore the local plan has no real impact on agriculture or forestry. Finally the financial base required for a proactive long-term strategy is circumscribed by central government policies towards local authorities' expenditure. In spite of these limitations the Loch Lomond plan has been a highly positive development, and represents a real base for future resource management.

Secondly, the Loch Lomond area was designated a Regional Park in 1989. This is a park within the system for recreational land proposed by the C.C.S. in its strategy `A Park System for Scotland' (CCS, 1974). It is funded by the relevant local authorities involved, which in turn receive substantial grants for park expenditure from the central government body, Scottish Natural Heritage (SNH). It has already proven to be a highly effective agency in tackling local problems, such as impact damage at heavily used recreational sites. However its remit is much more limited than that of National Parks in England and Wales, so that it lacks some of the key management powers required to pursue an effective strategy. Strengthening these powers is an absolute priority if the long term future of the area's environment is to be safeguarded.

Thirdly, just before its merger with the Nature Conservancy Council (Scotland) to form S.N.H., C.C.S. published The *mountain areas of Scotland* (CCS, 1990). In this important document National Park status for four of the most important recreational areas in Highland Scotland was proposed. This action was advocated as much on the need for conservation as for recreational development. A very strong case was made for all four areas, but the Loch Lomond area had a quite unassailable claim. (Dickinson, 1991b). Working parties created by the Secretary of State for Scotland have reported on the 2 areas requiring most urgent action, Loch Lomond and the Cairngorms. However the signs that positive actions will result , are not promising. Present government policy, in so far as any policy can actually be discerned, appears to be against National Parks for Scotland. This seems to be on the base of putative short-term financial savings, and cannot be defended by any longer term perspective. Present prevarication will entail greater future expense, and the real risk of permanent damage to the resource base.

11.6 Conclusions

The underlying problem for resource management for recreation and tourism (and indeed for all land uses) in the Loch Lomond area, is the lack of integration and planning at the national level of government. Land use policies for Scotland are handled by a series of independent agencies which act exclusively for a single activity, generally in competition with the other agencies. This is wholly inappropriate for a resource which is not only widely used in a multi-purpose manner, but is also susceptible to environmental degradation when used inappropriately. Damage to this fragile resource base is all the more likely in times, as at present, of rapid land use change. Furthermore,resultant land use conflicts are likely to become more contentious, and result in further damage to the resource base. The case for an integrated approach to land management in rural Scotland has been argued eloquently by Mowle (1988).

National Park status for this area is required immediately, for the following reasons. Firstly such a system can provide the much needed integrated approach to resource management, including agriculture and forestry. This will not only allow resource conservation to have a higher priority than at present, but also be much more cost-effective than the present resource utilisation planning vacuum. Integration would allow limited inputs of money and labour to be targeted more efficiently, and in line with clear long-term priorities. Indeed the type of integrated approach to resource planning which would stem from creation of a National Park in the Loch Lomond area, could have beneficial implications for resource management in Scotland as a whole.

A second sound reason for the establishment of a National Park lies in return of responsibility for resource management to local people, through their major role in the park's controlling authority. Presently it is apparent that many local people feel remote from environmental decision making, and are disenchanted with the current system. The management of the park must have a significant local dimension, drawing heavily not only on local labour, but also on the large pool of local knowledge about the area.

Although the Loch Lomond region, in common with many other designated National Parks throughout Western Europe, does not meet all international criteria for designation, a park is the best solution to reconciliation of conflicting pressures on its resource base at a time of rapid change. The outcome of the pressures for change cannot be predicted with any confidence. What is required in this area of international importance for recreation and tourism is a vision for the future. A park is the best way of ensuring that there is such a vision, and that the vision is one which accords with the aspirations of both local people and visitors. It is the starting point for sustainable tourist development, and a means of safeguarding this national asset for visitors from near and far.

References

Adams, C.E. and Tippett (1990), *Status of the fish community of Loch Lomond*, Report to the Scottish Development Agency, Glasgow.
Aitken, R. (1988), *Scottish Mountain Footpaths*, C.C.S, Perth.
C.C.S. (1974), *A Park System for Scotland*, C.C.S, Perth.
C.C.S. (The Countryside Commission for Scotland) (1990), *The mountain areas of Scotland: conservation and management*, C.C.S, Perth.
Dickinson, G. (1982), An assessment of pathway damage and management: The West Highland Way, *Department of Geography, University of Glasgow, Occasional Paper Series*, No. 10. Glasgow
Dickinson, G. (1988), Countryside Recreation in Selman, P.(ed.) *Countryside Planning in Practice: the Scottish experience*, pp 89-104, Stirling: S.U.P.
Dickinson, G. (1991a), Recreational Impacts, pp 39 - 49, in Dickinson, G., Jones, G. and Pender, G. (eds.) *Loch Lomond 1991*, Symposium Proceedings, Glasgow: CREST, University of Glasgow and Strathclyde University, Glasgow.
Dickinson, G. (1991b), National Parks - Scottish Needs and Spanish Experience, *Scottish Geographical Magazine*, 107, 2, pp124-129.
Dickinson, G. (1993), Environmental Degradation in the Loch Lomond Area: A Case Study of the Roles of Human Impacts and Environmental Changes, in Dawson, A.H., Jones H.R., Small, A. and Soulsby, J.A. (Eds), *Scottish Geographical Studies*, Universities of Dundee and St Andrews.
Dickinson, G. (1994), Vegetation and land use in the Loch Lomond catchment, *Hydrobiologia*, in press.
Dickinson, G. and Pender, G. (1991), *Flooding and Flood Damage around Loch Lomond January to April 1990*, Commissioned Report to the Loch Lomond Park Authority, Balloch G83 8SS, U.K.
Liddle, M. (1975), A selective review of the ecological effects of human

trampling on natural ecosystems, *Biological Conservation*, 7, pp. 17-36.

Loch Lomond Planning Group (1982), *Loch Lomond The Loch Lomond Local (Subject) plan for tourism, recreation and conservation*, Loch Lomond Planning Group, Glasgow.

Mowle, A. (1988), Integration: Holy Grail or Sacred Cow? in Selman, P (ed.) *Countryside Planning in Practice: the Scottish experience,* pp 247-264, Stirling: S.U.P.

Tivy, J. (1980), *The Effects of Recreation on Freshwater Lochs and Reservoirs in Scotland*, C.C.S, Perth.

12 Rural tourism development: Using a sustainable tourism development approach

B. Nitsch and J. van Straaten

12.1 Introduction

After the introduction of the concept of sustainable development by the World Commission on Environment and Development (1987), this concept was widely accepted by the vast majority of Western countries including the European Union as a starting point for their policies. The acceptance of this approach can be seen as an expression of the increasing environmental awareness at the end of the eighties. On the other hand, it can be argued that the introduction of such a concept was strongly related to the failure of traditional environmental policies in the previous decades. This failure necessitated the introduction of a general new approach aimed at realising a more sound environment.

When pollution of the environment comes up for discussion certain sectors are often seen as the main cause of environmental disruption. In most countries special attention has been given to the pollution of steel mills, oil refineries, traffic and intensive agriculture. Generally speaking, tourism was not seen as a real threat to nature and the environment. Recently, this picture has changed. There is an increasing awareness of the strong relationship between tourism and the quality of nature and the environment. One of the results of this development is that the concept of sustainable development has been accepted in tourism studies (Farell and McLellan, 1987; Farell and Runyan, 1991, Briassoulis and Van der Straaten, 1992). In addition, authorities took this approach as a starting point for their environmental and economic policies (Van der Straaten, 1992). Recently, the European Union accepted the Fifth Action Programme 'Towards Sustainability' in which tourism is given special attention (1992).

However, the acceptance of the concept of sustainable development does not mean that this concept is implemented in all concrete policies of countries and of the European Union. It has to be said that nobody is *against* sustainable development. It can be accepted by every polluting industry as a starting point for realising a sound environmental situation. However, as soon as vested interests become aware that authorities have the intention to introduce strict norms and standards in their sector, they generally have a different opinion. They argue that in this special case the economic position of the polluting sector is too important to be confronted with strict norms. From many investigations it becomes clear that vested economic interests are, in many cases, able to neutralize the implementation of strict norms (see for example Kasperkovitz, 1992; Opschoor and Van der Straaten, 1993; Dietz and Van der Straaten, 1992).

The aim of this chapter is to investigate the implementation of sustainable tourism in La Sierra in La Rioja in Spain, and in the Northern Pennines in the United Kingdom. These regions have many characteristics in common. They are typical rural regions in which employment has decreased for a long period and in which traditional agriculture has taken a dominant position for many decades. The regions include mountain areas with stock-farming, in particular sheep, and forestry being the major sources of income. Both regions can be defined as peripheral which implies that the intensification of agriculture has not been so dominant as is the case in the more centrally located agricultural regions. The average income is relatively low in both regions, emigration figures are high, and unemployment figures are high (Mellors, 1990; Commission of the European Community, 1990; Fernandez, 1993). Last century both regions were relatively prosperous. In La Rioja, wine, ceramic and textile industries were the main sectors, whereas in the North Pennines lead ore mining was the major economic activity. However, in this century the agricultural activities became more significant. Nowadays, agricultural restructuring (Common Agricultural Policy initiated by the European Union) result again in a decline of the local economy. Alternative economic activities, including tourism, are being sought in order to revitalize the local economy in the long tern (Commission of the European Community, 1990b and 1992).

After the Second World War, as the rural economy declined, many people emigrated to the nearby industrialized regions. For instance in the 1970's more than fifty villages in La Sierra were abandoned as Logrono, Pamplona and Bilbao industrialized. It is a similar picture in the North Pennines region where high levels of average employment can be found, in particular amongst the younger population.

Both areas are rich in cultural heritage as they were both economic centres in previous centuries. Lead ore mines in the North Pennines and mineral mines in La Sierra are recently reopened as a tourist attraction. Additionally, La Rioja has become well-known for its wine and agricultural products. In both areas well preserved remnants can be found of old cultures, such as the Celts and the Romans, while Christian and Arab civilization played a significant role in La Rioja (Elias, 1992).

Both regions are, for different reasons, attractive as a tourist destination. However, tourist infrastructure does not meet the conditions of mass tourism. Of course, there are many differences between these two regions. The most significant is that La Rioja is located in 'sunny' Spain, while the Northern Pennines are often associated with clouds, fog, and low temperatures.

Rural areas such as La Rioja and the Northern Pennines have become potential tourist destinations as they characterize the authentic rural life and the peace and quietness of the natural landscape. Visitors search for places to relax, to break away from daily routines and to sense a kind of freedom and escapism. In these regions tourism can be promoted as a major source of regional income. However, due to the many examples of uncontrolled tourism development in other areas of Spain and in Italy, and the increasing relevance of environmental issues, sustainable development and segmented marketing have been regarded as most important in order to manage tourism successfully in the countryside. Within sustainable development the environmental and cultural integrity of the area is maintained for the benefits of tourists and residents.

The objectives and strategies of the regional authorities in these two mountain regions within the European Union, which focus on sustainable tourism, have been studied. In both regions partnerships between the major funding organizations and the public authorities have been established. In La Sierra in La Rioja the European Union is directly involved; in the Northern Pennines tourism facilities and attractions are being developed by the existing regional and national organizations. This has been stimulated in La Sierra by subsidies which are based on objective 5B of the Structural Funds of the European Union: areas lagging behind in economic development. In the North Pennines no direct funding has been allocated. Some projects in this area, however, have received funding from adjacent regions according to Objective 2 of the Structural Funds of the European Union: areas in industrial decline.

Both regions show similar approaches in the development of tourism, which include:

*   Marketing strategies to increase the awareness of tourists that the region is a potential destination and to convince the local population of the benefits of tourism for the rural community (building image).
*   The organization of training courses in management and administration for local small-scale enterprises.
*   An increase and improvement of accommodation facilities.
*   The encouragement of local associations and partnerships to set up projects in order to establish organizational structures within the development of tourism such as farming holidays.
*   A direct involvement in developing and initiating projects through an overall coordinating management team.
*   The promotion of agro-tourism while encouraging farmers to start offering tourist accommodation.
*   The improvement of the communication between the tourism industry and the organizations involved on the conservation of the environment.

European Union funding has been allocated in order to diversify the economical activities in the region which includes the promotion of traditional craftswork, the production of 'green' agricultural goods and the development of tourism facilities and attractions. In doing this, the Union tries to increase employment, to halt migration from local villages, to improve the quality of life and to create another source of income for people living in the region. However, there are rural regions that do no receive Union funding directly in the development of sustainable tourism. In this case, financial resources can be obtained from the existing institutions and sustainable tourism will be pursued through different organizational structures. In both regions tourism development is not regarded as the only key to regenerate the local economy. This implies that other projects which are beneficial to the environment are being promoted too. This promotion includes the production of 'green' products, local crafts and artisans. These issues are not only promoted by the

European Union; in the North Pennines the same development can be recognized.

However, it is questionable whether this development will be successful. Many obstacles and barriers are present. A relevant question deals with the relationship between the aims of the European Union in the field of regional development on the one hand, and the implementation of sustainable tourism on the other. Generally speaking, regional and social funds from the European Union aim at 'developing' rural and peripherally located regions. These funds are very often used for improving the quality of the infrastructure. The central point is whether this regional 'development' frustrates the implementation of sustainable tourism. In addition, the influence of the Common Agricultural Policy of the European Union has to be given special attention. This policy aims at modernizing agriculture by focusing on special products for the European regions. The European market can absorb these products at a low price when specialization takes place. However, this specialization on certain products will undoubtly have a negative influence on the ecological qualities of the agricultural areas. By doing this, the tourism attractiveness of these regions will be reduced.

In this chapter a description is given of field studies undertaken in the two regions by the first author in 1992 and 1993. It was investigated how far sustainable tourism could be realized in these regions, what the initiatives of regional authorities were, and which role the European Union played in these regions. Finally special attention is given to the obstacles and barriers for realising sustainable tourism in these regions.

12.2 The LEADER programme in La Sierra

Tourism in La Sierra in La Rioja, Spain, have been developed by using subsidies which were received from the European Union to initiate a LEADER programme. It was funded by the ERDF (The European Regional Development Fund), the EAGGF (The Guidance Section of the European Agricultural Guidance and Guarantee Fund) and the ESF (The European Social Fund) according to objective 5B. Through CARREFOURS, a network organization of the European Union which provides information and documentation about the rural regions of the European Union, the government of La Rioja became aware of the possibility of receiving financial assistance from the European Union by presenting a working programme to the Ministry of Agriculture in Madrid (1990). The LEADER programme in general aims (Commission of the European Community, 1990 p.07):

- a diversification of agriculture and a specialization in traditional local agricultural products,
- the protection of nature and the environment by sustaining the traditional stock-farming and production of "green" products,
- a financial assistance to small-scale and local businesses, not only in the agricultural sector,
- education in all sectors of the economy,

- an improvement of the infrastructure. The economic problems in this area are the low population density, the decreasing local production, the high rate of emigration, the communication problems, and the restructuring of agricultural production.

The LEADER programmes throughout Europe focus on the creation of employment by increasing the traditional agricultural production and on the development of tourism within the area. Not all villages have been promoted, only those were selected which have potential economic opportunities by improving the infrastructure and those which are attractive to visitors.

The programme does not set up projects, but provides a model of local economic development through encouraging local people or associations to start their own activities and small firms by means of funding and advice, in order to provide a dynamic impulse for the local economy and to diffuse the benefits to form an 'alternative economy' (Gil Cordón, 1993).

12.2.1 The organizational structure of the LEADER programme
The programme has been established after approval by the European Union. Therefore, competent development strategies of the national and regional authorities and other organizations were presented to the national government of Spain. After approval, these plans were proposed to the Commission of the European Union which developed measures to implement the strategy according to the objectives of the European Regional Development Fund (Commission of the European Community, 1988). Finally, the regional government developed an operational strategy. Also, it had to ensure its implementation. This procedure is based on the Subsidiarity principle of the European Union.

Each LEADER programme has its own organizational structure and strategies. In general, the LEADER programme aims at a bottom-up approach, the local people are encouraged to participate in every phase of the programme (Chanan, 1992).

The main committee, consisting of representatives of the European Commission of Investing Partners, regional authorities, unions and departments of the government, sets out the strategies and management of special development programmes in La Rioja. It also approves and controls the projects assisted by the LEADER programme in La Sierra.

Through the representatives of regional organizations, LEADER has a strong relationship with CARREFOURS and the government of La Rioja. The chairman of the European Commission Investing Partners is also the chairperson of the Ministry of Agriculture and Infrastructure of the region. At the implementation level there is much consultation about and coordination between the government and LEADER. Also, informal communication between all levels of the organization is very important to solve conflicting issues concerning economic development.

Three coordinators are directly involved with tourism projects at the implementation level. Their activities can be regarded as the core of the LEADER programme. They travel around the area and encourage local people directly, many of them are older than 50 years of age, to start their own local enterprises. These coordinators set up courses, are involved with the development of public footpaths, give advice in administration and investment and guide the initiated developments. At first the three coordinators divided several tasks, but due to difficulties in communication and a lack in infrastructure they were forced to divide the regions into three areas of development, working closely together in undertaking similar activities.

12.2.2 Sustainable Tourism Development in La Sierra

The main objective of the European Union and the tourism department in La Rioja (Consejería del Turismo) is to manage tourists in a balanced and sustainable way in order to improve the economy and social life in La Rioja, while preserving the cultural heritage and the natural environment. This goal is reflected in the strategies of the LEADER programme in La Sierra. Tourism projects are integrated into the local economies; they focus upon environmental conservation projects and involve local residents.

The government of La Rioja considered three different strategies in order to develop tourism in La Sierra: by improving its position on the tourism market, by developing sustainable tourism to improve the economic sector and social life, and by preserving the natural environment and cultural heritage of the area. Therefore, five types of tourist attractions were considered as prime objectives in stimulating sustainable tourism in La Sierra: wine and gastronomy, palaeontology, cultural and natural heritage, mountain climbing and walking and the natural spas (Gobierno de La Rioja, 1989).

In La Sierra the LEADER programme has contributed to the development of tourism facilities and attractions as stated in the White Book of La Rioja of 1989. It has those persons included who have unprofitable enterprises and who therefore, cannot stay in the agricultural sector, or those who have worked in agriculture temporarily. The programme does not aim at changing the contemporary agricultural way of production. However, measures of the European Union concerning agriculture will change production. Therefore, the LEADER programme's aim is to establish 'model enterprises' for small-size farmers to diversify their economic activities; it does not aim to paternalize (Esteban Gil Cordón, LEADER coordinator, 1993). In doing this, the programme aims at convincing the local population of the benefits of tourism. The initiators have to apply for financial assistance under the condition that the LEADER coordinators may observe the project. There has been some resistance under the older population. However, the younger people are interested in starting a business in order to be able to live in the area. In addition, the attitude of the mayor of a municipality seemed to have a major influence on the initiation of tourism projects.

The LEADER committee sees tourism development not as the only way to success. It recognizes the potentials of some areas benefitting from visitors, but it also accepts the fact that there are regions where no tourism development is possible. Therefore, an evaluation of 'alternative', green and cultural products is considered to be important to the local economies in the future.

The first activities of the Leader programme have been to establish short courses, in order to establish a network of guides that can accompany groups of tourists and to educate rural people in palaeontology and environmental issues in group management. Also, there was a lot of interest for technical courses in Human Resource Management, business administration and business management. Another initiative of the LEADER programme, to promote tourism in La Sierra, resulted in a video about the "route of the Dinosaurs" which had been produced in collaboration with the association:"Amigos de Munilla". Furthermore, the LEADER programme has supported initiatives in accommodation facilities within this area. The establishment of a network of walking routes called "Sierras de la Rioja" in partnership with GR-93 has been created. In Enciso and the area around a holiday inn, Visitor Information Centre, restaurants and countryside visitor accommodations were funded (Fernandez Nantes, 1992; Izco, 1993). These 'model activities' have been very successful and more facilities have been developed to provide alternative recreation possibilities for the local people and to increase the number of tourism attractions for visitors.

La Rioja as a whole is promoted by the government. However, the LEADER programme provides information about the projects and new attractions solely in La Sierra by mailing to several businesses in the major cities of Spain. They organize tourist packages in order to diversify the tourist product of La Sierra and to extend the tourist season. In the strategies of the LEADER programme no segmentation of tourists have been made, but in future certain groups of tourists will be promoted in order not to create an oversupply of tourists in the tourist season.

The LEADER programme runs up to the summer of 1994, but in only three years it has been successful in encouraging, in educating and funding individual projects and local associations. Therefore, a LEADER II programme has been established, which will continue the activities of LEADER I. The LEADER II will finish, redevelop, enlarge and stimulate the projects started under LEADER I. Without a basic funding from the ERDF many businesses and organizations would not be able to continue during the years to come.

According to a new strategy proposal as stated in the Green Book of Rural Development, LEADER II will start from the same broad vision, in an attempt to encourage more people and associations to initiate projects benefitting the environment and the participation of the local population. It will also focus more on 'green' products that are locally produced. Furthermore, it will develop an impact study to measure the economic and tourism impacts on the environment; this can stimulate the evaluation of the effects and results of the LEADER II programme (Gil Cordón, 1993).

12.2.3 The financial structure of the LEADER programme
In total 442 million ECU's are allocated to the 212 Leader programmes by the Agricultural Structure Funds of the European Union (Chanan, 1992). Subsidies for projects are allocated after a presentation of an overall strategy and management plan. The projects need to include the production or activities beneficial to the natural environment, the participation of the local population and the guidance and evaluation by the LEADER coordinators. The LEADER programme, together with the government of La Rioja and local authorities, fund individual enterprises, but if the project has not been started within one year the money has to be returned.

1993 has been a 'pilot year' for the programme in which many activities have been promoted on an experimental basis. In the following years evaluation procedures will identify which activities will be continued.

12.3 The North Pennines Tourism Partnership

After the designation of the North Pennines as an Area of Outstanding Natural Beauty (AONB) in 1988, a full strategic tourism development plan was developed with the aim not only to increase the number of visitors to the North Pennines region, but also to encourage them to stay longer. The North Pennines Consultative Group and the existing tourism strategies set the context for a new tourism initiative. As a result of a seminar in the spring of 1989, the English Tourist Board (ETB), the Rural Development Commission, the Countryside Commission and the local authorities initiated the North Pennines partnership (English Tourist Board, 1992). Initially, the rural population was sceptical about the designation of the AONB and it took more than ten years to persuade the public that the designation would benefit the local economy in the long term (Countryside Commission, AONB policy, 1990a).

Before the North Pennines Tourism Partnership was established a marketing and management study had been completed in order to develop regional planning strategies and policies. Obviously, no direct measures where established in relation to conservation. Through the designation of an AONB the Countryside Commission became directly involved by appointing an AONB officer and the partnership started to sensitively promote and to guide tourism in the North Pennines. Also, the Countryside Commission and the Rural Development Commission participated in the activities of the partnership although to a lesser degree. From 1989 onwards the aims of the Countryside Commission have been primarily to conserve and enhance the natural beauty of the landscape and secondly: a) to meet the need for quiet enjoyment of the countryside; b) to have regard for the interests of those who live and work there (Countryside Commission AONB regulations, 1989). Mass tourism is not regarded as appropriate; it has negative impacts on the rural economy and may undermine the unique quality of the area (Countryside Commission, 1990b).

12.3.1 The organizational structure of the North Pennines Tourism Partnership
To develop a coherent strategic plan in order to promote tourism activities for a region that includes three councils and six districts is quite complicated. There are a multiplicity of agencies within the North Pennines region and all of them have other responsibilities besides tourism. Therefore, the tourism partnership has played a major role in managing tourism development successfully (English Tourist Board, 1991).

The organizational structure of the tourism partnership is quite simple. It is vertical and consists of three levels: the North Pennines committee, the management team and the working groups. Informal communication proved to be very important when conflicting issues between representatives appear.

The North Pennines committee forms the full partnership, comprising of local authorities, the Regional Tourist Boards, the Countryside Commission, the Rural Development Commission and representatives of the voluntary and private sectors in the region. The Regional Tourist Boards, the Countryside Commission and the Rural Development Commission delegate representatives to the meetings, which take place twice a year. The private and voluntary sector nominates up to eight individuals annually from as wide as a range of geographical and sectoral interests as possible. The committee approves or disapproves the working programmes in which budget, actions, priorities, future strategies, are stated. The decisions are more concerned with policy matters than with detailed practicalities.

The management team consists of the tourism partnership officer, representatives of the Regional Tourist Boards, the Rural Development Commission and the Countryside Commission. Its task is to prepare proposals for the Partnership Committee's consideration, to coordinate the operation of the working groups, to oversee the implementation of partnership decisions and to guide the partnership officer. In the meetings of the management team conflicts and strategies are discussed with the aim of consolidating any conflicts between the representatives of the different interest groups. Between the members, which are representatives of different organizations, agreement is sought.

Within the partnership the tourism officer's role is to coordinate meetings and initiate projects. Furthermore, the officer is an important intermediary between the management and implementation level. The action programmes and budgeting are major responsibilities and therefore the officer is very much involved with the implementation issues in the working groups. This person keeps in contact with local enterprises and is involved in other projects and local organizations.

There are two working groups, the Marketing Group and the Development Group which consist of expert members of the private and the public sector, and voluntary groups. The Development Group identifies small schemes of proposals that are beneficial to the industry, rather than providing capital incentives to individuals. Possible working areas are, business training subsidies, signing and interpretation, feasibility studies and market research. The Marketing Group is mainly responsible for publicity and promotion actions of tourism projects within the area.

Members, mostly women, volunteer to join the working groups but at the time of writing only the major business entrepreneurs were represented. Their tasks include drawing up detailed work programmes, budgeting and implementing decisions taken on such programmes with an agreed timescale. The working groups are the vehicle for the partnership, they are committed and involved with local businesses, which are not necessarily directly involved in tourism development. In the working groups possible conflicts with organizations, local people or environmental issues can be solved.

12.3.2 Sustainable tourism development in the North Pennines
Recreation and tourism have not been the primary reasons for designation of the North Pennines as an Area of Outstanding Natural Beauty, but it has been pursued in those areas where it can be compatible with conservation and the needs of agriculture, forestry and other uses. In addition the Countryside Commission sees its major task as one of protecting the quality of the typical English landscape and to increase the accessibility. Access to the countryside for tourists and residents has been one of the major programmes of the Countryside Commission over recent years (Countryside Commission, 1990a,b). In these programmes awareness of the residents to conserve and enhance their regional environment and the provision of information to tourists

is of considerable importance. Therefore, through the partnership the Countryside Commission has had a direct influence in the planning and management of the environment as a resource input for tourism.

To control projects in the countryside the Countryside Commission acts to evaluate the projects in order to establish whether the conditions of grant aid, set by the Commission, have been followed. At the time of research there was a project in consideration to have a Green Audit for the North Pennines Partnership. Its purpose is to evaluate, through desk research by an independent group of experts, the partnership's activities in environmental, economic and social terms. As this implies, the partnership aims at achieving 'green' or sustainable tourism. In May 1992, through the Secretary of State for Employment's Tourism and Environmental Task Force, seven principles to achieve sustainable development were stated. They form the basic idea underlying the activities that are implemented and future strategies that are being established (Branton, 1993):

1   The environment has an intrinsic value which outweighs its value as a tourism asset. Its enjoyment by future generations and its long term survival must not been prejudiced by short term considerations.
2   Tourism should be recognized as a positive activity with the potential to benefit the community and the place as well as the visitor.
3   The relationship between tourism and the environment must be managed so that it is sustainable in the long term. Tourism must not be allowed to damage the resource, prejudice its future enjoyment or bring unacceptable impacts.
4   Tourism activities and developments should respect the scale, nature and character of the place in which they are sited.
5   In any location, harmony must be sought between the needs of the visitor, the place and the host community.
6   In a dynamic world some change is inevitable and change can often be beneficial. Adaption to change, however, should not be at the expense of any of these principles.
7   The tourism industry, local authorities and environmental agencies all have a duty to respect the above principles and to work together to achieve their practical realization.

The tourism partnership provides information for individuals and businesses involved in tourism and covers areas such as access to expertise business advice, marketing, research statistics, viability of new projects, planning, photo library, local contacts and in depth knowledge of the tourism market in the North Pennines (Roger, Tym & Partners, 1988). Therefore, the tourism partnership is directly involved in research regarding visitors which is being conducted every two years. Also, the tourism partnership stimulates rather than subsidizes local projects that again can be considered as small partnerships of the public sector (English Tourist Board, 1992; Countryside Commission, 1990a). The aim of the partnership therefore is to establish cooperative structures between various groups and operators rather than to produce a real impact for two to three years.

In 1990 the tourism partnership launched several projects mostly aimed at improving the quality of the service of local tourism business and to coordinate local initiatives, in particular accommodation. A tourism training and recruitment coordinator was appointed to organize training for local business people.

The Youth Hostel Association and the partnership tried to initiate and coordinate camping barns (in old parts of the farm) on farms and estates in 1991. Also, a Farm Holiday Bureau, which is a network bureau of farming families, is promoted by the Tourism Partnership. The Durham Dales Centre in Stanhope was one of the projects promoted to encourage exhibitions and sales of local arts and crafts, to provide information about management of tourism enterprises, to establish a tourist information office and to promote art courses for residents.

In addition, the partnership provides information packages about the region for visitors, develops several walking programmes and stimulates a public transport partnership scheme to encourage public transportation within the region. Moreover, the partnership endorses green products of the local tourism enterprises. It introduced a 'Green Tourism Award' based around the principles for 'green' tourism development as stated in the "Maintaining the Balance" report of the English Tourist Board and the Employment Department Group (English Tourist Board, 1991).

12.3.3 Financial resources to develop sustainable tourism in the North Pennines

The most important funding source in developing tourism in rural regions for public and private organizations in England is the Rural Development Commission together with the Countryside Commission. The Rural Development Commission in general provides one-third of the core funding for projects up to 50,000 pounds. It also gives grants for local tourism development and funds for encouraging innovation and for small and medium business development. In landscape conservation schemes the County Council can provide financial and technical assistance. The AONB officer of the Countryside Commission is the adviser as to receive the most appropriate source of grant, whether from the Countryside Commission or the Rural Development Commission (Countryside Commission, 1990b).

The partnership is not involved in applying for grant aid from the European Union. However, small parts of the North Pennines region are eligible for Union funding by TAWSEN in Northumberland and IDOP (Integrated Development Operations Programmes) in Durham and Cleveland, under Objective 2 of the European Regional Development Fund. TAWSEN is a partnership, established in 1989 between the European Union, the United Kingdom Government, local authorities and a wide range of academic, training, voluntary, business and service organizations. The improvement of the infrastructure and communication has the highest priority together with training and education courses. Also, much emphasis is given to the development of small and medium size enterprises and tourism facilities, and to a lesser degree to improve the attractiveness of the landscape and promotion activities (Tawsen, 1993). In Durham and Cleveland, Union funding is available by the Integrated Development Operations Programme with one of the projects funded in the North Pennines region being the Durham Dales Centre and a number of training programmes (Durham and Cleveland Integrated Development Operations Programme, 1992).

The partnership was subsidized until April 1994. After this period the financial resources will be reconsidered for future activities. Without funding from the European Tourist Board and the Countryside Commission the partnership would not have been able to exist. There is not sufficient local recognition by local businesses to support the partnership completely, and in order to undertake major initial investments (advertising), public funding is vital. Furthermore, most enterprises are relatively small and their financial resources are not large enough to support the partnership completely.

12.4 Barriers in implementing sustainable tourism strategies

Both development programmes displayed similar objectives and strategies. However, the concept of sustainability was percepted differently. In La Sierra increased tourism activity was regarded as a part of the development of a healthy rural economy, whereas in the North Pennines tourism was developed in a more environmentally sensitive way. In the English case the environmental issues were regarded as most important, as a consequence of direct involvement of an AONB officer of the Countryside Commission. In La Sierra the improvement of the infrastructure, communication and basic needs were primary objectives as stated in the regional policy of the European Union. However, it must be recognized that there are many differences in landscape, including, the climate, economical position of the region, financial structure, the cultural and natural heritage and the differing needs of the tourists, which will result in very different implementation strategies.

In the implementation of the strategies of sustainable tourism in both regions many barriers and obstacles were present. Problems that can be categorized in organizational, social, political, ecological and financial issues.

12.4.1 Organizational and political barriers

Problems in communication have occurred in both regions. In La Sierra due to difficulties in communication networks and infrastructure. In the North Pennines regions due to the different regulation systems in the three counties and six districts. Conflicts between the parties involved in tourism issues are being solved through meetings of the partnerships, informal communication, overlapping partnerships and especially in the North Pennines through the Working Programmes in which local interest parties, not always in tourism, are confronted. Participation in local projects is on a voluntary base. Therefore, resistance of local organizations which have no direct interest can cause problems in initiating tourism projects. The LEADER programme in La Sierra does not have working groups at the lowest level. Therefore, conflicts are directly discussed among the development agents and the committee.

The LEADER programme, unlike the North Pennines region, does not have a major national organization such as the Countryside Commission. Union assistance, therefore, can provide a certain basic organizational structure which is necessary to manage tourism development successfully. To achieve this, the European Union can play an important role in setting up local (policy) structures through partnerships for the long term. However, it must be stated that existing local organizations can work against tourism projects. In the North Pennines case for example the Landowner Association has great influence over local policy-making with regard to, for example, grouse shooting (Wilson, 1992).

12.4.2 Social barriers

Before both tourism development projects were initiated, the local population was alarmed at the ways in which the traditional agricultural economy would change. The first activities of the programmes were to convince local authorities and organizations of the benefits of sustainable tourism development for the rural community. Also, the training programmes and direct involvement of the development agents in the management of local (partnership) projects awareness of the possibilities tourism can contribute to mutual understanding. Tourism development is seen as an economic stimulant for society. However, to achieve an alternative green economy more emphasis on local participation and education must be given.

To which amount tourism projects are initiated, depends on the attitude of the local authorities. In La Sierra the opinion of the Major is very important in developing projects. Also, in these regions mostly older people live, not always being interested in tourism profits. This needs more involvement of the development agents and education than the younger population that enthusiastic start projects in order to find an (alternative) economic activity within the region, which means that in the end emigration numbers are halted.

12.4.3 Ecological barriers

Both sustainable tourism development programmes have carefully selected areas where a certain type of tourism is being promoted and tourism projects are initiated. In both areas mass tourism is not regarded as an appropriate solution. However, only an evaluation procedure will demonstrate to which extent the activities have an impact on nature, landscape, cultural heritage and social life. In La Sierra, the LEADER programme is developing an evaluation and monitoring program to estimate the real environmental and cultural impact of the tourist activities and projects that have been established over the previous years. In the North Pennines the Countryside Commission is developing an independent research body to evaluate the activities initiated by the North Pennines tourism partnership. This may especially be relevant as measures have been taken to control the number of tourists in the future while the first phase of the development programmes is to attract as many tourists as possible. Moreover, what will happen when funding of environmentally sensitive projects ends and the partnerships have finished their guiding role? Economic issues still dominate the strategies which emphasize sustainable tourism development in both regions.

12.4.4 Financial barriers

The LEADER programme in La Sierra has direct funding from the European Union to allocate among the initiated projects. Depending upon the contribution of the regional authority additional funding is contributed to various extends.

The North Pennines tourism partnership only advices in funding with most grants coming from the Countryside Commission, the Rural Development Commission or the local government. As unlike in the Spanish case, almost half of the financial resources are provided by the private sector. Some Union funding has been allocated under Objective 2 to set up courses in business management and farm holiday accommodation facilities.

The European Union increases funding in La Sierra only after a financial contribution of the local authorities to projects and small medium sized enterprises. Sustainable development funding is only allocated to projects that preserve or enhance the natural or cultural environment. Projects or enterprises that produce traditional and environmental benefits (e.g. green products), goods or local craftswork and artisans are also promoted. The extend of funding is based on a detailed management plan.

Capital investment is crucial for those regions that are in an economic downstream development. It can provide a basis for the development of further economic activities and when this is managed successfully a healthy alternative economy can be realized. Funding is necessary, in particular, for the establishment of local and medium sized enterprises. However, it must be recognized that in the strategies of both regions developing tourism is not regarded as the only key to success. While encouraging the traditional way of production and traditional art, other economic activities are crucial to create a sustainable and alternative economy which does not over-use natural resources and which in the end may even become another input factor as a tourist attraction.

Both development programmes will receive funding until the end of 1994. However it is almost certain that the programmes will be continued. Regional tourism development in harmony with other regional activities, partnerships and the direct involvement in projects and additional funding have demonstrated to be successful in sustainable tourism development.

12.5 Conclusions

From the previous analysis some conclusions can be drawn:
*   Without the establishment of coordinating partnerships and basic financial resources sustainable tourism development can not be successful, as has been demonstrated in the two development programmes presented in this study. In England the tourism partnership works successfully through the well institutionalized local structures and national funding organizations such as the Countryside Commission and the Rural Development Commission, while in La Rioja, which has autonomy with regards to policy issues, no (national) organizations exist.
*   With regards to the tourism market rural regions will benefit from the increased demand throughout Europe. However, the tourism market rapidly changes. It is obvious that in the short term the rural economies will benefit from tourism development but without clearly set objectives, resource management, market segmentation, financial resources, a strong developed organization structure and a constant evaluation of resources the path towards sustainability will only take a few steps.
*   It is not clear what the relationship is between the supply and demand of

sustainable tourism. In other words: There are many depopulated areas in Europe suffering from a lack of regional resources. Only in a limited number of these regions tourism is a real option. How high is the level of demand on sustainable tourism related to this more or less fixed level of supply?

* Which type of economic development is feasible for those depopulated areas in which a touristic development - may it sustainable or not - cannot be seen as a real option? When sustainable development is taken as a guideline for all economic and environmental policies, which alternatives can be formulated for those regions?

* Is it possible to influence significantly the demand of people on sustainable tourism? The demand on sustainable tourism is concentrated in the urbanized European regions. What is the relationship between the living conditions in these areas and the demand on sustainable tourism?

* It is not clear what sustainable tourism is. In La Sierra and the North Pennines there is a general idea that the development of the last decades cannot be evaluated as sustainable, which leads to the conclusion that 'something' has to be changed. However, what are the criteria which can be used as a test for sustainable tourism?

* Funds from outside the region are relevant to start any form of sustainable tourism. It is not clear whether these funds are necessary in the long run. This point may be relevant as many functions of the ecosystems in remote areas such as watershed protection, the production of oxygen by green plants, and the presence of rare plants and animals are of national and international importance. The outside regions do not pay the rural areas for these functions of the ecosystems in the rural areas. This implies that the level of social costs and benefits related to this topic are not clear.

References

Branton, J. (1993), *Towards a Harmonious Triangle*, Workshop Proceedings, Centre for Travel and Tourism, University of Northumberland, Newcastle.

Briassoulis, Helen and Jan van der Straaten (eds.) (1992), *Tourism and the Environment*, Kluwer Academic Publishers, Dordrecht, Boston, London.

Chanan, G. (1992), Out of the Shadows, Strategies for Local Community Action in Europe. *LEADER Magazine*, A.E.I.D.L., Brussels, No.1.

Commission of the European Community [COM] (1988), *Regional Policy*, Office for Official Publications of the European Community, Brussels (CBNF870004ENC).

Commission of the European Community [COMEC] (1990a), *The New Structural Policies of the European Community*, Office for Official Publications of the European Community, Brussels (CCAD90008ENC).

Commission of the European Community [COM(438)] (1990b), *Community Action to Promote Rural Tourism*, European Community, Brussels.

Countryside Commission [CCP/289] (1990a), *The North Pennines AONB; Issues and Priorities*, Countryside Commission Publications, Manchester.

Countryside Commission [CCP/290] (1990b), *The North Pennines AONB; Grants and Advice available for Conservation and Development,* Countryside Commission Publications, Manchester.

Dietz, F.J. and J. van der Straaten (1992), Rethinking Environmental Economics; Missing Links between Economic Theory and Environmental Policy. *Journal of Economic Issues,* March, pp. 27-51.

English Tourist Board [ETB] (1991), *Maintaining the Balance, a Guide to Sustainable Tourism,* ETB, London.

English Tourist Board [ETB] (1992), North Pennines, the Last Wilderness. *Tourism Enterprise,* no.87, Nov/Dec. 1992, p.VII.

European Community Council [EEC(421] (1992), A Community Action Plan to Assist Tourism. *Official Journal of the European Community,* no. L 231/26.

Farell, B.H. and R.W. McLellan, 1987. Tourism and Physical Environment Research, *Annals of Tourism Research, 14(1), pp. 1-16.*

Farell, B.H. and D. Runyian (1991), Ecology and Tourism, Annals of Tourism Research,, 18(1), pp. 26-40.

Fernandez Nantes, J. (1992), Programma LEADER: Acciones en la Cuenca Alta del Cidacos. *VOZ, Boletin Informativo de la Asociación de Amigos de Munilla,* Asociación de Amigos de Munilla, Munilla, pp. 3-4.

Gil Córdon, E. (1993), El LEADER es el Desarollo Local Rural desde La Base. *Sierras de La Rioja, C.E.I.P.,* Logrono, No.2, pp. 10-11.

Gobierno de La Rioja (1989), *La Rioja Turística,* Déposito Legal, Logrono

Gobierno de La Rioja (1993), *La Rioja Turistíca,* Datos Profesionales, Déposito Legal, Logrono.

Integrated Development Operations Programme Durham and Cleveland [IDOP] (1992), *The Durham and Cleveland Integrated Development Operations Programme,* IDOP Secretariat European Section (DTI-NE), Newcastle upon Tyne, England.

Izco, P.(1993), Algo Mas que un Sendero. *Sierras de La Rioja,* C.E.I.P., Logrono, No.2, pp. 8-9.

Johanna M. Kasperkovitz (1992), 'Sustainable Development Against Vested Interests'. In: F.J. Dietz, U.E. Simonis and J. van der Straaten (eds.), *Sustainability and Environmental Policy,* Sigma Verlag, Berlin, pp. 138-149.

José Fernandez, M. (1993), El Terrirorio 5B, Algunos Datos sobre La Sierra. *Sierras de La Rioja,* C.E.I.P., Logrono, No.2, pp. 4-5.

Mellors, C. (1990), *A Guide to Regional Policy,* Routledge, London.

Opschoor, Hans and Jan van der Straaten, 1993. Sustainable Development: an Institutional Approach, *Ecological Economics,* Volume 7, pp. 203-222.

Straaten, J. van der (1992), A Sound European Environmental Policy: Challenges, Possibilities and Barriers, *Environmental Politics,* Volume 1, Nr. 4, pp. 65-83.

Roger Tym & Partners (1988), *Tourism in the North Pennines: Action Programme,* Roger Tym and Partners, London (no publication).

Tyne and Wear and South East Northumberland Integrated Development Operations Programme [TAWSEN] (1992), *TAWSEN,* Sunderland Borough Council, Newcastle upon Tyne, England.

Vicente Elías, L. (1992), *Guia de La Rioja,* El Pais, Madrid.

Wilson, O. (1992), Landownership and Rural Development in the North

Pennines: a Case Study. *Journal of Rural Studies,* Vol.8, no.2, pp. 145-158.

World Commission on Environment and Development (1987), *Our Common Future,* Oxford University Press, Oxford, New York.

13 Problems of tourism development in Spain

G.K. Priestley

13.1 Introduction

It is a well-known fact that the Spanish tourism industry is not as stable now as in the past. The purpose of this paper is to:
- identify the problems facing tourism in Spain;
- pinpoint the principal underlying causes;
- indicate the lessons that can be learned from the Spanish experience.

However, before analyzing the situation, it is necessary to outline the basic characteristics of Spanish tourism. The origins of mass tourism date back to the 1950s, although the period of most spectacular growth in the number of visitor arrivals was from the end of that decade until 1973. The number of annual visitor arrivals now oscillates between 50 and 54 million, of which approximately 70% are tourists (see Figure 13.1 and Table 13.1). The income from international tourism is approaching $20,000 million, which, in 1991, represented 7.9% of the GNP. Foreign exchange in that same year amounted to more than $4,500 million (Ministerio de Industria...., 1992). The economic benefits of tourism are not, however, evenly spread throughout the country. Tourist infrastructures are concentrated in certain regions, ranking in order of importance from the Balearic Islands, in first place, followed by Catalonia, Andalusia and the Canary Islands. Economic dependence on tourism likewise shows regional variations - the Balearic Islands, with over 50% of the region's income coming from tourism, are followed by the Canary Islands and Andalusia. Significant local variations also exist. In fact a high percentage of the total tourist accommodation supply is concentrated in a limited number of large resorts - Lloret de Mar, Salou, Benidorm, Torremolinos and Benalmádena on the Spanish mainland coast; ribbon development east and west of Palma de Mallorca; and the Canary Island resorts of Santa Cruz de Tenerife and Las Palmas de Gran Canaria.

The development of tourism since its early origins has not, however, followed a regular growth pattern throughout the period. The upward trend in visitor numbers suffered a serious setback in 1974 - 1976, and this situation was repeated on a lesser scale in 1979 - 1980. Since 1989, fluctuations have been constant. Nevertheless, there is a significant difference between the first two 'crises' and the present one. The first was caused by external factors as the tourist industry in general suffered the consequences of the worldwide economic crisis which originated in 1973. The second setback was the market's reply to the application of government policy, when considerable increases in hotel prices were introduced. The difference in the case of present instability in the tourist industry is that it is the result of an accumulation of adverse factors over a period of several years, rather than an immediate response to a single easily identified and unique cause.

13.2 Identifying the problem

The basic problem in Spanish tourism at present is its loss of economic viability. It is not simply a problem of the tailing-off of the upward trend in visitor numbers, nor of the quantity of foreign exchange acquired, as this continues to register small annual increases. It is a problem of the cost: benefit ratio, closely linked to the average spending per tourist which has gradually decreased in spite of rising prices paid by tourists, which almost doubled between 1983 and 1991 (Ministerio de Industria...., 1992).

The principal cause of this apparent contradiction is that Spain at present attracts a large proportion of its tourists from groups with low spending power or spending will. These include air and coach charter groups, campers and caravanners. In fact, 61% of foreign tourists entered Spain by road in 1991 (Ministerio de Industria...., op. cit.). This characteristic is related to the changes which have been taking place in the nature of tourism demand in general in recent years. These include the trend to more frequent, shorter-break holidays; new market sectors, such as old-age pensioners, those who have taken early retirement and the unemployed; more motorized tourists, with spectacular increases especially in coach travel. As a result, the low-spending tourist sectors have expanded considerably. Spain is well placed to cater for this type of demand, given that it is within easy reach of the principal generating centres.

Rapid and cheap access alone would not be sufficient reason to attract low spenders. The complementary condition necessary is the suitability of the type of product offered. In Spain, at the end of the 1980s, the price: quality ratio of tourist supply was low in the majority of the principal tourist destinations. In fact, quality was low in both absolute and relative terms. Serious structural defects negatively affected quality. Much of the existing accommodation, frequently unaltered since its construction in the early years of development, had become obsolete or, at best, in need of total renovation. Moreover, accommodation had been provided without a parallel development of adequate infrastructures and amenities, such as sewage treatment and disposal, provision of water supplies. Town planning was seldom contemplated and development was largely haphazard, anarchic and excessively dense. Urban amenity levels were therefore low: the provision and maintenance of gardens and parks, street lighting and paving, sea-front promenades and even beaches was often unsatisfactory. The overall result was the deterioration of both the natural and built environments.

Table 13.1
Tourism supply and demand in Spain, 1950-1991
(all statistics are expressed in thousands)

YEAR	VISITOR ARRIVALS	HOTEL BEDS	NON-HOTEL BEDS	CAMPSITE CAPACITY
1950	750			
1951	1263	78.8		
1952	1485	89.7		
1953	1710	98.7		
1954	1952	105.4		
1955	2522	109.7		
1956	2728	120.7		
1957	3187	122.8		
1958	3594	132.5		
1959	4195	142.5		
1960	6113	150.8		
1961	7455	162.1		
1962	8669	192.9		
1963	10932	263.9		
1964	14103	300.6		104.3
1965	14252	328.1		120.8
1966	17252	354.2		126.8
1967	17859	384.0		135.8
1968	19184	434.4		156.1
1969	21682	465.4		171.2
1970	24105	545.8	121.2	190.8
1971	26758	612.3		
1972	32507	657.7	179.0	208.1
1973	34559	699.4		211.6
1974	30343	732.9	190.9	221.2
1975	30122	785.3		224.0
1976	30014	799.0		230.4
1977	34267	803.7		232.2
1978	39970	808.0		227.9
1979	38902	806.6		246.4
1980	38027	814.4		272.2
1981	40129	811.7	270.9	280.6
1982	42011	826.0	277.9	303.9
1983	41263	834.5	292.7	344.3
1984	42932	835.2	295.5	356.3
1985	43235	843.3	298.0	385.4
1986	47389	864.8	290.0	406.5
1987	50545	886.7	304.0	438.0
1988	54178	907.9	328.4	457.4
1989	54058	918.6	335.8	470.4
1990	52044	929.5	384.9	571.3
1991	53495	972.8	402.7	575.3

Source: Ministerio de Industria ..., 1980-1992
Ministerio de Información ..., 1963-1979

189

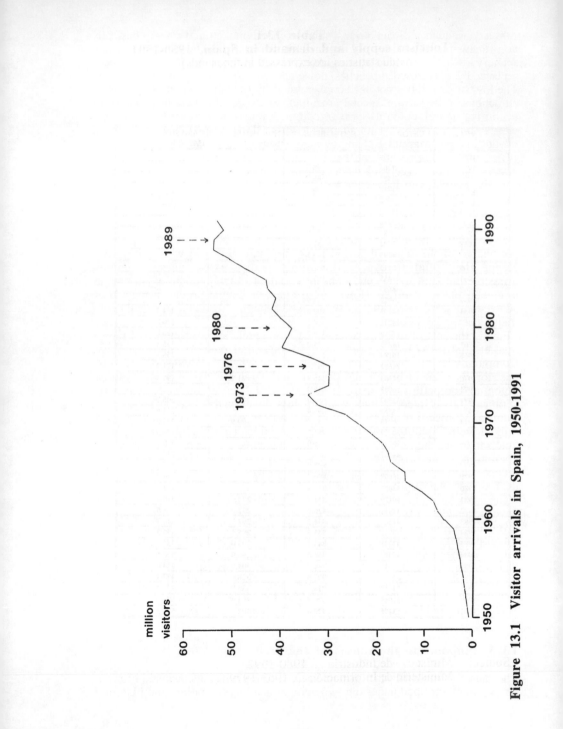

Figure 13.1 Visitor arrivals in Spain, 1950-1991

As a consequence, Spain has lost some of its original attractiveness - basically non-renewable natural resources, such as deserted beaches and spectacular scenery - which provided a tranquil and exotic atmosphere. These have been replaced by overcrowded beaches, noise and high density urban development. The loss of charm has not been compensated by the introduction of alternative attractions in the form of special amenities, or the development of other forms of tourism (rural, cultural, sport or congress tourism, for example). In other words, tourist supply has not adapted to either the changing characteristics of the destination areas or the changing motivations of potential clients.

By contrast, the natural market for Spanish tourism has not changed: the population of the largely urbanized countries of northern and western Europe. It is the people who have changed. They are more knowledgeable about the different options available as they are better informed and more widely travelled. They are also more discerning on matters which affect environmental quality. Moreover, their attitude to Spain as a destination has also changed, for it is no longer thought of as an "exotic" destination but rather the "pleasure periphery" of the political unit (European Community) in which they live. Hence they tend to expect the same quality of services, amenities, infrastructures and living conditions in both the natural and built environments as in their places of origin. However, in Spain the tourist product has not been adapted in accordance with the evolution of either motivations in general or the traditional market in particular.

Finally the cost of living in Spain, very low in relation to its principal tourist markets until 1973, has risen sharply since that date to equal European Community levels. The relation between quality which, as already pointed out, has not risen accordingly, and price is unfavourable. By way of contrast, potential competitors who, in the 1970s, had been either more expensive (France, Italy, Greece, Yugoslavia) or less developed (Greece, Yugoslavia, Tunisia, Morocco) (Cals, 1974) have been able to compete in recent years with a much better quality: price ratio. This situation has obliged many Spanish hotels to lower their prices in order to attract clients. This cannot be considered a solution to the problem as it induces a drop in the quality of service and reduces economic viability thus making improvement of the product through the reinvestment of profits impossible.

The crisis has not affected the country in a uniform fashion. Its repercussions have depended on the structure of tourism in each region, or even at resort level. The regions or resorts which depend most heavily on air charter or coach travel package clients staying at low category rated hotels have suffered the effects of the crisis most seriously. These include many of the resorts on the island of Mallorca, the Catalan resorts of Lloret de Mar, Platja d'Aro, Calella de la Costa and Salou and the Andalusian resorts of Torremolinos and Benalmádena. The higher quality tourism of the Canary Islands and part of the Andalusian coast has been less adversely affected.

13.3 Pinpointing the causes of the crisis

The causes of the difficulties which Spanish tourism has encountered in recent years can be grouped under the two general headings of policy and planning.

During the period of the dictatorship of General Franco, which lasted until his death in 1975, tourism policy was decided by the central government, while the municipal authorities were responsible for planning. After a three year transition period during which the establishment of a democratic constitution took priority over all other government matters, the responsibility for tourism policy was rapidly transferred to the autonomous regional governments which were set up. Thereafter, limited legislation introduced by both the central and autonomous governments affected planning. These measures included laws to restrict construction along the coastline and the regulation of the environmental impact of development projects. The municipal authorities remained responsible for all other aspects of town planning, and were obligated to revise existing urban master plans.

However, the basic structure of present-day Spanish tourism emerged during the early years of rapid expansion up until 1973, so it is therefore the policy and planning measures of this period which have had most influence on the present situation. The creation, in 1962, of a Subsecretariat of Tourism within the Ministry of Finance marked the official recognition of a tourism policy. The policy applied over the next decade could be summed up as one of 'numerical growth at all costs'. This was achieved through strict price control, to such an extent that annual price increases were kept below the rate of inflation. It could be said that this constituted the basic element of government policy throughout the period. Looking back, it is easy to condemn this policy as, at best, short - sighted. An explanation can be found in the authorities' mistrust of the long - term stability of the sector, which was in fact openly admitted (Oficina de Coordinación...., 1963). Tourism was never considered an integral part of the economy, and even less a priority sector. It was used as an instrument of development policy, but was not really a component of this policy.

This underlying philosophy conditioned other aspects of policy. For example, financial support for tourist enterprises, in the form of credits and loans, was also very limited, and different measures designed to encourage export sectors of the economy systematically excluded tourism. Likewise, government investment was concentrated on the establishment of a network of hotels aimed at opening up new areas to tourism (there were 82 of these 'albergues' and 'paradores nacionales' by 1971), but little attention was paid to the transport sector until after 1971, by which time companies from tourist-generating countries had already captured a large share and, consequently, control of the market. Nevertheless, the insufficiency of credits and loans was probably the most influential reason as to why a large number of hotel companies fell under foreign control.

The huge gap between public and private investment in accommodation and transport was paralleled by a similar deficit in infrastructure. Income from tourism was not reinvested to provide the necessary infrastructures alongside accommodation provision. Such investment was not seriously contemplated until 1972, and was mostly allocated to road construction, thus increasing congestion by improving access.

Government short-sightedness was also reflected in the absence of long-term planning. It was not until 1970 that minimum infrastructure requirements were established, and these went no further than basic necessities (such as electricity, drinking water, sewage and access). The fact that no Ministry has ever been set up to deal exclusively with problems of the tourism sector is further evidence of this mentality. Similarly, the structure of education was not adapted to prepare people for employment in the tourist sector and funding of research in this field was virtually non-existent. Consequently, the attitude of the population, after initial curiosity and enthusiasm, has tended towards apathy or even resentment, as people become more aware of the inconveniences of tourism than its economic benefits.

The second cause of the crisis in Spanish tourism lies in the domain of territorial planning. As has already been stated. planning is by and large a responsibility of the municipal authorities. Timid attempts at regional planning date from the establishment of the autonomous governments. Master plans for urban development existed in the 1970s, but were not strictly respected, and overdevelopment was permitted during this period of rapid tourism expansion. Construction tended to be on a piecemeal basis, and its extent depended mainly on local initiative. Moreover, the lack of legislation meant that not only was the quantity of construction largely uncontrolled, but also its quality. This is simply a reflection of the national policy of growth at all costs, which also operated at local level. Moreover, municipal revenues were negligible until the 1980s, making it impossible to keep the rate of provision of infrastructures, services and urban amenities abreast of that of accommodation. Even now, government controlled revenues are based on permanent population figures, making no extra allowance for summer visitors. This circumstance and the deficiencies inherited from the 1970s have made it difficult to counteract existing deficits.

New urban master plans were drawn up in the early 1980s. The majority tended to legalize the status quo, as practical difficulties - high density and sprawling land occupation, overdevelopment, haphazard urban layout - made other solutions impracticable. In fact, as each municipality had the authority to plan for future development, in the absence of overall regional plans, many even opted for further large scale tourism development. Only the recession in the tourist industry - i.e. market conditions - has served as a brake on development in these cases.

13.4 Conclusions

It could therefore be said that, in general, there has been a lack of coordination between the central government, local authorities and private enterprise. The central government was responsible for policy (policies which had no long - term projection and largely ignored the importance of tourism), while the local authorities were responsible for planning (although they lacked the financial capacity to implement projects). As a result, it was largely private enterprise that financed accommodation and amenity provision in tourist resorts, and the tendency was to speculate, looking for short-term returns, an easy task with such lax regulations.

Policy and planning in the 1960s and early 1970s had, therefore, far-reaching effects on the tourism product, because they eventually led to the loss of economic viability of international tourism, especially in large resorts which depended on organized mass tourism. A vicious circle was formed: a low

193

quality product had evolved, which could only be marketed at low prices, attracting low spenders and generating less and less profits, which, in turn, left little or no margin available for plant improvement, with the consequent further deterioration of the product - altogether, a self-destroying spiral.

13.5 Measures adopted in Spain recently

Since 1978, but especially after 1980, attempts have been made to remedy this situation, but modifying many of the characteristics of Spanish tourism laid down during the Franco era is not an easy task. Practical difficulties have made a rapid recovery impossible. These difficulties include the form and extent of urban development, infrastructure and amenity deficits, obsolete accommodation plant and low profit margins. An additional difficulty, which adversely affects demand, is the fact that Spain has lost part of its good 'image' as a tourist destination.

Some of the autonomous regional governments produced white papers on tourism during the 1980s (e.g. Miguelsanz, 1983; Aguiló, 1987) but it was not until 1990, in the face of the recession which began in 1989, that the Spanish government produced its own white paper (Fuejo, 1990). In it, the structural defects of Spanish tourism were finally recognized, and 30 different remedial measures were proposed. However, the appearance of this white paper was tardy and proposals concentrated on the provision of financial support for accommodation plant renovation and investment in transport infrastructures (roads, railways and airports) as a means to improving the quality of the product (Aranzadi, 1992). No solution was proposed for many of the basic structural defects.

Meanwhile many individual resorts are using their own initiative to correct errors committed in the past and thus counteract the recession. These consist mainly of: urban renewal; incentives to improve accommodation (tax rebates or free building permits for renovations); investment in infrastructures and amenities; more attention to the quality of service and selective marketing with a view to improving and individualizing the resort's image. Large resorts, such as Benidorm and Magaluf, have undertaken ambitious urban renewal programmes to reduce overcrowding and provide open spaces, thus greatly improving the built environment. Some resorts (e.g. Sitges, Sant Feliu de Guixols) have designed strategic plans to channel future development. Virtually all resorts have paid special attention to beach hygiene and amenity provision, as well as aesthetic considerations when laying out their seafronts.

Initiative at local level has generally surpassed measures implemented at a larger scale. Action by autonomous governments is restricted by the absence of adequate legislation in some cases, and in others, by the lack of financial means, for only a small proportion of their budget is allocated to tourism, as it is still not considered a priority sector of the economy.

The Spanish education system is currently undergoing a process of reform. However, tourism studies have not been included at university degree level, nor have significant changes been introduced in already existing lower level vocational studies programmes, which have not satisfied employers in the tourist sector in the past. Initiative in the sphere of education, as in other aspects of tourism, has been developed at a more local level. For example, the Catalan autonomous government is currently preparing a report on the needs for tourism-related education with a view to introducing changes in the education system. At local level, some individual universities are in the process of designing multidisciplinary degree courses in tourism studies, although, for the moment, recognition of degree status at national level is not guaranteed. It is hardly a coincidence that these initiatives come from the universities of Alicante (near Benidorm) and the Balearic Islands (in Palma de Mallorca).

13.6 The lessons to be learned

There is little merit in hindsight. It is easy to criticize the Spanish government's tourism policies of the 1960s and 1970s when the consequences are evident. However, they should be placed in their historical context: on the one hand, mass tourism was then a relatively new and unknown phenomenon worldwide and, on the other, environmental issues were not a preoccupation of the general public. Moreover, in the case of Spain, it must also be remembered that the country was still recovering, in relative isolation, from the devastation of its Civil War, and priority was given to the development of industry in the large cities in a period of mass rural depopulation. Little attention was paid to developments taking place on the undervalued coastal fringe, considered at this time to be of marginal economic value. The badly needed foreign exchange earned from tourism was simply welcomed with open arms.

For the benefit of regions where tourism is still in the early stages of development, the following recommendations should be considered, bearing in mind the lessons to be learned from the case of Spanish tourism.

1   The potential market segment of a proposed destination should be studied in a realistic manner. To do so, the first step is to identify the type of product that the destination can offer. An evaluation should be made of climate (length of season, for example), natural attractiveness, other attractions available, location with respect to the potential market. The product can then be designed in accordance with the type of tourist who would normally be attracted.

2   Quantity is not, by any means, the answer. Beware of large-scale developments, for their impact on the environment is very high. The environment should be considered a non-renewable natural resource, for which there exists a threshold of carrying capacity, which, once surpassed, makes sustainable development impossible. This problem has been encountered in many of Spain's large tourism resorts, where the deterioration of the natural environment has led to the disappearance of the original source of attraction. These typical mass tourism resorts can now be considered an obsolete form of development.

3   The product offered must have a high quality: price ratio; in other words, it must give 'value for money'. This concept should not, however, be confused with that of luxury tourism, for which the demand is very

195

limited. The average tourist's perception of quality rests nowadays on two considerations: the environment understood as both the natural and built environment, and the provision of services, including basic infrastructures and amenities, alongside accommodation. A low level of environmental impact together with efficient and pleasant service can be equated with high quality. This kind of 'high quality' product is not necessarily expensive to provide.

4   Diversification of the product is essential. The dangers of agricultural monoculture are well known, and similar dangers exist in the tourism industry. At a macro scale (national or regional level) different types of product should be developed in order to attract tourists from diverse social, cultural and geographical origins. However, at a micro scale (individual resort level), specialization in one market sector is recommendable. For example, it is impossible to cater adequately for the tastes of young people in search of a lively night-life, young family groups and old-age pensioners at the same time and in the same place. The tendency in many Spanish resorts has been towards specialization defined in terms of the geographical origin of the tourists, rather than their social composition. This is a consequence of the relative strength of the different tour operators in each resort. The inherent dangers of this form of dependence due to market concentration are obvious.

5   Flexibility in the evolution of the product is also essential. The supply must be able to adapt to changes in demand as a result of changes in tourist motivation. It is therefore necessary to establish mechanisms to make continuous investment possible: credits, loans, sufficient profits to encourage reinvestment.

However, in order to achieve the specific objectives outlined, two more general conditions must be satisfied in the fields of planning and education. In the first place, medium and long term development plans at both national and regional level must be designed. In the second place, the country's education system must be modified to prepare people for employment in the tourism sector, both at management and service level. Education should also incorporate the means for undertaking multi-disciplinary research in the field, and making the general public aware of the true significance of tourism in the country's economy. These measures together will provide the necessary mechanisms for the development of a high quality tourism product which is capable of evolving according to the dictates of demand.

References

Aguiló, E. (ed.) (1987), *Llibre Blanc del Turisme a Balears*, Conselleria de Turisme, Govern Balear, Palma de Mallorca. (2 vol.).
Aranzadi, J.C. (1992), Plan Marco de Competitividad del Turismo Español. *Estudios Turísticos* 115, pp. 3-10.

Bote Gómez, V. (1990), *Planificación económica del Turismo*, Trillas, México.

Cals, J. (1987), Turismo y polìtica turística en España 1974-1986, in: Velarde, H., Garcìa Delgado, J. and Pedreño, A. (eds) *El Sector terciario de la Economía española*, Economistas Libros, Colegio de Economistas de Madrid, Madrid, pp. 205-27.

Cals, J. (1983), El modelo turístico español. *Estudios Turìsticos* 80, pp.15-19.

Cals, J. (1982), *La Costa Brava i el Turisme: Estudis sobre la Política turística, el Territori i l'Hoteleria*, Kapel, Barcelona.

Cals, J. (1974), *Turismo y Política turística en España: una Aproximación*, Ariel, Barcelona.

Díaz Alvarez, J. (1988), *Geografía del Turismo*, Síntesis, Madrid.

Esteve Secall, R. (1991), *Un nuevo Modelo turístico para España*, Universidad de Málaga, Málaga.

Figuerola, M. (1983), Importancia del turismo en la economía española. *Estudios Turísticos* 80, pp. 21-30.

Fuejo, I. (ed.) (1990), *Libro Blanco del Turismo*, Ministerio de Transportes, Turismo y Comunicaciones, Secretaría General de Turismo, Madrid.

Gabinete de Estudios Económicos y Empresariales del Instituto Español de Turismo (1984), El papel del turismo en la estructura económica española. *Estudios Turísticos* 81, pp. 3-19.

Gaviria, M. (1990), España a la carta. *Estudios Turísticos* número extraordinario, pp. 77-85.

Gaviria, M. (ed.) (1974), *España a Gogo. Turismo Charter y Neocolonialismo del Espacio* , Ediciones Turner, Madrid.

Gibert, A. (1972), *El Crak turístico de la Costa Brava*, Càmara de Comerç, Girona.

López Palomeque, F. (1988), Geografía del turismo en España: una aproximación a la distribución espacial de la demanda turística y de la oferta de alojamiento. *Documents d'Anàlisi Geogràfica* 13, pp. 34-64.

Miguelsanz, A. (ed.) (1983), *Llibre Blanc del Turisme a Catalunya*, Generalitat de Catalunya, Departament de la Presidència, Barcelona.

Ministerio de Industria, Comercio y Turismo, Subdirección General de Planificación y Prospectiva Turística-Estadística (1980-1992), *Anuario de Estadísticas del Turismo, año 19...,* Ministerio de Industria, Comercio y Turismo, Secretaría General de Turismo - Turespaña, Dirección General de Política Turística, Madrid. (annual publication).

Ministerio de Información y Turismo, Secretaría General Técnica, Servicio de Estadística y Análisis de Datos, Sección de Estadística (1975-1979), *Anuario de Estadísticas del Turismo, año 19...,* Ministerio de Información y Turismo, Madrid. (annual publication).

Ministerio de Información y Turismo, Secretaría General Técnica, Servicio de Estadística y Anílisis de Datos, Sección de Estadística (1963-1974), *Estadísticas del Turismo, año 19...* Ministerio de Información y Turismo, Madrid. (annual publication).

Oficina de Coordinación y Programación Económica (1963), Informe del BIRF, in: *El Desarrollo económico de España*, Industria Turística Internacional, Madrid.

Palomino, A. (1972), *El Milagro turístico*, Plaza Janés, Barcelona.

Pearce, D.G. and Grimmeau, J.P. (1985), The spatial structure of tourist accommodation and hotel demand in Spain. *Geoforum* 16 (1), pp. 37-50.

Sanuy, F. (1983), El turismo y la crisis económica. *Estudios Turísticos* 80, pp. 67-76.

Vasalló, I. (1983), El turismo de masas en España. *Estudios Turísticos* 80, pp. 3-14.